'This is it! This is the one! The book I needed ᵥ
own capstone project. Jolanta and Majella have dᴏ.... ... ., ...,
understanding what a student needs to get the job done – all in a very effortless and
accessible manner. Bravo! *Undertaking Capstone Projects* is a must-have resource for students
and supervisors. It is clear, precise, uncluttered, and distils the significant experience of
the authors into a highly readable and practical companion for anyone working on a
capstone project. I wish that this book always existed. But – it will! This is a modern
classic. It will be remembered fondly by all who are guided by its wisdom and careful
support. Contemporary and future researchers will confidently remember this book as
that "one thing" that inspired them.'

Dr Conor Mc Guckin, *Associate Professor, University of
Dublin, Trinity College, Ireland*

'This book is a page-turner. At last we have a book that sets out a comprehensive
range of useful issues in planning, doing and reporting a capstone project. The authors'
experiences of working on capstone projects shines clearly. Its positive style and graphics
are first class for students and their supervisors: clear, down-to-earth, focused, practical
and thought-provoking for every stage and type of capstone project. The advice is
constructive, memorable and important. This book is a breath of fresh air, promoting and
rewarding reflective practice. It should be the number one call for students doing capstone
projects.'

Professor Keith Morrison, *Vice-rector and Professor of
Education, University of Saint Joseph, Macau, China*

'This is essential reading for psychology students completing research and capstone
projects. The book simplifies complex issues in research and is therefore clear, insightful
and easy to use.'

Professor Christian van Nieuwerburg, *Professor of Positive
Psychology and Coaching, RCSI, Ireland*

'At last, there is a comprehensive body of work on how to undertake capstone projects.
This much-needed resource not only fills a gap in the literature but also has a place in
addressing the knowledge gap of students and staff who seek to understand the purpose
and process of a capstone.'

Dr Kelly-Ann Allen, *Senior Lecturer, Monash University, Australia*

'This book is the meeting between the science of learning with the state of the art. If
you are a teacher or a student passionate about ensuring that your HE studies respond to
the needs of the real word, follow this book as a step-by-step manual for your final year
academic production.'

Professor Ilona Boniwell, *School of Psychology,
University of East London, United Kingdom*

Undertaking Capstone and Final Year Projects in Psychology

Undertaking Capstone and Final Year Projects in Psychology serves a seminal purpose in guiding its readers to create a capstone project. The text employs traditional and emerging methodologies and methods in order to posit an exhaustive approach that the psychology students can adopt to see their projects to fruition.

The text aims at fortifying the reader's skills through the structure of its chapters as they begin to work on their capstone or final year project. The chapters collectively explore the varied aspects that are involved in the completion of a final year project, that is, beginning from the inception of the idea to laying the foundation, designing the project, analysing the data, and, finally, presenting the findings. The text guides the reader through each step and provides further guidance on approaching the idea, coming up with the research question, positioning it within the epistemological and ontological context, and constructing the theoretical framework to arrive at the optimal design solutions.

The text will be useful for psychology students who are currently completing a capstone or a final year project. It is further aimed at psychology students who will subsequently be working on a project and are looking forward to gaining cognisance regarding the approach and the methodology to be adopted for the same.

Jolanta Burke, PhD is a chartered psychologist and an associate professor at the Centre for Positive Psychology and Health, RCSI University of Medicine and Health Sciences. She is an editor-in-chief of the *Journal of Happiness and Health*. Her latest books are *Positive Health: 100+ Research-based Positive Psychology* and *Lifestyle Medicine Tools to Enhance Your Wellbeing*, published by Routledge. For more information, please go to www.jolantaburke.com.

Majella Dempsey, EdD is an associate professor at Maynooth University. She is strand leader for the professional doctorate in curriculum studies and lectures on undergraduate and postgraduate modules. Majella supervises students at master's and doctoral levels. She is research active, leading large- and small-scale projects focused on teaching, learning, assessment, and curriculum.

Undertaking Capstone and Final Year Projects in Psychology

Practical Guide for Students

Jolanta Burke and Majella Dempsey

Routledge
Taylor & Francis Group

LONDON AND NEW YORK

Cover image: © Getty Images

First published 2023
by Routledge
4 Park Square, Milton Park, Abingdon, Oxon OX14 4RN

and by Routledge
605 Third Avenue, New York, NY 10158

Routledge is an imprint of the Taylor & Francis Group, an informa business

British Library Cataloguing-in-Publication Data
A catalogue record for this book is available from the British Library

Library of Congress Cataloging-in-Publication Data
Names: Burke, Jolanta, author. | Dempsey, Majella, author.
Title: Undertaking capstone and final year projects in psychology : practical guide
    for students / Jolanta Burke, Majella Dempsey.
Description: Abingdon, Oxon ; New York, NY : Routledge, 2023. | Includes
    bibliographical references and index.
Identifiers: LCCN 2022006564 (print) | LCCN 2022006565 (ebook) |
    ISBN 9781032201429 (hardback) | ISBN 9781032201443 (paperback) |
    ISBN 9781003262428 (ebook)
Subjects: LCSH: Psychology—Research—Methodology. | Psychology—Study and
    teaching (Higher) | Project method in teaching.
Classification: LCC BF76.5 .B87 2023 (print) | LCC BF76.5 (ebook) |
    DDC 150.7—dc23/eng/20220517
LC record available at https://lccn.loc.gov/2022006564
LC ebook record available at https://lccn.loc.gov/2022006565

ISBN: 978-1-032-20142-9 (hbk)
ISBN: 978-1-032-20144-3 (pbk)
ISBN: 978-1-003-26242-8 (ebk)

DOI: 10.4324/9781003262428

Typeset in Bembo
by Apex CoVantage, LLC

To our students, past, present, and future.

Contents

1 The foundation

Almost five million academic, peer-reviewed articles were published in the last decade about psychology. Researchers worldwide designed, conducted, and shared their studies on psychology. They discussed the research gaps. They addressed and reflected on the implications of their research for practitioners. Yet only a tiny percentage of them have been read and used by psychologists. Partially, it is because practitioners are not aware of most published research, or sometimes they find it difficult to discern which article is worthwhile reading and applying to practice. Another reason, however, is that the leap between theory and practice is often too difficult to take. It requires carrying out a capstone project or a similar practice-based research project to realise how psychologists can tap into the endless potential of academic research to improve their practice. In capstone project research, theory and practice come together in new and exciting ways with the practitioner at the heart of the endeavour. This is what this book is about, a journey of enhancing your skills to help you complete a final year project and become a research-informed practitioner for many years to come.

1.1 Structure of the book

Please note that although this book is about capstone projects and final year projects, we will primarily use the term "research" project throughout. However, we will refer to "capstone" instead of the generic "research" projects when referring to specific components of capstone projects.

Completing a research project is like building a house. When building a house, firstly, you need to set up solid foundations that you can rely on. Then, you need to review and enhance your skills to build it. Next, you need to decide the materials you wish to use, come up with a plan of action, and follow it through until the house is complete and ready to be used.

Similarly, this book is structured to help you build your skills and complete a research project. In Chapter 1, we will start by setting out the foundations for the research project. Next, you will find out what capstone and other research projects are all about and how they compare with each other. This chapter will also clarify the intricacies of capstone projects that will help you understand their role in research and practice. By the end of Chapter 1, you will have a helicopter view of what is required of you when embarking on a capstone and final year research project.

Chapter 2 will focus on you and your skills. When designing and carrying out a research project, you will need to ascertain how skills you already have developed can be

DOI: 10.4324/9781003262428-1

amplified and help you on your research project journey and what skills need a little bit of extra work to complete your project. Specifically, we will introduce you to a Perceive-Audit-Understand-Substitute-Edify (PAUSE) reflection model that will allow you to choose your topic, carry out your project, and apply it more effectively in psychological practice. We will also provide you with some evidence-based and practical guidelines on how best to make choices, engage in research-based practice, improve your critical thinking, and improve your project management skills. You will require all these skills to help you complete your research project.

In Chapter 3, we will introduce you to a step-by-step process, which will provide a helicopter view of your research project. We will also help you understand the differences between some of the most confusing concepts associated with research, such as empirical vs desk-based projects, quantitative vs qualitative research, inductive vs deductive reasoning, and research methodologies vs research methods. You will need clarity about these terms to make important decisions about the design of your research project.

Chapter 4 will delve deeper into the first step of the research project design, which is *the interest*. This chapter will guide you through techniques you can use to select a topic. We will then help you plan a strategy for reviewing the literature relating to a topic of your interest. Finally, by the end of this chapter, you will be able to create the most appropriate research question for your capstone project.

In Chapters 5, 6, and 7, we will discuss *the design* of your research project. Specifically, Chapter 5 will help you understand your ontological and epistemological positioning. In Chapter 6, we will introduce you to the methodology spectrum, which will allow you to select the best methodologies for your project. Finally, in Chapter 7, we will review various methods available that will help you carry out your project. By the end of Chapter 7, you will better understand how your research project will be designed.

Chapter 8 is dedicated to *the analysis* of an empirical research project. This chapter is only relevant to those who research with participants. First, we will review some of the important ethical considerations for your project. We will then discuss your data-gathering and data analysis strategies. By the end of this chapter, you will be able to make important decisions about the analysis aspects of your project.

Finally, in Chapter 9, we will discuss the presentation of your project. We will delve deeper into the artefacts you can create as part of your capstone project, which will help you in your practice. We will help you reflect on the implications of your project for practice and prepare your written and/or oral presentation of it. By the end of this chapter, you will know what steps you need to complete your capstone or final year research project.

The content of this book is the fruit of years of our experience of supervising students through capstone and final year projects. We have supervised students completing bachelor's and master's degrees and higher-level doctoral degrees and PhDs. What differentiates each level is the skills, topics, and research design you select and conduct. Regardless of whatever degree you are completing, the process remains the same.

1.2 How to read this book

We recommend that you read this book twice:

1   It is helpful to read it from cover to cover to familiarise yourself with the overall concepts and see a bigger picture of doing research.
2   We suggest you stop throughout and reflect on what you have read and how you can apply it to your practice.

3 When you read it the second time, we advise that you use your highlighter and fully engage with the book, stopping at relevant sections, re-reading them, and taking notes.

Engaging actively with this book will make it easier for you to complete your research project.

Have you ever run or watched someone running a marathon? There are several "water stations" where participants can stop, refill, and take a break on their route. Similarly, we have created a series of break-out sections, which aim to enhance your experience of engaging with the material. Each one of them begins with an image that symbolises the content. Here are the images and descriptions for them.

	Reflection time This image indicates reflection time. We encourage you to stop reading at this point and reflect upon the section so that you can make an informed decision as to what steps to take when designing your research project.
	Recap time When you see this image, it means that you stop and recap the most important parts of this chapter to help you make sense of what has been discussed.
	Self-assessment When you see this box, we ask you to complete a short survey to help you become aware of your strengths and areas for improvement.

Most importantly, however, don't forget to enjoy this experience, as the book will help you develop skills to tap into the limitless potential of research so that you can use it effectively in your psychological practice for years to come.

1.3 Final year projects

Final year projects come in various forms. The traditional approach to a final year project is a thesis, which is an extensive body of work to add value to research. An extension comes in the form of a research paper, whereby universities request that instead of a long 15k or 20k word thesis, students produce a concise research paper (6–7k words), which they can tweak afterwards for a publication. In recent years, many educational institutions have tried to find an alternative to a research project that is more practical and helps students apply their knowledge to their practice rather than add value to research; this is how e-portfolio and capstone projects came about. The interest in capstone projects continues to grow, with over 60% of psychological courses in the USA offering capstone projects as their preferred mode of assessment. This chapter will delve deeper into explaining what capstone projects are and then compare them to the more traditional final year projects.

1.4 Capstone project myths

Myths about capstone projects permeate the education system and prevent institutions and professionals from engaging with them fully. The most prevalent myth associated with a capstone project is calling it a mini-thesis, which does not do it justice. There are fundamental differences between these two final year assessments. Yet, we have heard both students and academics referring to it this way for years. Even though it is understandable, given that theses have been in the academic lexicon for centuries, it undermines the vital role that capstone projects play in professional practice, which relates to enhancing professionals' research-based practice capacity, instead of primarily adding value to a research base. This is why a concerted effort needs to be made in educational institutions to refer to it as a capstone project, not a mini-thesis.

Calling it a mini-thesis diminishes its impact and is conducive to students perceiving it as a lesser version of an academic thesis. This is yet another myth associated with capstone projects, as capstone projects are major pieces of work that culminate an engagement with an educational programme. Over the years, we have received many emails from students wondering whether they would be awarded the same quality of a degree if they chose to take a capstone project route instead of a thesis. Their question showed a fundamental lack of understanding of the differences between these two assessments, which we will explain further in this chapter. The award received for completing a capstone project is equally important, and it addresses a different need. While a thesis focuses on adding to the wealth of research, the cornerstone of a capstone project is to enrich the psychological practice.

These myths lead to only a relatively small percentage of students selecting capstone projects as their final year assessments (Henscheid and South Carolina University, 2000), highlighting an urgent need for change. Firstly, this change refers to how academics view capstone projects. The more they appreciate its value, the more likely they will recommend it to their students. Secondly, students need to understand better the intricacies involved in designing and completing a capstone project so that they are confident about their decision. Most importantly, however, there is an urgent need for a systemic change that allows for capstone projects to be seen as equal to traditional approaches to completing a final year project. Until myths are dispelled, and a better understanding of capstone projects is prevalent, they will not be used to their total capacity. This book aims to address this gap and provide an easy-to-use guide for both students and academics interested in it.

1.5 Capstone project: definition and benefits

Capstone projects are final year projects focused on enhancing evidence-based psychology practice. They are usually introduced in three- and four-year university degree programmes; however, they are also increasingly popular in one- and two-year postgraduate programmes (Hammer et al., 2018; Hauhart and Grahe, 2010) and doctoral capstone projects for those completing the highest level of education. They enable students to reflect on and apply to their daily practice the knowledge they have gained during their studies, as well as learn how to pose or solve work-related problems and enrich educational practice using evidence-based solutions. Capstone projects are a pinnacle of evidence-based practice.

What makes capstone projects particularly useful is that they encourage students to apply evidence-based solutions to their work-related issues (Lunt et al., 2008). Given the amount of psychological research being published each year, you need to learn how to read it, discern its value, and, most importantly, apply it in your daily practice to improve your outcomes further. Using research is an acquired skill, which you can learn by completing a capstone project. This is why capstone projects are often seen as particularly useful for preparing students for jobs after graduation (Beer et al., 2011).

Whether you are a student seeking a job after graduation, or an existing psychology professional, the skills you learn by carrying out a capstone project are invaluable for enhancing your career and your outputs. Think about it. If you have two surgeons to choose from to remove your appendix, both graduated ten years ago, but only one engaged in research-based practice, which one would you select to operate on you? We guess you would choose the one who has kept herself up to speed with all the latest research developments. The same applies to psychology professionals, who operate every day on people's minds by expanding their knowledge and changing their perspectives on their lives. We have a responsibility to society to keep ourselves informed of the latest developments in research and use them in education. This is why it is crucial to keep your knowledge and skills up to date and apply it effectively in your practice, and this is what capstone projects are designed for – to help you develop the competencies to do it.

Furthermore, third-level institutions are increasingly under pressure to create graduate and postgraduate programmes that provide participants with practical skills to use their knowledge at work. Partially, it is because nowadays, some government funding for universities depends on the number of graduates that have found gainful employment within two or so years from the programme completion. It is also because students are no longer interested in courses that provide them with unavailing knowledge that you cannot use in practice. Due to this systemic change, schools and departments of education worldwide have begun to depart from the traditional assessments of theses and dissertations and started to pivot towards more practical assessments, such as capstone projects. The same move is starting to happen in psychology departments. This is why capstone projects are needed now more than ever.

Most importantly, however, completing a capstone project will help you develop independent learning, solution-focused problem-solving, in addition to improving your research-based practice (Lee and Loton, 2015). For many participants, capstone projects have become high-impact activities in their academic journey, which added significantly to their professional development long term (Healey et al., 2012). We hope that engaging with a capstone project will help you achieve this too.

1.6 Defining features

Capstone projects are unique in the way they assess your knowledge and skills gained through an educational programme. A survey with hundreds of psychology departments offering capstone projects to students reported that the two main reasons for introducing projects were to help students review and integrate what they have learnt in their studies (85%) and help students extend and apply what they learnt in daily practice (Grahe and Hauhart, 2013). The following sections will find these and other defining features of designing and conducting a capstone project. In addition, we compared each one of the features to other final year projects in psychology to ease your understanding.

1.6.1 Practical

Capstone projects are the experiential component of students' academic experience, sometimes referred to as *practicum* projects because they refer to practice. Specifically, they are an application of academic knowledge in practice. They help students understand the importance of evidence-based practice and encourage them to continue expanding their knowledge.

At the same time, traditional final year psychology projects may include applying a theory in practice, but its main objective is usually to add value to research, not practice. This is one main defining and differentiating feature of capstone projects.

1.6.2 Coherent

Another defining feature of a capstone project is that it helps you create a sense of coherence relating to your studies (Carlson and Peterson, 1993; Durel, 1993). In other words, it integrates all your experiences, newly gained knowledge, and skills you have developed during your educational programme and churns them into your project, which is an outcome of your aggregated learning.

Coherence to consolidating knowledge can relate either to your own experiences or extend across the entire profession and beyond it. Some capstone projects draw from education and use other disciplines to inform them. They may tap into theories that have never been explored in the psychological context and transform them into usable ideas that can enrich psychological practice. Therefore, the coherence of a capstone project relates to both the depth and breadth of knowledge.

At the same time, this feature is not essential for traditional final year projects in psychology. While some theses or research papers may indeed cover the material from your educational programme, this is not a requirement. Students are often encouraged to follow their passion when deciding on their topic. They may, therefore, veer outside of the covered material into an aspect of psychology not discussed in the educational programme for as long as it fits into the remit of the degree.

1.6.3 Dual time perspective

Another crucial feature of capstone projects is their dual time perspective. Since its inception, capstone projects were focused on consolidating knowledge gained during studies (past) so that students can apply it in their future practice (Starr-Glass, 2010). In fact, consolidation is such an important aspect of it that in many institutions, it is recommended not to seek out new content when completing a capstone project, rather focus on what students already know and apply it in practice (van Acker et al., 2014). The duality of time perspective is evident as students need to review the past, consolidate what they have learnt, and negotiate the future.

An aspect of the dual time perspective refers to the focus on preparing students who are not yet employed to enter the workforce (Ryan et al. 2012). Capstone projects help them create a new professional identity, even when they have not had professional experience (McNamara et al., 2011). They allow them to integrate and make sense of all they already know and project into the future by bridging their knowledge with practice. That bridging provides a transformative experience whereby students learn not only the skill of reviewing their knowledge but also its application in daily lives.

Capstone projects, however, are also very useful for those already employed who aim to further develop their professional and personal skills (Blanford et al., 2020). For them, bridging these two time perspectives can be accomplished with skilful reflection on their practice (past) and engaging in activities that aim to develop a range of skills, such as confidence, self-belief, or independence that help them in their future practice (Lee and Loton, 2019).

Compared to capstone projects, other final year projects in psychology do not require students to draw from the past or the present to project into the future. Instead, they may focus on a one-time perspective in designing and executing their project. For example, they may identify a research gap (in the present) and address it as part of their research project with a view to enriching the research base. While they will mention the implications for future research and practice, as it is part of their inquiry, it will not become their primary objective. Whereby capstone projects prepare professionals or future professionals for improved research-based practice, so the dual time perspective feature is of utmost importance.

1.6.4 Research-based practice

Across educational institutions worldwide, two types of capstone projects have emerged. One type relates to a final year project, which is not underpinned by any research. Instead, it focuses on designing an artefact based merely on students' experiences or personal interests. The other type is a capstone research project which incorporates research as the foundation for practice. This book focuses solely on research-based projects and, as such, offers knowledge and helps you develop skills on how to do it.

Evidence-based practice is described as research-based knowledge, research-informed practice, evidence-based interventions, evidence-informed practice, or lifelong learning (Gibbs, 2003). Regardless of the term used, it refers to applying research findings to the daily practice of psychologists, therapists, coaches, social workers, teachers, researchers, learning and development practitioners, and others using psychology at work to improve their outcomes. Evidence-based practice is yet another defining feature of capstone projects. When students design their capstone research projects, their familiarity with evidence-based practice increases, thus allowing them to engage more actively in research-based practice (Peterson et al., 2011). Consequently, a capstone project becomes a stepping stone for improved psychological practice. We will discuss evidence-based practice skills in more detail in Section 2.3 of this book.

In contrast, while traditional final year projects in psychology appreciate the research-based practice, they usually inform the research-based practice rather than focus on it. However, papers and theses may be published that address the research-based practice. Therefore, while research-based practice is not a focus of a traditional final year project in psychology, it can undoubtedly become a topic and feature.

1.6.5 Creative

The essence of every one of us, without exception, is our creativity, which is expressed in various ways (Beghetto and Kaufman, 2007). Some of us have a "Big-C" creativity. For example, one of our students with Big-C creativity designed a research-informed, art-based project as part of his assessment. He wrote a script, directed it, and performed it in a theatre production to illustrate the application of *Growth Mindset* research in schools

(Dweck, 2006). His project resulted in standing ovations from his peers and further awarded him first-class honours.

Some of us have "little-c" creativity, which refers to formulating everyday-life creative solutions to problems. One of our students with this type of creativity immersed herself in a systematic literature review that aimed to answer one of her work-related questions: How *can a coach improve her listening skills?* This project allowed her to tap into the pragmatic aspects of problem-solving associated with her coaching practice. She systematically assessed studies relating to listening skills, especially in the context of coaching, which resulted in seven practical, evidence-based tools she could use to assist her when working with clients.

There are also some of us who boast a "mini-c" creativity, which refers to meaningful insights that lead to self-discovery and self-improvement. For one of our students, this type of creativity inspired her to carry out an action research project, the aim of which was to redesign her teaching practice in order to improve her students' experience with psychology. An essential aspect of this approach was her deep reflection on what has worked in the classroom and what changes she should make in her teaching practice. Her strength of perspective turned her project into a remarkable force of insightful practices.

Finally, another type of creativity is "pro-c" creativity, which stands for an expert-level creativity. One of our positive psychology students, who is a training consultant, redesigned her organisational approach to enhancing wellbeing. Her profound knowledge in positive psychology, coupled with her professional creativity, resulted in a unique approach to long-term organisational wellbeing adopted by many international organisations.

All four students had different strengths and displayed different types of creativity. However, what all of them had in common was that all these diverse projects were part of their capstone project assessment. The range of the projects they selected illustrates an immense potential that capstone projects have in education to enrich research-based practice regardless of your interests. This is why there is something for everyone in completing a capstone project in psychology.

While creativity is not exclusive to capstone projects, due to their flexibility of presentation (see Chapter 9 for details), it allows students to let their imagination go wild when conducting their projects. They go beyond the usual boundaries of the educational structure for as long as they are focused on research-based practice. In contrast, traditional final year projects need to be presented in a specific structure of (1) abstract, (2) introduction, (3) literature review, (4) methods, (5) results, and (6) discussion. This structure may restrict the creativity of some students.

Reflection time

What type of creativity do you have, and how can you use your strengths to design a project most suitable to your needs?

1.6.6 Flexible

What makes capstone projects particularly attractive is the flexibility of their design. There is only one component of a capstone project which is non-negotiable. All other aspects of it are flexible depending on students' needs and/or the institutional requirement. The only non-negotiable part of the project is its practical dimension.

The practical dimension of a capstone project comes in various forms. Your project may be beneficial because it applies to psychological practice, meaning it helps you become a better psychologist. It can also be practical, as the knowledge you have gained while conducting your research applies to other psychologists and researchers. Perhaps it adds to previously acquired knowledge. Alternatively, it is practical because it serves a specific purpose you have; for example, it allows you to prepare psychological guidelines for your organisational practice or assess a new strength-based approach to counselling. Apart from the practical aspects of it, the capstone project is flexible.

Its flexibility is associated with the methodology you select; therefore, you can conduct quantitative or qualitative research that adopts various ontological and epistemological views. You can also choose various data collection methods, or you may choose to do a desk-based project instead of empirical research. A capstone project offers you a variety of options for your project design. Finally, the format you choose to present your project may also vary. In essence, the project can be as flexible as you desire to answer the practice-based question you have.

1.7 Online capstone projects

The COVID-19 pandemic has affected over 1.6 billion students worldwide (UN, 2020). While there were a lot of negative consequences associated with it, it has inadvertently forced educational institutions to move online. This resulted in exponential growth of skills among educators and more ease in delivering remote learning (Dempsey and Burke, 2021). In post-COVID-19 education, we predict that more programmes will be provided online, many of which will apply capstone projects as part of their final year assessment.

While, to date, many online capstone courses are delivered, they are not fully integrated with the ethos of online learning (Arthur and Newton-Calvert, 2015). This is why five critical components for a specific authentic online capstone experience have been created to help students embrace it fully (Devine et al., 2020). They include (1) choice and empowerment, meaning that students should be allowed to direct their learning while completing a project; (2) real-world problem, the topic of a capstone project referring to a practical aspect of their profession; (3) reflection and inquiry, which is an opportunity for students to engage in reflective practice and critical thinking; (4) support and coaching developed by their supervisors to help them integrate their knowledge and practice; and finally (5) community and collaboration, allowing them to connect with organisations and colleagues outside educational institutions. These five components are the basis for online capstone project practice.

1.8 Differences between capstone and traditional projects

Capstone projects are offered to students either to choose between the traditional end-of-year assessment or a compulsory element of their educational programme. To fully comprehend the unique facets of a capstone project, let us review the three most frequently deployed final year approaches, such as (1) thesis/dissertation, (2) research paper, and (3) e-portfolio, and discuss how they compare with a capstone project.

1.8.1 Thesis/dissertation

According to some scholars, we should use theses and dissertations interchangeably due to their academic similarities. However, others consider theses assessments for a bachelor's or master's degree and view dissertations in the context of a doctoral-level piece of work, although in some universities, the opposite is applied (Pemberton, 2012; Paltridge and Starfield, 2007). For ease of understanding, we will refer to both as a thesis in this book.

A thesis is a traditional assessment used in universities, which denotes a written exploration of a subject or topic of research (Walsh and Ryan, 2015) and may include a thesis defence, otherwise known as viva, which is an oral aspect of it. A thesis is designed to contribute to an academic field, with its primary audience being the academic community. Therefore, it often follows a typical academic structure that consists of an abstract, introduction, literature review, methodology, results, and discussion. On the other hand, a capstone project is more relaxed concerning the structure. While some follow strict academic guidelines, especially when designed as an empirical capstone research project, most have a practice-focused structure, either negotiated by students and their supervisors or recommended by an institution. Please see Chapter 9 for the structure we recommend for an educational capstone research project.

One of the components of a thesis and dissertation is a section about the implication of research for practice. However, the pragmatic aspect of research is not the quintessence of a thesis; the main aim is to add to the existing body of research. This is one of the main differences between theses and capstone projects, which mainly focused on the practical aspect of using research to enhance educational practice.

Another difference between a thesis and a capstone project is the size of the project. Educational institutions worldwide have established guidelines about credits awarded for each module, which vary across the board and require a specific number of words to be produced as part of the project. It may be, for instance, 15k or 20k words for a bachelor's degree, 20k or 30k for a master's degree, and between 50k to 120k for a doctoral or a PhD dissertation. Capstone projects, however, produce considerably thinner volumes. This is yet another difference between a traditional thesis and a capstone project.

Finally, over the last decade, a drive to enhance research-based practice resulted in many universities encouraging students to do school-based or practice-based research as a final year assessment. This approach is a pivot towards designing a capstone project. It encourages students to consider their practice when designing a study; however, it retains the academic structure of a thesis. Whereas a capstone research project has practitioners and their work at the heart of its design, and its structure is negotiable depending on the praxis needs.

1.8.2 Research paper

In recent years, many universities worldwide have replaced their traditional theses with a requirement for students to write and/or publish research papers. Their rationale is that research papers may reach a wider audience than theses. Even if a study is excellent and provides a significant contribution to research, unless it is transformed into an academic paper and published, it may not see the light of day. Sadly, by the time students complete their degrees, they may not be motivated to transform their research into a publication. This is why some institutions have decided to encourage students to submit a 6k-word research paper instead of a 20k-word thesis and then tweak it for submission to an academic, peer-reviewed journal. Similarly, some PhD students are encouraged to publish two or three academic papers instead of writing a 100k-word thesis. This is how a research paper has become yet another format for a final year assessment.

While it is possible to have two foci in carrying out research – i.e. contributing to the research field and practice – writing a research paper pivots towards an academic contribution. In contrast, a capstone project moves towards a practical contribution. Furthermore, a capstone research project has the practitioner in mind. While similar methodologies and methods are used for both approaches, the outcomes are focused on educational practitioners and how the research may add value to their practice, not how research may add value to an academic inquiry.

It is vital to notice that writing a capstone research project does not exclude the possibility of publishing it as a research paper. Several capstone projects in education have been published. When research that is carried out can help researchers and practitioners, you can quickly transform a capstone project into a research paper, or if the university guidelines permit, the final project may consist of a research paper submission. This is where the flexibility of the capstone project comes into play.

1.8.3 E-portfolio

This is yet another approach to assessing students' work, and it relates to a collection of artefacts, which demonstrate students' learning journey and upon which they are assessed. An e-portfolio, as the name suggests, is an electronic portfolio, which is an amalgamation of pieces of work over a period that creates evidence for students' development. Often the portfolio denotes a pragmatic approach to knowledge creation, which makes it similar to the capstone projects. However, the capstone project provides a more research-based practice than an e-portfolio and is often informed by theoretical frameworks, which is not a requirement for an e-portfolio.

Hopefully, by now, you have a better understanding of what a capstone project is and how it differs from other traditional approaches. Let us now reflect on what you have read to help you assimilate your knowledge.

Reflection time

In what way can completing a capstone project help you develop your educational practice?

Recap Time

This chapter clarified the definition of capstone projects and reviewed the central myths associated with them. We have also compared them to the traditional approaches to final year assessments and discussed some of the defining features of capstone projects. By now, we hope you have a better understanding as to why you would want to engage with a capstone project.

References

Arthur, D.S., and Z. Newton-Calvert. 2015. "Online Community-Based Learning as the Practice of Freedom: The Online Capstone Experience at Portland State University." *Metropolitan Universities* 26(3): 135–157.

Beer, M., R.A. Eisenstat, N. Foote, T. Fredberg, and F. Norrgren. 2011. *Higher Ambition: How Great Leaders Create Economic and Social Value.* Cambridge, MA: Harvard University Press.

Beghetto, R.A., and J.C. Kaufman. 2007. "The Genesis of Creative Greatness: Mini-c and the Expert Performance Approach." *High Ability Studies* 18(1): 59–61. doi: 10.1080/13598130701350668.

Blanford, J., P. Kennelly, B. King, D. Miller, and T. Bracken. 2020. "Merits of Capstone Projects in an Online Graduate Program for Working Professionals." *Journal of Geography in Higher Education* 44(1): 45–69. doi: 10.1080/03098265.2019.1694874.

Carlson, C.D., and R.J. Peterson. 1993. "Social Problems and Policy: A Capstone Course." *Teaching Sociology* 21: 239–241. doi: 10.2307/1319018.

Dempsey, M., and J. Burke. 2021. *Lessons Learned: The Experiences of Teachers in Ireland during the 2020 Pandemic.* Maynooth: Maynooth University.

Devine, J.L., K.S. Bourgault, and R.N. Schwartz. 2020. "Using the Online Capstone Experience to Support Authentic Learning." *TechTrends: Linking Research & Practice to Improve Learning* 64(4): 606–615. doi: 10.1007/s11528-020-00516-1.

Durel, R.J. 1993. "The Capstone Course: A Rite of Passage." *Teaching Sociology* 21: 223–225. doi: 10.2307/1319014.

Dweck, C.S. 2006. *Mindset: The New Psychology of Success.* New York: Random House.

Gibbs, C. 2003. "Explaining Effective Teaching: Self-efficacy and Thought Control of Action." *The Journal of Educational Enquiry* 4(2): 1–14.

Grahe, J.E., and R.C. Hauhart. 2013. "Describing Typical Capstone Course Experiences from a National Random Sample." *Teaching of Psychology* 40(4): 281–287.

Hammer, S., L. Abawi, P. Gibbings, H. Jones, P. Redmond, and S. Shams. 2018. "Developing a Generic Review Framework to Assure Capstone Quality." *Higher Education Research and Development* 37(4): 730–743.

Hauhart, R.C., and J.E. Grahe. 2010. "The Undergraduate Capstone Course in the Social Sciences: Results from a Regional Survey." *Teaching Sociology* 38(1): 4–17.

Healey, M., L. Lannin, J. Derounian, A. Stibbe, S. Bray, J. Deane, S. Hill, J. Keane, and C. Simmons. 2012. *Rethinking Final Year Projects and Dissertations.* York: The Higher Education Academy.

Henscheid, J.M., and Columbia National Resource Center for the Freshman Year Experience and Students in Transition South Carolina Univ. 2000. "Professing the Disciplines: An Analysis of Senior Seminars and Capstone Courses." The First-Year Experience Monograph Series No. 30.

Lee, N., and D. Loton. 2015. "Integrating Research and Professional Learning – Australian Capstones." *Council on Undergraduate Research Quarterly* 35(4): 28–35.

Lee, N., and D. Loton. 2019. "Capstone Purposes across Disciplines." *Studies in Higher Education* 44(1): 134–150. doi: 10.1080/03075079.2017.1347155.

Lunt, B.M., J.J. Ekstrom, S. Gorka et al. 2008. "Information Technology 2008: Curriculum Guidelines for Undergraduate Degree Programs in Information Technology." New York: Association for Computing Machinery.

McNamara, J., C. Brown, R.M. Field, S.M. Kift, D.A. Buttler, and C. Treloar. 2011. "Capstones: Transitions and Professional Identity." WACE World Conference, Philadelphia, USA.

Paltridge, B., and S. Starfield. 2007. *Thesis and Dissertation Writing in a Second Language.* New York: Routledge.

Pemberton, C.L.A. 2012. "A 'How-to' Guide for the Education Thesis/Dissertation Process." *Kappa Delta Pi Record* 48(2): 82–86. doi: 10.1080/00228958.2012.680378.

Peterson, S.M., A. Phillips, S.I. Bacon, and Z. Machunda. 2011. "Teaching Evidence-Based Practice at the BSW Level: An Effective Capstone Project." *Journal of Social Work Education* 47(3): 509–524. doi: 10.5175/JSWE.2011.200900129.

Ryan, M.D., N.M. Tews, and B.A. Washer. 2012. "Team-Teaching a Digital Senior Capstone Project in CTE." *Techniques: Connecting Education and Careers (J3)* 87(2): 52–55.

Starr-Glass, D. 2010. "Reconsidering the International Business Capstone: Capping, Bridging, or Both?" *Journal of Teaching in International Business* 21(4): 329–345.

United Nations. 2020. "Education during COVID-19 and Beyond." *Policy Brief.* www.un.org/development/desa/dspd/wp-content/uploads/sites/22/2020/08/sg_policy_brief_covid-19_and_education_august_2020.pdf

van Acker, L., J. Bailey, K. Wilson, and E. French. 2014. "Capping Them Off! Exploring and Explaining the Patterns in Undergraduate Capstone Subjects in Australian Business Schools." *Higher Education Research and Development* 33(5): 1049–1062.

Walsh, T., and A. Ryan. 2015. *Writing Your Thesis: A Guide for Postgraduate Students.* Maynooth: Mace Press.

2   Developing skills

The first skill we will discuss is reflection. Without developing it further, you may struggle to connect the dots between all the knowledge you have gained in your educational programme and your lifelong experience and relate it effectively to your research project. Connecting these dots will allow you to make a new meaning from your academic experiences and enrich the outcome of your project.

The second skill we will delve deeper into is making wise choices. As you are designing your study, you may be overwhelmed with the number of options you can choose. In this section, we will help you make decisions and find ways to reduce your feelings of anxiety and doubt about the choices you will have at your disposal.

The next skill we will discuss is practice. As you already know, applying research in practice is an essential component of research projects. This section will provide you with an easy process that will enable you to make research more applicable to practice.

We cannot discuss research project skills without introducing you to critical thinking. As you are reflecting on your experiences and making your practical choices, you will need to discern the quality of the work you read and produce. In this section, we will provide you with an easy-to-understand step on doing this.

Finally, let us not forget that it is a project; therefore, it requires good project management skills. Some of you may be great at applying theory to practice but might be less efficient about your project management skills. This section will provide you with an easy-to-follow structure on how you can manage your research project more effectively.

Figure 2.1 provides you with all the fundamental skills you require to engage with a research project.

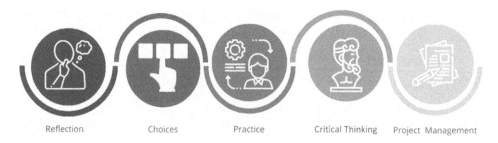

Reflection   Choices   Practice   Critical Thinking   Project Management

Figure 2.1 A range of skills that enable the completion of a research project.

DOI: 10.4324/9781003262428-2

2.1 Reflection

 *Self-assessment*

Please identify your level of agreement with the following statements:	Strongly disagree	Disagree	Neither agree nor disagree	Agree	Strongly agree
I am interested in analysing my behaviour					
I frequently examine my thoughts and feelings					
I need to think about the world around me and make sense of it					
I am usually aware of my thoughts					
I usually have a clear idea why I have behaved in a particular way					

Scoring:

Assign the following numbers to your responses: 1 for strongly disagree, 2 for disagree, 3 for neither agree nor disagree, 4 for agree, and 5 for strongly agree. Calculate your total score by adding all the numbers. If you scored:

5–10 points – you need to develop your reflective skills. Please read and re-read this section making sure that you understand it well. Take a notepad and practice reflecting on your day every day for ten minutes. Complete this assessment again in two weeks and see how you have progressed.

11–17 points – you are doing very well in some aspects of reflection and need some extra work in others. As you read this chapter, identify what additional skills you need to further develop, and over the next two weeks, make the extra effort to develop these skills. Consider practising reflection by carving spare time every day to sit and think about your day, or practice some expressive writing that will help you develop your reflective skills further.

17–20 points – you are doing brilliantly. Keep up the excellent work and reflect on what else you can do to improve it.

Reflection is an essential aspect of carrying out a research project. It is like gardening. The more effort you put into reflecting on practice, the more robust your crops will be. The reflection method is inherent to teaching; however, it is often done ad hoc. This reflection type does not go deep enough and might not lead to lasting change. To develop a robust and meaningful research project, we need to put effort into our reflective practice.

During your research project completion, you will engage in reflective practice throughout the entire cycle that starts with selecting a topic, carrying out your research, and then reflecting on the implications of the research for your practice. However, one of the main goals of engaging in a research project is to help you develop a research-based practice to build your knowledge and skills as a professional. There are many approaches to research-based practice, which you can start employing during your research project development. The following section will go deeper into it.

2.1.1 Models of reflection

As you progress through the research project, you will need to use reflection to help you make sense of your experience. Sometimes as we work with our students, we find that reflection can be particularly challenging, and they often confuse it with a description. Read these two paragraphs and see the difference between a description and reflection.

Descriptive: Today, I experienced a difficult situation at work. I am a trainee therapist, and one of my clients walked out of the room in the middle of the session. It all began five minutes earlier when I challenged him about his relationship with a friend. He sat still without responding to me or saying another word. I let the silence fill the room and waited until he felt comfortable responding to me. Then suddenly, he stood up and walked out of the room without saying a word. I called after him, but he didn't even turn his head and rushed off quickly, banging the door behind him. I felt frustrated with the situation and disappointed with myself. What did I do wrong? On reflection, I may have challenged my clients too soon. I need to make sure they are ready to be challenged in the future.

Reflective: Today, I experienced a difficult situation at work, a case that challenged my skills as a therapist. I questioned my client about his relationship with a friend. Instead of responding to me, he sat still and then walked out in the middle of the session without a word. My instant reaction was to blame myself for my inexperience. I wonder if my client was also blaming himself for his argument with a friend. He didn't seem to, as he spoke derogatorily about him. However, it may have been because he felt partially guilty about it and could not voice it yet. My client and I were blaming ourselves for something different, except I opened up about it in my diary while he shut off. Maybe writing about it before speaking with me next time may be helpful for him. I will buzz him later and remind him of this helpful tool. It is difficult for everyone to be challenged. Sometimes, when challenged, we become so overwhelmed that we cannot cope with this feeling, which may have happened to my client. This is something I might need to bring up at our next session. I hope he is ok, and I hope that our work together will help him deal with challenges more easily.

Both situations depicted the same incident, yet the reflective example went considerably deeper and resulted in different, more specific, and potentially more lasting improvements in therapeutic practice. When we are used to a descriptive assessment of situations we find ourselves in when we present a problem and then quickly conclude what we should do differently without a proper in-depth analysis, it is challenging to develop more meaningful practice. This is why models of reflections have been created to help us.

Table 2.1 An example of models for reflection used in education.

Citation	Content
Burke and Dempsey (2022)	The PAUSE model of reflection: Perceive-Audit-Understand-Substitute-Edify. The model is used for simultaneous reflection about self, clients, peers, scholarship, and system.
Bassot (2020)	Metaphorical mirrors: the bathroom mirror (reflecting on self), the rear-view mirror (reflecting back), the wing or side-view mirror (reflecting on feedback from others), the magnifying mirror (reflecting on detail), the funfair mirrors (reflection can be distorted), the shop window reflection (reflecting naturally while we are in practice).
Brookfield (2005)	Lens of their own autobiography as teachers and learners – Lens of students' eyes – Lens of colleagues' experiences – Lens of educational literature.
Johns (2002)	Reflection-influencing factors – Could I have dealt with it better – learning – description of the experience.
Rolfe, Freshwater, and Jasper (2001)	Reflexive Learning: What? – So what? – Now what?
Atkins and Murphy (1993)	Awareness – Describe the situation – Analyse feeling and knowledge – Evaluate the relevance of knowledge – Identify any learning.
Schoen (1987)	Reflection in action (during the event) and Reflection on action (after the event).
Gibbs (1988)	Description-Feelings-Evaluation-Analysis-Conclusion-Action Plan.
Kolb (1983)	Reflective Cycle: Concrete experience – Reflective observation – Abstract conceptualisation, Active experimentation.

They guide us through thinking and learning from our experiences, which can ultimately enrich our practice. Table 2.1 provides a list of the best-known reflective models that you can use to reflect on your experience in your final year assessment. Alternatively, you may apply the PAUSE model that we created specifically for reflecting throughout the journey of your research project. The PAUSE model of reflection is described in detail in the next section.

We encourage you to find out more about each model of reflection and identify which one speaks to you the loudest. Whichever model you choose, you need to feel comfortable with it, and it needs to serve you well. Learning about models will allow you to engage with your practice on a higher level and start noticing actions that have until now remained in your blind spot.

The PAUSE model of reflection

This model was created as an amalgamation of various models and upon the extensive experience of our reflective practice. It consists of a cyclical process that you can use to PAUSE and reflect on your daily experience. The word PAUSE is an anagram, which stands for P-perceive, A-audit, U-understand, S-substitute, E-edify. Each one of the PAUSE components is described in Table 2.2.

Table 2.2 The cyclic components of the PAUSE model of reflection.

PAUSE components	Explanation
Perceive	Become aware of the situation, notice what has been happening for you and your environment.
Audit	Analyse the situation in more detail.
Understand	Understand how and why the situation occurred and the rationale of all parties involved in it.
Substitute	Substitute your previous way of thinking with a new way of thinking based on the process of reflection in which you engaged.
Edify	Edify your practice by implementing what you choose to improve morally or intellectually.

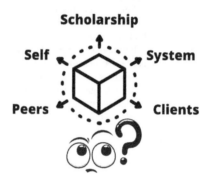

Figure 2.2 The PAUSE reference points for reflection.

At the heart of the model are the reference points for reflection adapted from Brookfield (2005), who asserts that our reflection should include:

1   Self, which relates to our internal experiences, autobiographies.
2   Students, meaning that we should reflect on how they perceive the world.
3   Peers, incorporating our colleagues' experiences.
4   Scholarship, which relates to the past literature, research-based practice.

However, we have replaced "students" with "clients" given that psychologists' perspective is wider than education professionals, for whom the model was created. Also, what was missing for us in Brookfield's model was the (5) system, which refers to the complex mechanism of the environment within which our work and organisation are placed. As a psychology professional, it is necessary to consider the context of systems and their usefulness for all parties involved. Therefore, we encourage you to follow a PAUSE process while reflecting on various reference points. For example, when auditing, look at the situation from multiple viewpoints – i.e. self, clients, peers, scholarship, and system. This comprehensive reflection will allow you to develop more meaningful practice. Figure 2.2 provides a pictorial representation of the PAUSE reference points.

The PAUSE model of reflection is an amalgamation of process and reference points, as illustrated in Figure 2.3. Please note the cyclical nature of the PAUSE model. Reflection is a continuous process and requires constant attention. Therefore, we continue to repeat the reflective activity over and over again. However, what is also important to remember is

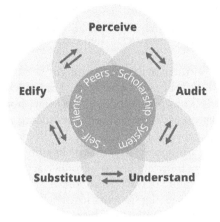

Figure 2.3 The PAUSE model of reflection.

that it is a fluid undertaking that often does not follow the order set in the PAUSE model because we go backwards and forwards through this process. Sometimes we skip a step, only to go back to it later. For example, after we reach the stage of substituting our past behaviour with new behaviour, we may go back and try to understand its impact on others. Equally, we may initially skip auditing and go straight into trying to understand why something happened and then go back to further audit it. Therefore, please practice flexibility when engaging with this model. Let us now go into each part of the model one by one.

PERCEIVE

Perceiving is about becoming aware and noticing the situation and its intricacies. We perceive it through the eyes of everyone involved in the process, be it ourselves, clients, peers, scholarship, and the system. Unless we can perceive the situation and view it from various points of reference, we cannot change our perspective. A changed attitude enriches our understanding and practice. Here is an example of how it works.

You, a trainee clinical psychologist, are shadowing a senior clinical psychologist who is carrying out an early intervention with a child diagnosed with autism. Halfway through the intervention, the child becomes distressed. The senior psychologist helps him calm down and, during a debrief, asks you to tell her what happened in the room. Your view is that the child became aware of his parents leaving the room, which upset him. The senior clinical psychologist's view is that the noise from the other room bothered him. This is what typically happens when two people witness the same event. They sometimes perceive it differently, depending on their knowledge or experiences.

Our brains are built to discern information essential to us and ignore what is not crucial. Perceiving everything in our environment would not be possible nor valuable, as it might lead to confusion, cognitive overload, and an inability to take action. What helps us ignore unimportant information is familiarisation. The more familiar we are with something, the less we notice it. So, we start taking it for granted. For example, two psychologists work with children in a school. Psychologist A works in a school where rarely ever there are behavioural issues with their students; psychologist B works in a school for children from disadvantaged backgrounds and dealing with behavioural problems of their students has become a norm. While psychologist A started to take their students' good behaviour for granted, psychologist B starts each day wondering what issues they will be dealing with today. If they spoke to each other, they might see the situations they are familiar with very differently. However, when reflecting, the trick is to recognise the familiarity on their own.

As psychologists reflect on their practice, they might work off autopilot, doing what they have been doing before, just because they are used to it. However, when they PAUSE and actively engage in reflection, psychologist A may start noticing her students' good behaviour, delving deeper into auditing it and understanding it, which may lead her to a conclusion that the good behaviour is a sign of groupthink, according to which people desire group conformity to such an extent that they find it challenging to think for themselves. This, in turn, may motivate her to introduce activities in the school that will encourage students to share unique perspectives about the topics discussed. On the other hand, psychologist B may start noticing students' negative behaviour despite being used to it. After a more profound process of reflection, he may focus on identifying the situations when students behave well and replicating them to improve students' behaviour. These are two examples of how the P of the PAUSE model can initiate a transformative process for educational psychologists who have stopped noticing common school behaviours.

AUDIT

The next step of the PAUSE model is to audit what we have perceived. Auditing refers to analysing our feelings, thoughts, and behaviours associated with them. When auditing our emotions, we need to consider the emotional impact of the situation on ourselves and other people involved, as per the PAUSE reference points we discussed. It is crucial to delve deeper into our emotions instead of simply stating the obvious. For example, we may feel upset, but what does upset feel like for us? Is it anger? Is it disappointment? Is it sadness? Is it hurt? Say that we go for hurt. We are upset because we are feeling hurt. We can also delve deeper into this emotion by trying to figure out why we feel hurt. Is it because we are jealous, betrayed, or perhaps rejected by others? Say we feel rejected. Now that we know we feel rejected, it is easier for us to do something about it, as we may be able to analyse our thoughts associated with feeling rejected. If we stayed at "feeling upset", we might not have realised that it was due to the rejection. Table 2.3 provides further examples of how to delve deeper into our emotions.

When analysing our thoughts about feeling rejected, we may notice that we blame our school leader for not intervening in a situation that has caused us upset. Instead of focusing on ourselves, our thoughts have taken us on a journey that puts a spotlight on a

Table 2.3 Going deeper into feelings. Adapted from David (2017).

Initial emotion	Deeper-level emotion
Sad	Disappointed – Regretful – Depressed – Disillusioned – Dismayed
Anxious	Afraid – Stressed – Worried – Cautious – Sceptical
Embarrassed	Guilty – Ashamed – Self-conscious – Inferior – Pathetic
Hurt	Jealous – Betrayed – Shocked – Victimised – Deprived
Angry	Frustrated – Grumpy – Defensive – Spiteful – Offended
Happy	Thankful – Excited – Relieved – Confident – Trusting

principal. "She is inconsiderate, and she is inexperienced, she is bad" – we are thinking – "I don't want to work for her anymore". As a result of these thoughts, we notice that we don't want to work there anymore. Now, we are auditing our emotions again, and anger has replaced our hurt, and we are feeling rejected.

Reflection time

Think about an emotion you felt this week and audit it. Maybe discuss your thinking with a friend or colleague as you try to make sense of it.

The next stage of the process, understanding, allows us to explain why the situation happened. Now that we know we feel rejected by our team and angry with our school leader for not intervening, we may try to put ourselves in their shoes and understand why people behaved the way they did. Perhaps they did not like our idea, and they dismissed it quickly. Or maybe it is the end of the week and everyone on the team, including the school leader, has a short fuse. As we dwell on the reasons for it and start feeling a little calmer and more understanding of the situation, we receive an email from the principal asking how we are. Regardless of the outcome of the situation, the process of auditing opens up a door for a deeper understanding, which can help us deal with situations differently.

Auditing allows us to take control of a situation and our reaction to it. We do it by labelling our emotions, considering our subsequent thoughts and automatic behaviours. According to cognitive behavioural therapy, these three processes are connected. When our feelings are negative, our thoughts become darker, leading to us behaving in ways that are not useful. For instance, when we feel rejected, we may think that our leader is useless, and consequently, we may march into their office the next day to offer our resignation. Lack of reflection may lead us to act on autopilot and out of control. However, when we PAUSE and start reflecting on a situation, we audit our emotions, audit our thoughts, and realise that selecting the behaviour we automatically feel like choosing might not be the best option. Pausing and auditing our thoughts can lead to a wiser decision. Even if the behaviour we displayed was not the most appropriate, auditing our emotions, thoughts and behaviours might lead to an alternative action that can undo the damage we created. This is how a PAUSE reflective model can put us in control of our lives.

This section discussed only one reference point – i.e. the situation from the self-perspective. However, auditing can relate to what we believe our clients or peers have felt or thought of. Also, we may do the same with the system, which does not have thoughts or feelings; however, it does take a life of its own. Actions cause reactions, and they can be edited in the personification of the system. For example, going back to the situation of feeling rejected, we may audit the processes available in the school that may prevent this situation from reoccurring. These processes may involve the policy, monitoring systems, or feedback processes that allow for an honest discussion between an employee and a leader.

UNDERSTAND

After noticing the situation and auditing it, the next step is to understand why it has occurred. This requires a deeper-level reflection that draws from our lifelong experience of similar situations. Understanding is about asking yourself why? Why did it occur? Because I allowed it to happen. Why did I let it happen? Because I didn't think about the consequences. Why did I not think about the implications? Because . . . This process of asking why can go as deep as you wish, and the deeper you go, the more life-changing experiences you may have with a PAUSE model for reflection.

Another way we can understand is by considering the motivation people have for doing what they do. Sometimes when two people are motivated by different things, they may clash, or a problematic situation may occur. It may be easier to understand why a crisis has happened by analysing people's motivation. There are many models of motivation; however, one that can be useful with the PAUSE model comes from the Choice Theory, according to which we have five genetically driven needs (1) survival, (2) love and belonging, (3) freedom, (4) fun, and (5) power (Glasser, 1999). We can explain our behaviour as a degree to which our needs were infringed upon. For example, when we feel rejected, we strongly need love and belonging, and our colleagues' actions make us feel isolated.

Similarly, the leader did not stand up for us, as she was driven by survival. She did not want to take sides. This model can help us understand the situation more effectively.

SUBSTITUTE

After we have audited our feelings, thoughts, behaviours and tried to understand why the situation happened, we may consider substituting our past thinking with new beliefs or our past behaviour with new behaviour. This stage indicates the outcome of our learning from this situation. For example, after analysing it thoroughly, we may decide that in the future, when our team does not take our idea on board, instead of getting upset and refusing to offer any more suggestions, we will continue engaging with our team and stop taking any such refusal to heart. After all, our feeling of isolation came from a deep need to belong, and as soon as we felt this way, we stopped talking and withdrew. However, everyone on the team can suggest ideas, but not all ideas will be taken on board. Next time, we try to come up with several ideas and not take them as a personal affront when colleagues don't select our suggestions.

In this step of the PAUSE model of reflection, we need to consider substituting our initial thoughts and feelings with more valuable ideas. The initial reaction was formed as a consequence of autopilot. A decision about a substitute reaction is due to the process of self-reflection. These substitute thoughts, feelings, and behaviours will lead us to different results, and to do it, we need to be clear as to what they are.

EDIFY

In the final stage of the PAUSE model of reflection, we need to edify – i.e. implement the change we set out to action. All change will be difficult until it becomes a habit. Yet, it sometimes takes many weeks to develop a habitual behaviour. This is why edifying the difference and reflecting further upon it is the final part and the beginning part of the process, which continues to cycle as we learn.

Whether you choose to engage in the PAUSE model of reflection or any other models of reflection, your ultimate objective is to help you improve your professional practice. When describing the PAUSE model, we have used as an example a situation at work, which you reflect on to help you change your future behaviour. However, this model can be used at all stages of completing your research project. For example, you may reflect on various incidents in professional practice in this manner to help you decide on the topic of your interest. You may also reflect on the process of your research using this model. Finally, you may use the model to help you develop a list of implications for practice as you review your research findings or the literature you have read. Whatever your intention, the PAUSE model can help you engage in your research project practice and enrich your outcomes.

2.2 Making choices

As you are preparing to carry out your research project, you will need to make many choices. These choices will involve selecting a topic of enquiry, the literature you read and choose to use, the research design, methods, and many other important decisions. It is sometimes overwhelming for students to make these choices. Here are a few things you need to remember about making choices that can help you move smoothly towards your research project completion.

2.2.1 Reduce your expectations

All research has limitations, and as researchers, we need to reduce them but cannot eliminate them. This is why, no matter what choices you make, they will not be perfect, as it is not perfection we are looking for, but a *good enough* approach to designing a research project. Therefore, as you make your choices, try and reflect on what alternatives you have and whether they are doable with the resources you have at your disposal. If not, consider it a limitation of your study and recommend that future research consider a different approach. Remember, there are no perfect research designs, participants, or approaches to analysis. All research has its limitations.

2.2.2 Reduce your choices

It is suitable for us to have choices, but too many of them make us unhappy and prevent us from making decisions (Schwartz, 2004). An ability to decide is essential when designing a research project. Your choices for the project are almost limitless. If you try and explore all possibilities before making a decision, you will be stuck in an indecisive limbo, unable to move on. Worse yet, you may also regret the choices you have already made (Schwartz et al., 2002), which distract you from what is essential when completing your research project. When you start experiencing challenges halfway through your research, you may regret the topic you selected or a specific design, wondering what it would be like if you took another direction. We have had students who wanted to change their topic a month before their submission, as they felt they had made the wrong decision about it. This is why it is essential to reduce your choices. Here is how we help our students do it:

- When you can't make up your mind about a topic, spend a week searching the literature and come up with your top three choices, which are good enough. Remember that you are not changing the world with your research project, just adding to your practice. If you are having difficulty doing it, write a list of seven to ten choices and come up with your criteria based on what is important to you. For example, you may be guided by your interest, so on a scale from 1–10, evaluate each choice and then select the three topics that have scored the highest. Or, your criteria may be based on how useful they are for your work, how easy they are to do, how much they can help you become a confident professional. First, you need to figure out your criteria, which will help you narrow it down.

- To narrow down your topics from three to one, it is helpful to consider the research design that would be most applicable to each of your topics and then reflect on your access to participants. Say you are trying to decide whether to evaluate an existing wellbeing programme for children or explore the wellbeing of children. The first option calls for an experimental design and focuses on accessing children. If you don't have access to children, this option is automatically out. On the other hand, the second option calls for a quantitative survey or an interview. For the survey option, you will need at least 100 individuals to participate, whereas, for an interview, you will need between five to ten. Depending on your access to participants, you may select one option or another.

- When you can't make up your mind about your research design, start with some basics. Do you want to do a desk-based or empirical study? Say you choose empirical research. Do you like words (qualitative) or numbers (quantitative)? Say you choose qualitative research, decide how objective or subjective you would like your study to be, and select your three main options from the spectrum we provided in this book. Read about these three approaches and make sure you understand the process and differences between them. Now, write pros and cons for them concerning you and the topic of your enquiry, and choose one approach you think will be good enough for your research project. Dividing your decision into binary or at least limited options will help you cope with the number of choices you need to make.

- When you spend too much time reviewing academic databases and are taken off the beaten track with your enquiry, set up a time limit for yourself – e.g. I will spend three hours exploring this topic and then move to the next one. Otherwise, the abundance of articles in the academic database may seem overwhelming.

2.3 Research-based practice

An essential component of a research project is its implication for practice. When completing a project, the skills you will develop will help you become research-based or evidence-based practitioners. Training research shows a weak connection between the knowledge gained in initial education and professional practice (Jakhelln et al., 2021). This means that many practitioners, despite engaging in further education, cannot tap into the resource that research offers. One of the objectives of a research project is to help practitioners use research in their work and feel comfortable doing it.

This is a difficult skill to learn, as we often draw our practice from the habits developed through our initial training and what we observed others doing. Yet, research keeps growing year on year. There may be tens, hundreds, or even thousands of academic journal papers published on any given topic of your interest. The ability to tap into this incredible resource allows us to continue growing after completing our initial education.

When we think about research, there is often a trilemma of three different worlds and how they speak to each other. On the one hand, you have the researchers who may be very knowledgeable in one specific area, for example, psychological assessment practices, but not knowledgeable about the intricacies of the environment in which their clients work or live. On the other hand, you may have policymakers who want to change mental health; however, they may not be familiar with the research in the area. Finally, you have the psychology practitioners navigating the complexity of daily practice as they enact policy (McKenney and Reeves, 2019). Research projects seek to link these worlds and, in doing so, impact practice. All problems are multifaceted, and often no one theory can encompass the variety of factors that must be considered.

All the skills you learn when working on your research project prepare you to engage with research-based practice. However, for this skill to be honed, you need to apply research in practice. There are many barriers to doing this (Snell, 2003; Hewitt-Taylor et al., 2012). For example, access to a journal is not available for some people, or they find it difficult to understand an academic paper. Further on in the book, we will give you a few tips on reading scholarly articles to get the best out of them. Other reasons include the demands of time. Professionals are busy, so devoting weekly time to learning about the research and its potential application is a challenge. We hope that the research project practice will help you hone your skills to such an extent that this process will become easier and more accessible to you so that it will not take too much of your time. Finally, another important obstacle to a research-based practice is the lack of professionals' confidence in applying what they have read to practice. Critical thinking that you develop as part of the research project will hopefully help you overcome this obstacle, as you will be more confident about the new research you read. Let us now delve deeper into this crucial skill.

2.4 Critical thinking

One of the primary skills that third-level education helps students develop is critical thinking. It is a concept that is easily misunderstood. You can use it when reviewing your literature, designing your research project, or when you write about it. To simplify it, let us consider it the process of wearing magical hats. Your attitude, behaviour, and outcomes change every time you put them on. To best illustrate it, let us imagine you describe your work as a psychologist to someone. You can do it in a descriptive, positive, negative, or critical way.

When you put on a descriptive hat, you talk about the work you do as a process – e.g. as a psychologist, I carry out the following tasks daily, a, b, and c. When you put on a positive hat, you talk about all the beautiful things about our job. When you put on a negative hat, you share some of your disappointments about the job. However, when you put on a critical hat, you offer a more balanced and objective perspective on your job. Figure 2.4 provides a depiction of the thinking hats. The same applies to your research project, reading the literature about your topic of interest, or writing your project.

| Descriptive | Positive | Negative | Critical |

Figure 2.4 Thinking hats.

When you review the literature, you may write it descriptively, whereby you tell the readers all the interesting literature you have read one by one. You focus on passing on information without much reflection about it. You describe one text after another and let the readers draw their conclusions. Here is an example of writing a literature review with a descriptive hat on:

> Smith (2019) claimed that critical thinking is one of the most difficult skills for students to learn. Murphy (2020) said this might be due to a lack of understanding about what it means to be critical. Williams (2018) explained that the reason for it might be due to the way it is introduced at third level.

Therefore, in the previous example, a student merely described what they have read and summarised its main points. One text follows another. Even if the thoughts and ideas are well organised, the student's voice is not evident from it, nor is there any evidence of reflection on the read material.

When you put on a positive hat, you take on board everything you read and believe in its merits without any doubts. You follow a fallible logic according to which "if it is written by an academic, it must be true". However, as you engage with the literature on any topic, you will see that academics have many different views they argue. Therefore, for one topic, you may have many perspectives, theories, models. When reviewing the literature, you need to acknowledge various perspectives and find the rationale for selecting the most applicable one to your research. Reading texts and writing about them with a positive hat on will not capture the complexity of the matter. Here is an example of writing a literature review with a positive hat on:

> According to Smith (2019), a literature review requires critical thinking. Unfortunately, it isn't easy for students to think critically. The author says it is a skill, and students find it difficult to develop. The author also warns that if students want to develop it, they need to work hard on it.

This is an example of a literature review carried out by a student who describes what they have read and fully believes it to be true without coming up with any counterarguments. There is no critical thinking involved in writing these statements, and the student takes it for granted that whatever the researcher wrote must be true.

In contrast, we may put a negative hat on, whereby we decide we do not like a specific topic and want to provide evidence for its shortcomings through our lectures. We, therefore, go on a journey of finding fault in everything that the authors published about it, without much balance. Even though we are being critical, we do not practice critical thinking, as we see only one side of a story. Critical thinking, however, is about being objective and making rational conclusions from the literature we have read. Here is an example of a literature review written with a critical hat:

> Literature review is a complex process that requires critical thinking (Smith, 2019). Students find critical thinking challenging for various reasons, such as the lack of understanding of what it means or inadequate introduction to critical thinking at the third level (Murphy, 2020; Williams, 2018). However, some have expressed ease of engaging in critical thinking when certain foundations are established (Bryan, 2009). The differences in students' critical thinking skills need to be considered when designing a programme.

In this example, we can see that a student has thought of creating an argument and reflected on patterns of the literature he has read and their relationship to each other. Section 4.2.3 provides further information about critical engagement with literature.

2.5 Project management

Another vital skill that you will develop further during your research project completion is managing a project. Depending on your educational institution, you may have less than one academic year to design and execute your project or as much as two or three years to do it. Regardless of the time you have, the project's complexity makes it challenging for many students.

GRIT is your ability to persevere and keep your interest going over a prolonged period (Duckworth et al., 2007). GRIT helps you regain your motivation for the project when it keeps dwindling and put effort into it to progress it. While some of us are naturally gritty, and a project like this comes easy to us, others may need a little bit of help. Based on our former students' experiences, we will share some ideas illustrating what you can do to keep your interest going.

- Regular meetings with your supervisor or a study group. Nothing can help you motivate yourself better than other people. Supervisors are helpful to bounce ideas off and help us deal with challenges. Study groups are also instrumental. We compare our progress to others, and when we feel we are falling behind, we put in more effort to catch up. We listen to the peer group challenges and see that we are not on our own. Also, if we get stuck on one stage of the project, we may ask others for advice which will help us keep going. Most importantly, however, knowing that our meeting is coming up soon motivates us to dust off our last meeting notes and try to make some, albeit minor, progress before our encounter. Organising regular meetings with others can help you keep the project progressing.
- A Project Plan is yet another tool in your toolbox that can help you succeed at a research project. Try to spend some time drawing up a plan of what you need to complete to meet your deadline. Some say that we need to start from the end and work backwards. Figure out your submission date, list all the steps you need to complete, and figure out how many weeks you have for each step. It is always helpful to add some extra time to your steps, so you will still have the time to complete the project if you run over. Also, if you know that you will have some time off during the academic year during which you can focus on the project, it is helpful to incorporate the workload around your calendar. Drawing up a plan may take some time, but it is suitable for many reasons. Firstly, it gives you peace of mind when you know you have it all under control. Secondly, as your milestones approach, your body will subconsciously react to the deadline, making you feel you need to put more effort to make it or review your deadlines. Finally, it will stop you from meandering and staying too long on some parts of your project. Not planning your research project is like heading into the mountains without a map. Chances are, you may get lost or miss your deadline.
- Procrastination is not helpful when completing a research project; therefore, you need to ensure you reduce it as much as possible. There are four different approaches you take towards achieving a long-term project: (1) planning, (2) procrastination, (3) trifling, and (4) incubation (Biswas-Diener, 2010). Most good students choose

to plan, strategise and start working on their long-term projects immediately. On the other hand, procrastinators put off their work until the last minute. Usually, they produce mediocre quality work, and often, their excuse is that they did not have the time to come up with something of high quality. Triflers are students who start immediately and are highly motivated to complete the project, but as it progresses, they lose interest. They are similar to those whose GRIT is not high, and due to their lost focus, they tend to come up with mediocre quality of work. Finally, some students completing a research project are incubators. This means that they behave like procrastinators in that they tend to put their work off until the last minute and need deadlines to motivate them. However, unlike procrastinators, they do not bury their heads in the sand and pretend they do not have a research project to complete; instead, they think a lot about it, even though they start writing and producing work later in the process.

This incubation allows them to come up with great ideas, which are then further developed as the project continues. Due to the incubation period, they often produce high-quality work, which is sometimes better than the planner's output.

Of all the students, procrastinators fare the worst. This is why we need to do everything in our power to notice we are procrastinating and do something to stop it. There are many reasons for procrastination. We do it sometimes because we are disorganised, and planning is not our strength, meaning that we don't know where to start. If you are in this situation, ask someone to help you plan your project and offer you some ideas. Alternatively, you can do it yourself. Later in the book, we provide you with Figure 3.60, which provides a step-by-step process for completing a research project. Each part of the process can be your milestone, and you need to decide how much time for each step you have.

Sometimes we procrastinate because we are afraid we will not do well in our project. This is a typically fixed mindset attitude, whereby we associate our successes with who we are (Dweck, 2006). If we don't do well, we may think we are not intelligent enough or not talented enough. What would people think?! Self-sabotaging, such as procrastination, will give us an excuse for not being good. We can tell everyone: "If only I had more time, I'd do better". When this is your reason for procrastination, start seeing your project not as an evaluation of who you are but as an opportunity to master your skills. You are not good at it YET, so you need to practice. Research projects are less related to your talent and much more to the hours you put in. Your effort will give you the best results. Focus on the process, not the outcome. Research projects are a process that helps you develop your skills and improve your practice.

Reflection time

Of all the skills discussed in this chapter, which ones will come easy to you, and which ones will you need to put more effort into to develop? What steps will you take over the next few weeks to do it? How can you use your strengths to help you achieve them?

Recap time

This chapter discussed some of the skills you require for completing your research project. One of the most important ones is reflection. We provided you with a list of reflective models that can help you reflect effectively on your practice and project. We also introduced you to our PAUSE model for reflection, which includes the following steps: Perceive, Audit, Understand, Substitute, Edify. We encourage you to reflect in the context of self, clients, peers, scholarship, and system. We then listed a range of tips that can help you make choices, engage in research-based practice, critical thinking, and project management. Finally, we asked you to reflect on which one of the skills required to carry out your research project needs more effort to develop.

References

Atkins, S., and K. Murphy. 1993. "Reflection: A Review of the Literature." *Journal of Advanced Nursing* (Wiley-Blackwell) 18(8): 1188–1192. doi: 10.1046/j.1365-2648.1993.18081188.x.

Bassot, B. 2020. *The Reflective Journal.* 3rd ed. London: Macmillan Education.

Biswas-Diener, R. 2010. *Practicing Positive Psychology Coaching: Assessment, Activities, and Strategies for Success.* Hoboken, NJ: John Wiley & Sons Inc.

Brookfield, S. 2005. *Becoming a Critically Reflective Teacher.* San Francisco: Jossey-Bass.

Burke, J., and M. Dempsey. 2022. *Undertaking Capstone Projects in Education: A Practical Guide for Students.* Abingdon: Routledge.

David, S. 2017. *Emotional Agility: Get Unstuck, Embrace Change and Thrive in Work and Life.* London: Penguin Books Ltd.

Duckworth, A.L., C. Peterson, M.D. Matthews, and D.R. Kelly. 2007. "Grit: Perseverance and Passion for Long-Term Goals." *Journal of Personality and Social Psychology* 92(6): 1087–1101. doi: 10.1037/0022-3514.92.6.1087.

Dweck, C.S. 2006. *Mindset: The New Psychology of Success.* New York: Random House.

Eisner, E. 2003. "Educational Connoisseurship and Educational Criticism: An Arts-Based Approach to Educational Evaluation." In *International Handbook of Educational Evaluation. Kluwer International Handbooks of Education,* edited by T. Kellaghan and D.L. Stufflebeam. Dordrecht: Springer.

Gibbs, G. 1988. *Learning by Doing: A Guide to Teaching and Learning Methods.* London: Further Education Unit.

Glasser, W. 1999. *Choice Theory: A New Psychology of Personal Freedom.* New York: HarperPerennial.

Hewitt-Taylor, J., V. Heaslip, and N.E. Rowe. 2012. "Applying Research to Practice: Exploring the Barriers." *British Journal of Nursing* 21(6): 356–359. doi: 10.12968/bjon.2012.21.6.356.

Jakhelln, R., G. Eklund, J. Aspfors, K. Bjørndal, and G. Stølen. 2021. "Newly Qualified Teachers' Understandings of Research-based Teacher Education Practices–Two Cases From Finland and Norway." *Scandinavian Journal of Educational Research* 65(1): 123–139. doi: 10.1080/00313831.2019.1659402.

Johns, C. 2002. *Guided Reflection: Advancing Practice.* Oxford: Blackwell Science.

Kolb, D.A. 1983. *Experiential Learning: Experience as the Source of Learning and Development.* Englewood Cliffs, NJ: Prentice Hall.

McKenney, S., and T. Reeves. 2019. *Conducting Educational Design Research.* 2nd ed. Abingdon: Routledge.

Rolfe, G., D. Freshwater, and M. Jasper. 2001. *Critical Reflection in Nursing and the Helping Professions: A User's Guide.* Basingstoke, UK: Palgrave Macmillan.

Schoen, D. 1987. *Educating the Reflective Practitioner.* San Francisco: Jossey-Bass.

Schwartz, B. 2004. *The Paradox of Choice: Why More Is Less.* New York: HarperCollins.

Schwartz, B., A. Ward, and S. Lyubomirsky. 2002. "Maximizing versus Satisficing: Happiness is a Matter of Choice." *Journal of Personality & Social Psychology* 83(5): 1178–1197. doi: 10.1037/0022-3514.83.5.1178.

Snell, M.E. 2003. "Applying Research to Practice: The More Pervasive Problem?" *Research & Practice for Persons with Severe Disabilities* 28(3): 143–147. doi: 10.2511/rpsd.28.3.143.

3 Getting ready, set, go

3.1 Empirical vs desk-based

There are two types of research projects that you can develop: an empirical project and a desk-based project (Deepamala and Shobha, 2018). Empirical projects refer to projects carried out in a real-life environment with participants, so in designing your research, you need to make sure that it follows the ethical guidelines of your educational institution. Empirical projects create new data, test theories, and apply knowledge. On the other hand, desk-based projects can be carried out in the comfort of your home, without involvement from any participants. The main objective is to review existing data or theories and make new meanings. Table 3.1 lists the characteristics of empirical and desk-based projects.

Reflection time

What are the advantages and disadvantages of empirical and desk-based projects? Which one are you more attracted to?

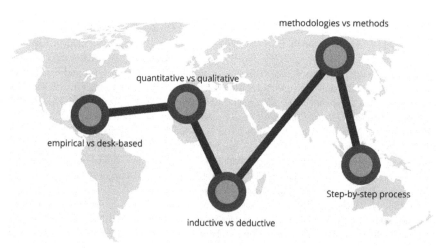

Figure 3.1 The map of the journey we will take in this chapter.

DOI: 10.4324/9781003262428-3

Table 3.1 Characteristics of empirical and desk-based studies.

Empirical	*Desk-based*
Participant involvement	No participants
Ethical review necessary	No ethical review required
Test and create theories	Create theories
Apply knowledge	Gather knowledge
Create new data	Make new meaning of existing literature and data

3.2 Quantitative vs qualitative

Quantitative research refers to research that concerns numbers. Specifically, it aims to quantify participants' attitudes, opinions, and behaviours and analyse numerical patterns from data. For example, you may carry out a survey that assesses employees' attitudes towards applying positive leadership. You ask them to answer a series of questions designed for them and then analyse their trend response. Your data may show that the vast majority of them (93%) have heard of positive leadership; however, half of the participants (52%) have difficulty understanding its practical applications. From your data, you may conclude that more clarity is needed about the concepts, and your implications may include designing a programme, training event, or intervention that aims to provide employees with case studies and other practical examples of how authentic leadership is used effectively in organisations. This is an example of how a short quantitative survey may be designed for a research project.

On the other hand, qualitative research refers to the narrative, observations, and visual (non-numerical) data. You try to understand how participants behave in their context. It involves the researchers collecting data using qualitative methods such as interviews, focus groups, observations, and art-based research to build an understanding of a phenomenon in context. In qualitative research, you analyse data by categorising it and organising it into patterns that produce a descriptive, narrative synthesis. For example, you might want to look at how leaders communicate with their teams. You observe a small number of leaders over time. In your observations, you note the number of times leaders ask questions and the number of times they tell their team what to do. Next, you video team meetings and analyse the video and observation notes looking for patterns in practice. You then interview each leader about their experiences. In this way, you build up a narrative about how leaders communicate with their staff and how effective their communication is. Many research projects use a mix of both quantitative and qualitative methods.

Reflection time

What would interest you more:

- Searching for patterns in numbers? Why/why not?
- Reading transcripts of interviews? Why/why not?

3.3 Inductive vs deductive

Inductive and deductive approaches refer to our search for understanding. We all view the world differently; therefore, we use various ways to understand what is happening around us. We take deductive, inductive, and hybrid inductive-deductive approaches (Cohen et al., 2018).

The deductive reasoning approach derives from Aristotle. It helps us argue our stance by firstly stating our view (hypothesis) and then providing an example of it and making a conclusion. For example, say that my view is that cognitive behavioural therapy (CBT) is helpful. Given that CBT is a therapeutic approach, I conclude that therapy must be beneficial (Figure 3.2). Or, I further make a generic statement about therapy being helpful, then provide examples showing that it has helped many clients change their attitudes; therefore, I may conclude that therapy changes attitudes.

Another type of reasoning used mainly in qualitative research is inductive logic, meaning that we provide several facts that create a hypothesis (Figure 3.3). Again, going back to the CBT example, we can conclude that therapy is beneficial by providing several examples of the usefulness of CBT and other therapeutic approaches such as Solution-Focused Therapy (SFT) and, from them, concluding that therapy is helpful. Therefore, the steps for inductive reasoning include (1) example, (2) example, (3) conclusion.

The hybrid inductive-deductive approach is an amalgamation of both, whereby examples follow presuppositions, and then, if necessary, the hypotheses are revised (Figure 3.4). Therefore, in our therapy example, we may start our inquiry by stating that therapy is beneficial, provide an example that CBT is part of therapy, and instead of concluding that therapy is helpful, we may note that there is evidence that some types of therapies are useful

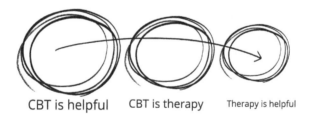

CBT is helpful   CBT is therapy   Therapy is helpful

Figure 3.2 An example of deductive logic.

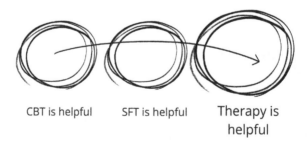

CBT is helpful   SFT is helpful   Therapy is helpful

Figure 3.3 An example of inductive logic.

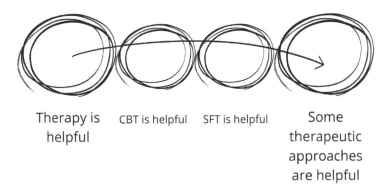

Therapy is helpful   CBT is helpful   SFT is helpful   Some therapeutic approaches are helpful

Figure 3.4 An example of the inductive-deductive approach.

Reflection time

Which approach do you usually use for viewing the world? Consider an argument you have recently had with someone. What were the differences in your reasoning?

Inductive and deductive reasoning is also applied in the research process. In deductive research, you are testing an existing theory, while in inductive research, you are trying to develop a theory. The steps in inductive research are usually (1) observation, (2) searching for a pattern, and from this, (3) you develop a theory. With deductive reasoning, you start with an existing theory, formulate a hypothesis based on that theory, collect data to test the hypothesis of your theory, and analyse the results to see if the results support or reject the hypothesis. While researchers mainly select either an inductive or deductive research approach, combining both inductive and deductive reasoning in one research project is not uncommon. Figure 3.5 provides a summary of inductive and deductive research approaches.[

3.4 Methodologies vs methods

As you continue on your research journey, you may come across the concepts of methodology and methods, which some students find confusing. Methodologies refer to the collection of research design approaches you use to complete your research project. This includes your overall research design, what data you have retained and excluded, if your study is empirical, who your participants are, your ethical considerations when working with them, and what data you collect and analyse. All this information falls under the category of methodology.

On the other hand, a method is just one component of methodology, as it is a tool and procedure for collecting and analysing your data in an empirical project. For example, you

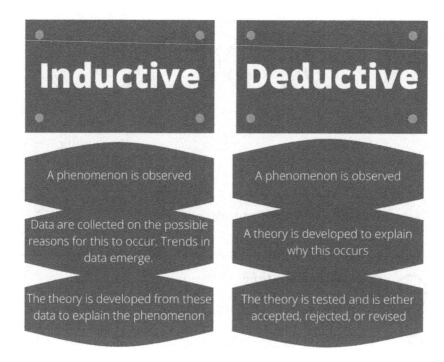

Figure 3.5 Characteristics of inductive and deductive research.

may choose to design a quantitative research project (methodology) and collect your data using a questionnaire (method). Alternatively, you may decide to do a qualitative project (methodology) and collect your data through focus groups (method). For more information about methods, go to Chapter 7.

3.5 Step-by-step process

In order to make life easier for you, we divided the process of a research project completion into four easy steps (Figure 3.6). By the end of each step, you will be able to achieve the following:

- Step 1: create the contours of your interests and decide on your research question.
- Step 2: design your research project.
- Step 3: collect and analyse your data.
- Step 4: present your project and artefact (if applicable).

In step one, you will need to identify a list of potential interests you have and, after reflecting on them, narrow it down to your topic. Then, you will be asked to scope the literature about the topic of your interest and make sense of it. Finally, you will write up the research question to guide your research project.

In step two, you will attempt to design your research project by figuring out your positioning. Then, we will guide you through a range of approaches to carrying out an

Step-By-Step Process

FOR CAPSTONE PROJECTS.

STEP 1: **THE INTEREST**	**TOPIC CHOICE**	**LITERATURE SCOPING**	**RESEARCH QUESTION**
STEP 2: **THE DESIGN**	**POSITIONING**	**RESEARCH DESIGN SPECTRUM**	**METHODS**
STEP 3: **THE ANALYSIS** **(EMPIRICAL ONLY)**	**ETHICS**	**DATA GATHERING**	**DATA ANALYSIS**
STEP 4: **THE PRESENTATION**	**ARTEFACT DEVELOPMENT (OPTIONAL)**	**CONTRIBUTION TO KNOWLEDGE & PRACTICE**	**PRESENTATION (ORAL OR WRITTEN)**

Figure 3.6 Step-by-step process for completing research projects.

empirical or desk-based project. In the end, you will decide what options you want to take on board and why. Finally, we will introduce you to various methods you can use in your project.

Step three is relevant to you only if you are interested in an empirical study. Firstly, we will review some of the ethical considerations when working with human participants in detail. We will then delve into the process of gathering data and analysing it.

In the final step, four, we will introduce you to a range of artefacts that you can create as part of your research project. Next, we will discuss ways to review your implications for practice, regardless of whether your project was empirical or desk-based. Finally, we will delve deeper into the process of presenting your project as part of your assessment and after that.

Reflection time

At first glance, which part of the step-by-step process do you find most challenging and why? What can you do to ease your research project journey?

Recap time

This chapter has clarified some of the main concepts you need to know when embarking on a research project. Firstly, we reviewed the differences between empirical and desk-based research. Secondly, we contrasted quantitative and qualitative research. Thirdly, we explained the difference between inductive and deductive research and methodologies and methods. Finally, we introduced you to the step-by-step process for conducting research projects in psychology. We will follow this structure throughout the remainder of the book.

References

Cohen, L., L. Manion, and K. Morrison. 2018. *Research Methods in Education*. Abingdon, UK: Routledge.

Deepamala, N., and G. Shobha. 2018. "Effective Approach in Making Capstone Project a Holistic Learning Experience to Students of Undergraduate Computer Science Engineering Program." *Journal of Technology and Science Education* 8(4): 420–438.

4 The interest

Some educational institutions help students narrow their interests by specifying which aspect of psychology to focus on. For example, in a psychotherapy course, the focus of students' research projects may be applying a specific therapeutic approach, which the school of psychotherapy recommends. In a work/organisational psychology programme, the project may relate to a case study in an organisation. Every educational institution is different, which is why, when selecting a topic and subsequent research questions, you need to identify the parameters within which your institution allows you to work and then explore your options.

4.1 Topic choice

There are three main approaches to selecting a topic for your research project:

1   Inward deficit approach
2   Outward deficit approach
3   Inward abundance approach
4   Outward abundance approach
5   Hybrid approach (mix of two or more approaches)

4.1.1 Inward deficit approach

Reflect on your practice (inward) and identify some of the challenges and problems (deficits) you experience. For example, if you are still in training and have not yet had an opportunity to practice, you may reflect on which part of the course content is most challenging for you or which one you don't know enough about and would like to explore further. Alternatively, you may consider the feedback you've been given about an aspect

Figure 4.1 Outline of chapter 4.

DOI: 10.4324/9781003262428-4

Table 4.1 Examples of inward deficit approach for selecting a topic.

Example of problems/challenges	Possible topic
I am struggling to say "no" to people. When they ask me to help them, I do it, even if it doesn't suit me. Afterwards, I resent them and beat myself up for agreeing to it.	Assertiveness
I feel a little out of place in the canteen. All my colleagues have worked with each other for a long time. They created little groups to which I don't feel I belong. I want to find out how I can join an in-group.	Building relationships at work
I struggle to pass on to my students the passion I have for maths. They don't seem to engage with the activities as enthusiastically as I would. I want to come up with a way of introducing maths that would make them feel more interested in it.	Teaching methods
I need to learn how to stay quiet. I tend to fill spaces, and I'm anxious every time the client becomes silent, so I say something nervously after a few seconds, which feel like minutes.	Giving clients space
I often feel exhausted. I go home and crash on my sofa. I would like to find out what I can do to mind myself better to have the energy to have a life after work.	Wellbeing

of your practice that you need to improve on. Whatever your starting point is, the objective of this approach is to identify issues and allow your research project to address them. Table 4.1 provides examples of some of the challenges you may experience at work and research project topics associated with them.

Reflection time

For the next few weeks, reflect daily on the challenges you are experiencing in your job/education programme. Read them back at the end of the week and identify one topic that you may wish to explore further as your research project.

4.1.2 Outward deficit approach

Examine some of the issues (deficits) that your colleagues are experiencing in their practice or the gaps in research findings you have read about in academic papers or books (outward) related to educational practice. The outward nature of this type of topic selection means that your research project does not aim to help you in your practice. Instead, its purpose is to help other educators with their practice. Table 4.2 provides examples of sources you can use when searching for a topic of an outward deficit research project.

Each of the sources provides you with rich information about the issues educators experience and potential solutions to them. Watch out for the most frequently reoccurring issues, and once you find them reflect on how they would help you in your practice. This type of approach to finding a topic can indirectly impact your practice. This is also a typical approach to quick literature search used in the traditional thesis (Wilson, 2015).

Table 4.2 Information sources for carrying out a literature search. Adapted from Wilson (2015).

Source	Purpose
Fellow psychologists	Listen carefully to their discussions for any exciting issues they have mentioned or challenges. Is there any topic of a debate you find particularly attractive?
Social media (Twitter, Facebook, blogs, etc.)	Start following some of the influencers or organisations that discuss or mention topics that may interest you to develop further.
The media (TV, radio, podcasts)	Search for an interesting discussion about some of the contemporary issues in psychology, which your research project could further explore.
Professional organisations (magazines, websites, pictures, conferences)	Communication from any professional organisations that invite guests and speak of some of the topical issues and their limitations may be a great source of information when exploring a potential topic of your research project.
Academic sources (journal papers, books)	Searching for an academic database is yet another source of information that can help you identify both a topic of your research and make choices about your methodology.

Reflection time

For the next few weeks, engage with all the resources at your disposal and make a list of the most interesting topics you have come across. Then, reflect on how researching these topics can help you improve your practice.

4.1.3 Inward abundance approach

Another approach to identifying what you wish to study is the abundance approach, which focuses on what is working in psychology instead of what is problematic and needs fixing (Cameron and Lavine, 2006; Cooperrider et al., 2018). This perspective is very different to the deficit process, which is concerned with problems in psychology. You can use the abundance approach to review other people's practice (outwardly), your practice (inwardly), or as a hybrid approach (inwardly and outwardly). Given that "bad is stronger than good" (Baumeister et al., 2001), this is a less natural process of inquiry, which is why we need a model to help us work through it.

The most prevalent abundance model comes from the Appreciative Inquiry (AI), parts of which are recommended to use in research (Shuayb et al., 2009). We have tweaked it to best suit the topic selection for your research project for this exercise. In step one, we review best practices and consider what is working well, what we do, or what other practitioners do that gives us positive outcomes. In step two, we focus on a specific best practice and identify the resources (people, actions, props, etc.) that contributed to its success. In step three, we create an image of the best-case scenario. Finally, we select a topic that best helps us get there in step four. Figure 4.2 provides a pictorial representation of this approach.

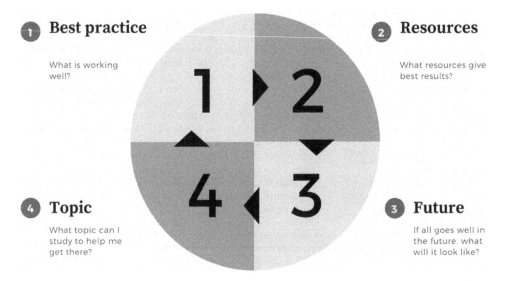

Figure 4.2 An abundance model of reflection to identify a research project topic.

The reason this approach may be more effective for some is that recent research demonstrates that when working on a project, too much focus on a problem may slow down progress (Pavez, 2017), whereas focusing on what is working well helps us acknowledge our strengths and build upon them more effectively. Furthermore, given that a research project is based on research-based practice, we must maximise, not reduce, our potential. Also, when our starting point is what is going well, our research may lead to more impactful outcomes than our focus on fixing (minimal effort) what is not working well.

Here is what the inward abundance approach looks like in research:

Best Practice: You reflect on your knowledge, experience, or long-term practice using a reflective journal. As part of your reflection process, you complete a character strengths assessment (www.viacharacter.org) and realise that one of your top character strengths is "perspective". This means that you are particularly good at seeing the same situation from different viewpoints, whereby other people might not have the same cognitive flexibility to consider it. So you decide to create a project which allows you to use your strength of perspective.

Resources: Upon further reflection, you realise that what often helps you consider a situation from various viewpoints is standing in front of a whiteboard and letting your imagination run wild. You start by coming up with unrelated ideas, creating a mindmap, and slowly, you organise them into succinct perspectives. You also realise that you enjoy completing this process independently and with classical music playing in the background. You will make sure that when the time comes, you will replicate this environment to help you maximise the use of your strength of perspective.

Future: If all went well, your project would therefore involve perspectives. You could either take one topic, say "wellbeing", and design a research project considering various perspectives. Perhaps a multidisciplinary review of wellbeing would inform your psychological practice. Alternatively, you could develop a project that studies the topic of views. You could identify various evidence-based approaches in exploring perspectives and test their effectiveness with clients, which would provide you with practical tools to teach others something that comes naturally to you.

Topic: You, therefore, select the topic of assessing the effectiveness of three tools (to be confirmed) that help individuals view situations from various perspectives.

4.1.4 Outward abundance approach

In the previous section, we reviewed ways to use an inward abundance model of reflection to identify your topic. You can apply the exact process for the outward-focused topic selection.

Here is what the outward abundance approach looks like in research:

Best Practice: As part of your health psychology degree, you have read a lot about how to help individuals change their habits to engage in healthy eating. You realise that there is a lot of good research about this topic, which taps into various aspects of behavioural change. There is so much variety, maybe because not one size fits all. To design your research project, you would like to explore this pluralism of healthy eating. Some of the more recent theories of healthy eating employ an integration of various approaches. You would like to tap into them. Also, you realise that changing a habit is not enough and you need to help clients maintain their newly altered routine, so you would like to consider this too.

Resources: Experience showed you that the best way to start exploring different models is by reading a recent book that reviews models of change. This is one resource you can use. Concerning the approaches you can apply, another thing that worked in the past is to inquire with your family and friends what had worked for them when they were trying to eat more healthy food. You decide you would use both approaches when exploring this topic.

Future: By the end of this project, you want to see a simplified process of behavioural change that you would be able to use with your clients. Perhaps it would be an amalgamation of various models or working through a selected model and ways in which you can instigate change.

Topic: Identify one approach and test it with clients to help them develop healthy eating habits.

4.1.5 Hybrid approach

The hybrid approach to identifying a topic incorporates two or more of the approaches discussed earlier. These approaches can be a mixture of abundance approaches or deficit and abundance approaches. Table 4.3 provides an example of how abundance approaches can be used separately (inward or outward) or as a hybrid in your research project.

Table 4.3 Example of applying an abundance approach for selecting a research project topic.

Examples	Best practice	Resources	Future	Topic
Example 1 (inward)	One of your strengths is creativity. You are a corporate trainer, and your trainees told you last week that your training sessions are different and more fun than others'. Your leader praised you at the staff meeting for your ingenuity.	You usually use lots of props and colours when designing students' handouts. You try to do something different for every training event, not to repeat your activities.	In the future, imagine you have higher-level creativity, something like lateral thinking you've read about before that goes beyond using colours and props but thinking outside the box in a more sophisticated way.	Lateral thinking by Edward de Bono is your project focus. You want to design Action Research to help you apply the "six thinking hats" theory (Bono, 2017) in your training practice.
Example 2 (outward)	Research shows that positive leadership can help leaders get extraordinary results.	Some of the topics mentioned in books related to leaders' ability to build trust, enhance staff wellbeing, spot team's strengths as vehicles for boosting their performance (Burke, 2020).	As a future leader, you see yourself as a positive leader, working closely with your team who trust you and work hard together to ensure your department or organisation is a success.	You now wonder how to create a trusting environment for your future team and decide to take it on as your topic. You want to interview colleagues to identify what makes them trust their leaders more and hope to learn what you can do in the future to become a leader with extraordinary results.
Example 3 (hybrid)	You have been chatting with your colleagues about how lucky you were to work in an organisation with high staff morale. You began to reflect in your diary about what enhances staff morale, and you can't put your finger on it, but you know that you feel it.	When your morale is at its best, you tend to feel supported by your colleagues, have a good time with students, and feel that your personal life is going well too.	In the future, you would like to see more consistency of feeling high morale levels so that your arguments with your wife don't affect it as much as they do nowadays.	As part of your research, you would like to do an online survey to find out how employees' personal lives affect their sense of staff morale and how they compartmentalise their work and energy not to influence each other.

Reflection time

In this chapter, we discussed five approaches to selecting a topic. Take a piece of paper and, for ten minutes, write down which approach you would like to use for your research project and why:

1 Inward (deficit or abundance) approach
2 Outward (deficit or abundance) approach
   or
3 Hybrid approach?

4.2 Literature scoping

There are two stages of engaging with the literature, the first is a quick literature search that can help you identify the topic, and the second is a more careful approach to scoping the relevant literature to help you delve deeper into what research is available on the subject of your interest (Wilson, 2015). In this section, we will focus on the literature scoping, which includes selecting and reading the correct texts and making sense of them and recording them effectively so that you are not overwhelmed by all the literature you read.

4.2.1 Information management

Like most students, you may find it challenging to manage large amounts of information (Walter and Stouck, 2020). Many graduates have stories to tell of how they have read something interesting but could not find a citation for it later. This is why an effective strategy for managing information before engaging with the literature is essential.

One of the most effective techniques for managing information is to create an Excel sheet comprising columns that refer to the information you require for your literature review. We usually recommend that students include such headings as the following:

1 References with the author's details.
2 Key findings from the article.
3 Exciting results from the literature review of the article.
4 Comments, where you can put your reflections about an article.

In addition to these four main headings, you can enter whatever other information is relevant to your research. For example, if your topic is to identify the best ways to motivate school children, you may include a heading about the theories of motivation discussed by authors of various academic papers; if your topic is about ways in which you can practice gratitude in a classroom, you may include a heading about the specific gratitude interventions used in past research. Table 4.4 provides an example of a basic sheet for information management.

What is excellent about a note-taking sheet like this is that it encourages us to think about what we read and enter only the most relevant information. Also, it reduces

Table 4.4 Example of a note-taking sheet for literature review.

Citation	Key findings	Literature review	Comments
Paper 1			
Paper 2			
Book 1			
Report 1			

the volume of data we collate and helps us organise it better. For example, before you write a literature review, you may reflect on what themes you need to explore. Then, you create a separate sheet for each theme where you enter 10, 15, or 20 papers. This way, before you write a section in your literature review, you can print out two to three sheets of paper, put them right in front of you, look at the bigger picture of the literature you've collated and organise your arguments well. Also, this way, you will not lose any of the essential and relevant citations as they are nicely organised in this Excel filing system.

4.2.2 Sourcing literature

To carry out a good literature review, you need to draw it from the latest research. Some books are good for providing you with a helicopter view of a topic. However, before an average book is written and published, at least a year passes; therefore, many books published two or three years ago contain research that is over five years old. Yet, there are at least one million new academic articles published in psychology each year. In addition, some books delve deeper into one specific perspective, ignoring other viewpoints, so the most effective way of sourcing literature is usually by reading academic articles.

Many of the academic articles are accessible via open access. You may be able to source them via Google Scholar, ResearchGate, and other open-access platforms. However, they are not exhaustive, which is why it is helpful to draw from some of the academic databases available through the library of your educational institution, such as Education Research Complete, PsycInfo, ERIC, British Education Index, Australian Education Index, International Education Research Database, CUREE – Centre for the Use of Research and Evidence in Education, and many more. Ask your librarian for the most suitable databases available in your educational institution.

A significant advantage of using academic databases is that you can narrow down your search to whatever topics you require. For example, many of them allow you to refine your search using various categories, such as source type (e.g. academic journals, reports, books), major heading or thesaurus term, participants' age, geographical location, and many more. This allows you to focus on the most relevant 20–30 articles out of the many available online.

Another great advantage of using academic databases is the quality of their articles. Google Scholar and ResearchGate have algorithms that allow you to tap into as many resources as possible, regardless of their quality. However, academic databases are more selective in what they offer. Mind you, this doesn't mean that all the articles published in academic databases are of high quality; it just means that they have met specific quality criteria to be included.

4.2.3 Reading articles

Given that university professors and researchers read academic literature for a living, it is always helpful to learn some of their techniques. When reading a book, or a book chapter, academics are much more selective in what they read. Similarly, when reading an academic paper, academics focus on the argument, empirical evidence presented in an article and how the research contributes to the community. In contrast, practitioners are more focused on enriching their professional practice (Bartels, 2003). They often trust that the academic who wrote the article knows what they are discussing and tend to take it on board indiscriminately. However, this type of reading is not very useful in a research project, where critical thinking is required to discern the quality of the literature read.

There are two types of reading, (1) surface and (2) deep reading, and most students practice predominantly surface reading (Hermida, 2009). When you surface-read academic articles, you focus on the text itself rather than its meaning. You tend to take on board everything you read uncritically and do not connect it with your prior knowledge. This makes retaining knowledge more problematic and impacts the quality of critical engagement you practice. On the other hand, when we practice deep reading, we question the authors' arguments and consult additional texts to understand alternate views. Table 4.5 provides an example of how you can read an academic article deeper.

Table 4.5 Deep reading strategies. Adapted from Hermida (2009).

Strategies for deep reading	Practical considerations
Reading purpose	Reflect on why you are reading this specific article. What is your objective for doing it? Consider at least one question you would like answered by the end of reading the article.
Context	Learn about the author and their general views. Are they representative of mainstream thinking, or are they radical? What experiences have they had that could have influenced their writing. What were their previous articles about?
Author's thesis	What does the author intend to do with this article? What is their purpose for writing it? Are they trying to challenge the current views about the topic, or have they identified a research gap or a variable that needs further exploration? What are the author's main arguments?
Deconstruction of assumptions	You must be aware of some of the assumptions associated with the field of research you are reading about. They are the concepts, debates, and principles that the author takes for granted and needs to understand to engage with their argument fully. This is a problematic aspect of deep reading, and it becomes easier the more we read.
Evaluation of author's data (in empirical texts)	It is crucial to evaluate the author's research design. How did they collect their data? What sampling technique did they use? How are they presenting their data? What kind of reasoning are they using? Are there gaps in the information provided?
Evaluation of author's arguments	This section is about assessing the validity of the author's arguments. Not all authors follow logic. Ideas proposed by the author need to be questioned. How compelling is the author's rationale in arguing a stance? Did the author provide convincing examples to make their argument stick? Can you think of contra-arguments?
Consequences of author's arguments	How can the author's findings, their stance be implemented in practice? How can each one of the author's views affect the practitioners? How does the author's conclusion compare with other findings or other authors?

4.3 Research question

One of the primary purposes of conducting a comprehensive literature review is to establish a research question. Research questions inform the literature review section of your research project, methodology, and how you derive and present your research. While having a good question is not a guarantee of a good study, having a poorly constructed question may create a series of issues that will prevent you from completing your research project (Agee, 2009).

For research questions to be practical and ease the design of your research project, they need to be succinct and adequately narrowed down. Table 4.6 provides examples of research questions for both qualitative and quantitative methodologies. Please note that a question varies concerning the purpose it serves. For example, the goal of one research project may be to *describe* participants' experiences, another one to *explore* their

Table 4.6 Examples of research questions for qualitative and quantitative methodologies.

Methodology	Purpose	Research question example
Qualitative	Descriptive	• What is the lived experience of leading an organisation undergoing structural changes? • How does the physical environment impact inclusion? • How does children's self-concept develop over the first year in pre-school?
Qualitative	Explorative	• How does attending after-school study club impact on students' perceptions of learning? • How does performance review impact on employees' motivation? • How does self-compassion impact intergroup discrimination?
Qualitative	Comparative	• What are the wellbeing challenges of stroke vs cancer patients? • Is the behaviour change process of losing and gaining weight different for participants? • Is student engagement better in face-to-face or in the online environment?
Quantitative	Descriptive	• What proportion of call centre workers intends to leave this sector? • How many positive emotions do individuals with dysphoric mood disorder experience daily? • What is the prevalence of individuals scoring high in intuitive eating among weight management clients?
Quantitative	Explorative	• What is the relationship between GRIT and passion? • Is there a relationship between age and wellbeing, after controlling for gender? • How much of the variance in accountants' perceived stress can be explained by their job satisfaction, motivation, and passion for work? Which one of the three variables are the best predictors of teachers' stress?
Quantitative	Comparative	• Are females more creative than males? • Is there a difference in wellbeing before and after completing a programme? • Which intervention was more effective to enhance self-efficacy?

experiences. In contrast, a third research project may *compare* participants' experiences. They all pertained to all participants' experiences, but what they do with those experiences differs. Other words that can be used when creating a purpose of your research project include: investigate, determine, examine, explain, provide, develop, ascertain, assess, unravel, establish, shine a new light, clarify, and others. Clarity about your research purpose can help you create your research question.

When deciding on a research question, it is essential not to settle for the first option that comes to mind. Instead, delve more profound as it will help you narrow it down. You can take easy steps (Booth et al., 2008). Firstly, select a topic. Then, create an initial, indirect question that will help you focus on what you do not know or want to know more about your topic. Then, ask yourself: *"so what?"* as this will help you to get to the bottom of what is important about your research and how you can narrow it down further. You can keep asking yourself, *"so what?"* many times to delve deeper and deeper into your topic. This process will allow you to construct a specific question. Share your question with a colleague or a supervisor to check for coherence and adequate depth. Next, identify the keywords or areas you will need to review in the literature related to your question. You can start with broad areas and then use more specific words to do it. While reviewing the literature, note how other researchers designed their research questions and revise your question accordingly. This process will take you to the stage of planning your research design based on the question you created (Figure 4.3).

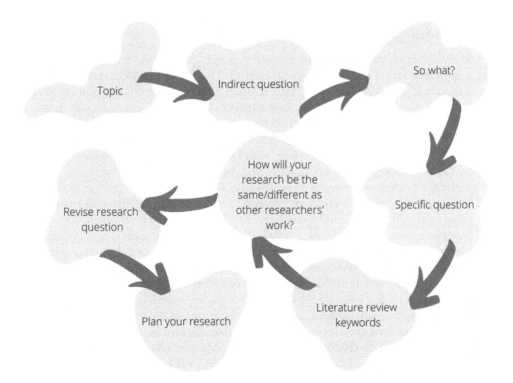

Figure 4.3 Clarifying research questions. Adapted from Booth et al. (2008).

Here is an example of the research question clarification process:

I am interested in how young people learn in the online environment. In particular, I am thinking about motivation for learning in this environment. Therefore, I am working on learning online to impact students' motivation.

> **My indirect question is:** because I want to find out if students' motivation for learning online is lower than if they are learning in a face-to-face environment.
>
> **So what?:** This is important because we need to identify ways to keep students motivated for learning in the online environment, especially in language education.
>
> **Specific question:** How does online learning impact students' motivation for learning languages at the lower secondary level?
>
> **Keywords for literature review:** Learning, distance education, language education, motivation, self-regulation, learner autonomy, relatedness, cognitive and metacognitive strategies.
>
> **How are other researchers designing their studies?:** Researchers use various measures for motivation. Many studies link cause to student self-regulation and relatedness of the content. Most of the studies are carried out at further education and third level.
>
> **My revised research question:** How do students describe the intrinsic motivation for speaking and writing practice in an online course in French at the lower secondary level in Ireland?

Now you can start to plan your research project.

4.3.1 Hypothesis (quantitative research)

Qualitative research projects aim to explore concepts (inductive), whereas quantitative research projects aim to test hypotheses (deductive). This is why many quantitative research projects include a hypothesis apart from a research question. Instead, a hypothesis is created based on the theoretical foundations (Cohen et al., 2018). For example, your research question may state: *What is the relationship between students' physics results and GRIT?* Your hypothesis derives from the theory of GRIT, according to which higher GRIT levels can predict students' performance. Therefore, your hypothesis would state: *Students with high levels of GRIT report higher physics SAT scores*, and your null hypothesis would state: *Students with higher GRIT levels do not report higher physics SAT scores*.

Our starting point when creating a hypothesis is deciding on the null hypothesis, according to which the relationship between two or more variables is independent. The null hypothesis assumes no difference between our participants concerning their attitude, knowledge, personality, and other test variables. The objective of conducting statistical tests is to accept the null hypothesis or reject it. A rejected hypothesis means that a change post-experiment occurred, or that there is indeed a difference or a relationship between variables. Therefore, it is essential to consider both the hypothesis and the null hypothesis.

When constructing a hypothesis, make sure it is written in the present tense. It is typical for the abstract, literature review, results, and discussion to be written consistently in the past tense, e.g. Smith (2020) claimed that . . . , Murphy (2020) concluded that . . . . However, some academic journal editors are often put off by an article that is written in the present tense, e.g. Smith (2020) claims that . . . , Murphy (2020) concludes that . . . ; or worse, mixes up past and present tenses, e.g. Smith (2020) contended that . . . ,

Table 4.7 Examples of hypotheses and basic statistics used in research design.

Hypothesis example	Statistics used in research
There is a relationship between leaders' motivation and employees' outcomes.	Correlation (Pearson or Spearman)
Leaders' motivation predicts employees' outcomes.	Multiple regression
After controlling for years of experience, there is a positive relationship between leaders' motivation and employees' outcomes.	Partial correlation
There is a difference between male and female leaders in their levels of motivation for work.	Chi-square, Independent t-test, or Mann-Whitney U test
There is a difference between new, experienced, and very experienced leaders in their levels of motivation for work.	ANOVA or Kruskal-Wallis
Leaders' motivation increases after they engage with employees meaningfully.	Paired samples t-test or Wilcoxon test

Murphy (2020) concludes that. Yet, one thing that you should always write in the present tense is your hypothesis.

Hypotheses relate to various types of statistics used in research. Table 4.7 provides examples of them.

Recap time

This chapter discussed the first part of research project design, which refers to exploring and narrowing down your interests. Specifically, we went through the steps you can take to decide on your topic. We gave you three options. The first is via the inward deficit approach; the second is via the outward deficit approach; the third is via the mixed abundance approach. We then delved into best practices for literature scoping. We encouraged you to decide on your information management technique and recommended that you use a brief excel note-taking system for it. We then gave you tips on how to best source your literature and engage with it critically so that you can have a great head-start for your research-based practice. Finally, we helped you create your research question. For those who chose to design a quantitative research project, we helped you make the most suitable hypotheses.

References

Agee, J. 2009. "Developing Qualitative Research Questions: A Reflective Process." *International Journal of Qualitative Studies in Education* 22(4): 431–447. doi: 10.1080/09518390902736512

Bartels, N. 2003. "How Teachers and Researchers Read Academic Articles." *Teaching and Teacher Education: An International Journal of Research and Studies* 19(7): 737–753.

Baumeister, R.F., E. Bratslavsky, C. Finkenauer, and K.D. Vohs. 2001. "Bad Is Stronger Than Good." *Review of General Psychology* 5(4): 323–370. doi: 10.1037/1089-2680.5.4.323.

Bono, de. 2017. *Six Thinking Hats*. London: Penguin.

Booth, W., G. Colomb, and J. Williams. 2008. *The Craft of Research*. Chicago: University of Chicago Press.

Burke, J. 2020. *Positive Psychology and School Leadership: The New Science of Positive Educational Leadership.* New York City: Nova Science.

Cameron, K.S., and M. Lavine. 2006. *Making the Impossible Possible: Leading Extraordinary Performance – The Rocky Flats Story: Lessons from the Clean-up of America's Most Dangerous Nuclear Weapons Plant.* San Francisco, CA: Berrett-Koehler Publishers.

Cohen, L., L. Manion, and K. Morrison. 2018. *Research Methods in Education.* Abingdon, UK: Routledge.

Cooperrider, D.L., M. McQuaid, and L.N. Godwin. 2018. "A Positive Revolution in Education: Uniting Appreciative Inquiry with the Science of Human Flourishing to 'Power Up Positive Education'." *AI Practitioner* 20(4): 3–19. doi: 10.12781/978-1-907549-37-3-1.

Hermida, J. 2009. "The Importance of Teaching Academic Reading Skills in First-Year University Courses." *International Journal of Research & Review* 3: 20–30.

Pavez, I. 2017. "An Empirical Understanding of Appreciative Organizing as a Way to Reframe Group Development." 5th World Congress on Positive Psychology, Montreal, Canada.

Shuayb, M., C. Sharp, M. Judkins, and M. Hetherington. 2009. *Using Appreciative Inquiry in Educational Research: Possibilities and Limitations.* Slough, UK: National Foundation for Educational Research.

Walter, L., and J. Stouck. 2020. "Writing the Literature Review: Graduate Student Experiences." *The Canadian Journal for the Scholarship of Teaching and Learning* 11(1). doi: 10.5206/cjsotl-rcacea.2020.1.8295

Wilson, E. 2015. "Reviewing the Literature and Writing a Literature Review." In *School-based Research: A Guide for Education Students*, edited by E. Wilson. London: Sage.

5 Positioning

The next stage of the process of conducting research is the design. The design refers to the conceptualisation of your research project. There are three parts to this process:

1 Positioning helps you clarify your philosophical perspective that guides your decision-making process.
2 Methodology spectrum, which is the approach you take to discover your knowledge.
3 Methods, which refer to the instruments we use for data collection.

In other words, the design is the conceptual thinking behind your final year project (Figure 5.1).

Let us begin with positioning.

5.1 Positioning

We all view the world differently because our life experiences have been different. We make assumptions about the reality of the social world (ontology) and how we acquire our knowledge about it (epistemology). Becoming aware of the perspective from which you view the world is important for research, as it allows you to understand yourself better, clarify your thinking about your project, and help you align your research project to a particular research paradigm that best suits your views. A research paradigm refers to your philosophical assumptions that guide and give direction to your thinking and action (Kuhn, 1962). In the context of your project, it is useful to understand your own set of beliefs, as it will help you select a methodology, collect your data and analyse it effectively. It is also important that you continue reflecting on your paradigm as you progress your research to see if your perspective has changed, or whether it needs to change. In this section, we will discuss six main perspectives (sets of beliefs) relating to your project

Figure 5.1 The outline of the design part of the research project.

DOI: 10.4324/9781003262428-5

(1) positivism (2) post-positivism, (3) pragmatism, (4) constructivism, (5) interpretive paradigm, and (6) critical paradigm. All paradigms have strengths and limitations and are part of an ongoing discussion by the psychological community.

In addition to the paradigms, we will also review how your theoretical framework informs your research design. We will contrast it with the conceptual framework and theories, all of which need to become a fundamental and explicit part of your research design.

5.1.1 Positivist paradigm

Positivism is traditionally associated with research taken up in the natural sciences. When you are positioned in the positivist paradigm, your ontological position is that of *realism*, meaning that you believe that reality exists independent of the knower; the truth is out there to be discovered. At the same time, your epistemological position is that you as a researcher can access the independent reality through valid and reliable collection and analysis tools. These two views lead you to believe that truth or knowledge is out there for you, as a researcher, to discover in responsible ways.

One of the most significant limitations in designing research within this paradigm is our challenge in controlling the variables (factors) that we study. A key goal in positivist research is to isolate and control the influence of all factors or variables so that only the key variables of interest are examined (e.g. only X could have caused Y). In this regard, positivist researchers are most interested in the study's internal validity – how well the study design and evidence gathered support claims for causal inference.

For example, imagine sending out two project surveys during a particular year looking at work-life balance, one at the beginning of the year in January and another one after the summer holiday break. Think of how different life would be at these two points in time. The timing of your research will impact your findings. But this is not the only thing that will influence your results. Say that your country's government announces a new, controversial budget creating upheaval among the citizens halfway through the year. All these factors will impact your research results, and there is very little control you have over them as a researcher. Some claim that it is almost impossible to guard against fluctuating individual factors (Scotland, 2012). The positivist paradigm privileges analytical tools and processes external to the researcher. The assumption is that these are neutral, which is one of the more significant limitations of research design within positivism.

Here are some of the research characteristics located within the positivist paradigm (Kivunja and Kuyini, 2017).

- Conclusions from the positivist position are seen to be objective and enduring. This is difficult to defend in research because knowledge is regarded as separate from the person.
- The belief is that cause and effect are distinguishable and analytically separable.
- There is an assumption that the social world can be studied in a value-free way, the same way as the natural world. There is also a belief that explanations of a causal nature can be made (Mertens, 2010).
- The belief is that the results of inquiry can be quantified. The use of numbers and statistics are objective tools we use to access reality and are free of interpretation.
- Rests on formulation and testing of hypotheses. To test a hypothesis, it is essential to have a reasonable hypothesis.

- Pursues an objective search for facts.
- The methodology must be objective, empirical, and scientific.

Methodologies and methods

The methodologies positioned in the positivists' paradigm are quantitative, such as experimental, quasi-experimental, randomised control trials, or comparative designs. Therefore, the methods you can use in this paradigm are predominately quantitative, including surveys and questionnaires.

Challenges

One of the challenges of this paradigm is that describing and controlling variables in social settings is not always possible. Research design can guard against challenges, so a straightforward well-developed design is crucial. Reducing complex social research questions to quantifiable results can also present some challenges. A lot of human experience is not quantifiable, such as feelings and attitudes. Applying the scientific method to research where you cannot control the variables is flawed. Many researchers moved from adopting a positivist position to post-positivism.

5.1.2 Post-positivism

As a response to some limitations of positivism, post-positivism is another position where claims to an understanding of knowledge are based on probability rather than certainty. The ontological views of positivists and post-positivists are the same; where they differ is in terms of the level of confidence to access reality, your epistemological perspective as a post-positivist is that knowledge is tentative and open to refutation (Popper, 1979). This view of the world helps you design research that must be as objective as you can make it, yet mindful of factors that may influence it, for example, contextual factors. You can do it by using "thick descriptions", which help you analyse research participants' behaviours and their context, which is a missing element from the purely positivist approach. Taking these extra precautions will make your research "robust to empirical refutation" (Scotland, 2012, p. 12).

For example, Borman et al. (2018) studied a self-affirmation intervention and examined whether initial academic benefits in middle school carried over into high school. They tested for differential impacts moderated by school context and assessed the causal effects of student engagement with an intervention on self-affirming writing. They reported on data from a randomised controlled trial of a self-affirmation intervention implemented at scale in an entire urban school district in the midwestern United States. They stated their results in tentative open to refutation terms: "Our results imply the potential for powerful, lasting academic impacts from self-affirmation interventions if implemented broadly; however, these effects will depend on both contextual and individual factors" (p. 1). This post-positivist stance eliminates alternative explanations by making a solid case for their claim.

Methodologies and methods

The methodologies positioned in the post-positivists' paradigm are quantitative, such as quasi-experimental, randomised control trials, or comparative designs. The methods you can use in this paradigm are predominately quantitative with some qualitative aspects including surveys, questionnaires, observation, and interviews.

Challenges

The challenges for designing research with a post-positivist stance are not unlike those in positivism, that of controlling variables. In presenting the findings of research as tentative and open to refutation, this can lead to competing explanations of findings.

Reflection time

Think about the variables in your research. List all variables and describe how you might control and measure them. If your research does not have variables, you will need to consider other positions.

5.1.3 Constructivism

Within this paradigm, your view is that knowledge is socially constructed by individuals lived experiences within complex social worlds. You the researcher are part of this world within which you carry out your research; unlike the positivist paradigm, you are not independent of the process (Raskin and Bridges, 2002). You and your participants are intertwined and influence each other. Within this paradigm, there are multiple socially constructed realities (Mertens, 2010). For example, do you believe that fortune tellers can advise you on the future? If you do, then this is your reality, and it can exist alongside the person who does not believe this. In constructivism therefore reality is constructed through human interaction. Knowledge is a human creation and is socially and cultur-ally constructed. Individuals create meaning through their lived environment and their interactions with each other. Constructivism emphasises the importance of culture and context in the process of knowledge creation. Truth lies in the individual's experience. This truth is culturally, historically, and context dependent, and therefore your research is value-laden and value-bound. You will, therefore, report your values and biases related to the topic you are researching.

This philosophical stance grew out of the work of Husserl on phenomenology and the study of interpretive meaning called hermeneutics (Mertens, 2010; Shaw, 2019). In constructivism the researcher is striving to understand the world of the participants and to look at their experiences of their lived world. In trying to understand their experi-ence, the researcher is interpreting their experiences and constructing a reality from this. However, by being in their world, the researcher is influencing it.

Methodologies and methods

The methodologies used in this paradigm are phenomenology, hermeneutical, case study, ethnographic, grounded theory, and narrative. The methods used for data collection are all concerned with getting at the participants' experiences, such as observations, interviews, pictures, diaries/journals, and document analysis. In most research projects, you will use multiple qualitative methods to gather data. You need your data to help you to construct a reality from how the experiences are described. Mertens (2010) describes this as being like an anthropologist trying to decipher meaning from observations, journals, and interviews with participants while keeping the cultural context in mind at all times.

Challenges

This kind of idiographic research that is focused on the individual experience can be challenging for a novice researcher. The positioning means that you cannot have a well-defined question at the start of the research process, the question will evolve and change as the study progresses. The question will be open-ended and descriptive (Creswell and Poth, 2018). This can be challenging for researchers working within tight time frames. Your closeness to the research process may bring complex ethical issues that need to be addressed ahead of and during the research.

5.1.4 Pragmatism

Pragmatism is unique because it avoids discussion about ontology or epistemology and instead focuses on what works first (Tashakkori and Teddie, 2003), and its position on knowledge considers the claims of trial-and-error truths (Lukenchuk, 2017). Although both can also be considered under other paradigms, it provides a practical foundation for thinking about action research and mixed methods. It also offers an epistemological anchor that allows you to get outside the interpretive cycle. In particular, pragmatists emphasise creating knowledge through lines of action with effectiveness as the criteria for judging the values of research (Mertens, 2010). The emphasis is on the problem being studied and the questions you ask about this problem, allowing for greater possibilities in your research (Biesta, 2014; Creswell, 2013). Kelly and Cordeiro (2020) argue that pragmatism offers a practical framework for organisational research. It allows for abductive, inductive, and deductive reasoning, thus allowing new ways of knowing and understanding.

In summary, here are the characteristics of research located within the pragmatic paradigm (Kivunja and Kuyini, 2017).

- An emphasis on what works in research, the concept of actionable knowledge. Pragmatism is not committed to any one reality, and therein lies the freedom for the researcher. Your methodology will depend on your research question.
- The use of "what works" allows you to address the questions being investigated without worrying as to whether the questions are wholly quantitative or qualitative in nature. The questions determine the methods used (Hall et al., 2020). You could decide to use a mixed-methods design with quantitative questionnaires and interviews.
- They utilise lines of action best suited to studying the phenomenon being investigated. You use the best approaches to gaining knowledge using every methodology that helps that knowledge discovery. Pragmatists search for points of connection (Mertens, 2010).
- This search for useful points of connection within the research project facilitates understanding of the situation, acknowledging that research always occurs in social, historical, political, and other contexts (Creswell, 2013). Researchers recognise the interconnectedness of experience, knowing, and acting (Kelly and Cordeiro, 2020).

Methodologies and methods

The methodologies in this paradigm include both qualitative and quantitative, including case studies, phenomenology, ethnography, action research, mixed methods, grounded theory, and causal-comparative methodology, among others. The methods used are decided by the purpose of the research.

Challenges

The researcher's values and politics influence the research outcomes in this paradigm; therefore, they can lead to questions about what works for whom and to what end (Mertens, 2010; Hall, 2020).

Reflection time

Thinking about your research project, what is the phenomenon you are interested in?

What is your research question? How can you best answer this question?

5.1.5 Interpretive paradigm

Suppose your research project is under the interpretivist paradigm. In that case, your ontological stance is on a spectrum between that of *relativism* where truth is relative to some broader context, so true here and now or is culturally constructed, and *subjectivism* where truth is individualistic, so true for me or constructed by me alone. The distinction is one of the scope of reference. They can be understood as a spectrum within the interpretivist paradigm. Our senses mediate our realities. Individuals construct realities, and there are as many realities as individuals (Scotland, 2012). For example, two people could observe a phenomenon, and both could have very different views of what is happening depending on their world views.

Your epistemological stance would be that knowledge is culturally derived and historically situated. Knowledge is always a matter of some level of interpretation. How you interpret knowledge is influenced by various factors, it is co-constructed by our interaction with the world. In this paradigm, you seek to understand phenomena from the individual's perspective. You are looking at the interactions between individuals and the cultural and historical context (Creswell, 2013), the context is always essential, and the phenomena are thickly described (Scotland, 2012). Unlike the post-positivist paradigm, thick descriptions seek to illustrate and not explain.

In summary, here are some characteristics of research positioned within the interpretivist paradigm (Kivunja and Kuyini, 2017).

- We cannot understand the social world in ways that are entirely divorced of interpretation.
- The belief is that realities are multiple and socially constructed.

- The acceptance that there is inevitable interaction between the researcher and their research participants.
- The acceptance that context is vital for knowledge and knowing.
- The belief is that knowledge is created by the findings and likely to be value-laden, and the values need to be made explicit.
- The belief is that causes and effects are mutually interdependent. You will have a rigorous research design that other researchers could apply in their contexts. The issues of causal direction and generalisability are distinct. You might be able to accurately postulate cause and effect (maybe via grounded theory) in one context but still not generalise to another context.

Methodologies and methods

The methodologies positioned in the interpretive paradigm are qualitative, such as mixed methods, case study, phenomenology, hermeneutics, or ethnography. You can use any methods, including open-ended interviews, focus groups, questionnaires, observations, autoethnography, narrative, content, text or discourse analysis, visual, and arts-based methods, such as think-aloud and role-playing. Think about which method will allow you to gather data to make thick descriptions and make meaning of the phenomena being researched (Scotland, 2012; Lukenchuk and Kolich, 2013).

Challenges

One of the challenges of this paradigm is that it is not always possible to generalise your findings to other settings. In addition, one of the methodological challenges that apply to interpretivist approaches is how to check interpretations (and to escape the interpretive cycle). So, researcher and/or data triangulation's added demand applies even more in this paradigm.

Reflection time

Thinking about your research project, what is the phenomenon you are interested in?
Who are the individuals who you want to participate in your research?
What is the cultural and historical context of your research?

5.1.6 Critical paradigm

When you position yourself in a critical paradigm, your ontological stance is *critical realism*, whereby you believe that realities are socially constructed and the tools of construction all involve power (Scotland, 2012). Your epistemology is that knowledge is always a matter of power, so coming to know must acknowledge power or interpret it in terms of power. In this paradigm, language is essential and carries its power. In the critical paradigm, you will find a range of theories, such as critical theory, neo-Marxist theory, feminism, critical race and ethnic theories, queer theory, disability studies, social re-constructivism, and social and political activism, among others (Lukenchuk and Kolich, 2013).

In summary, here are the characteristics of research located within the critical paradigm (Kivunja and Kuyini, 2017).

- The concern with power relationships within social structures.
- The conscious recognition of the consequences of privileging versions of reality.
- The treatment of research as an act of construction or de/construction rather than discovery. Feminist approaches are collective, women-centred, and grounded in the lived experience (De Saxe, 2014).
- A central focus of the research effort is on uncovering agency, which is hidden by social practices, leading to liberation and emancipation. You seek to turn critical thought into emancipatory action (De Saxe, 2014).
- The deliberate efforts of the researcher to address issues of power, oppression, and trust among research participants through thoughtful, critical conversations as you endeavour to understand individuals' social realities. You deliberately use methodologies and methods that help you address these issues.

Methodologies and methods

The methodologies positioned in this paradigm include critical discourse analysis, critical ethnography, (participatory) action research, critical narrative inquiry, or ideology critique. The methods can consist of open-ended interviews, focus groups, questionnaires, observations, autoethnography, narrative, content, text or discourse analysis, visual, and various art-based methods.

Challenges

A challenge for you as a researcher is to manage the power relations within this type of research. It takes a lot of practice and significant experience to carry out many methods, such as participatory action research and ensuring that all voices are heard. You will need to be very clear at all stages about managing this.

Conclusion

In this section, we have presented six leading positions you can take when completing your project. You must begin your project by identifying your positioning, as it is the lens through which you view the world, which can therefore affect the decisions you make about your research. However, we encourage you to revisit positioning as you continue on your journey of conducting a research project. You may decide to embrace a different perspective if it better suits your research and allows you to address your research question more effectively.

Also, the five perspectives are some of the main ones that you can reflect on. However, there are other positions that you can explore, such as transformative, post-structuralist, and transcendental. Please consult Cohen et al. (2018), Creswell (2013), or Lukenchuk (2013, 2017) for further information.

Reflection time

Thinking about your research project, is your focus on bringing about change? If so, what change are you hoping to bring? How might you work with your participants in the research?

5.2 Theoretical framework

A theoretical framework is a structure upon which your research project sits in the context of developing or testing theories (Ravitch and Riggan, 2017; Jabareen, 2009). Let us illustrate it with a metaphor of grocery shopping. You walk into a store (e.g. field of psychology) and go towards a specific section, i.e. vegetables (e.g. the field of health psychology). In the vegetable section, you are particularly interested in tomatoes (e.g. research relating to behaviour change), you have many different kinds of tomatoes there, such as Beef tomatoes, Cherry tomatoes, Roma tomatoes, Green tomatoes (e.g. various theories of behavioural change, such as Skinner's Operant Learning Theory (1953), Bandura's Social Cognitive Theory (1997), Model of Goal-Directed Behaviour (Perugini and Bagozzi, 2001), or Transtheoretical Model (Prochalska and DiClemente, 1983)). You decide to buy Beef tomatoes (e.g. you choose the Transtheoretical Model – TM). Now, you take your tomatoes home. They become the basis for your Caprese Salad, meaning you present other ingredients in the context of tomatoes you've purchased (e.g. discuss the topic of your research project and the methodological decisions you have made in the context of the TM).

According to the TM, there are five distinct stages of behaviour change:

1   Pre-contemplation, i.e. not aware that the behaviour needs to change
2   Contemplation, i.e. considering pros and cons of change
3   Preparation, i.e. planning change
4   Action, i.e. starting to change behaviour
5   Maintenance, i.e. sustaining behavioural change

Let's say that your topic of research is weight management. If you choose to base your research on the TM of change, you might decide to collect qualitative data (interviews with people who have lost weight) and establish your questions on the TM. As such, you will be asking them when they become aware of the need to lose weight. Then explore how they prepared for this change, what action they have taken, and what tools helped them sustain their behavioural change. If a model you selected has a scale, you may design quantitative research to test hundreds of people and assess their behavioural change.

Selecting a theoretical model can also, in part, inform your literature review. While you will need to explain what models of behavioural change you considered and the reasons why you selected the TM in particular, a section in your literature review will probably delve into the content of the model, such as the review of the literature concerning the preparation for changing behaviour, taking action, etc. Similarly, the theoretical framework you select for your research project will inform your findings and discussion. This is an example of how a single theory can become a framework for the discussion of your project.

At the same time, one of your friends from the educational programme is also interested in researching weight management. However, her theoretical framework is different, as she chose to adopt the Social Cognitive Theory (SCT: Bandura, 1997), thus considering weight management in the context of SCT. Therefore, her literature review will delve into Bandura's concept of self-efficacy and its relevance for people who wish to lose weight. According to the SCT, there are four sources of information individuals use to develop self-efficacy:

1   Mastery experiences, i.e. practising behaviour.
2   Vicarious experience, i.e. modelling behaviour.
3   Social/verbal persuasion, i.e. others expressing confidence that someone can change their behaviour.
4   Physiological experience, i.e. reframing beliefs from harmful to useful.

When this theory is adopted as a framework for weight management, the research project's focus becomes losing weight in the context of self-efficacy. Your friend may also conduct interviews with participants, but the SCT will inform her questions; thus, she will ask participants how they practised their behaviour change, what exactly they did to lose weight, what they modelled it on, how they modelled what they did, etc. Your friend's results will also be different, as she had additional questions asked and a different focus when analysing her data. Finally, this framework will inform your friend's discussion and implications for practice.

This is an example of how the same topic with the same research question can take a diametrically different direction depending on what theoretical framework you apply in your research project. This is why care needs to be taken when deciding on your framework, and its implications need to be considered.

Here is a simple process of identifying theoretical framework, adapted from Ravitch and Riggan (2017).

Step 1: Identify the theory cluster, i.e. a range of theories that fall into a similar category, e.g. wellbeing theories.
Step 2: Identify the main theories and their propositions or ideas that constitute each theory.

See Table 5.1 as an example.

Step 3: Identify the theory selected for your research project.
Step 4: State clearly the contribution of the project to the knowledge related to the theory. Table 5.2 provides an example of theories and how a topic of wellbeing relates to them.

To sum up, we think of a theoretical framework as the application of a theory, or a set of concepts drawn from the same theory, to offer an explanation for a research problem, or "shed some light on a particular phenomenon" (Imenda, 2014, p. 189). A theoretical framework is 'a very general theoretical system with assumptions, concepts and specific social theories' (Neuman, 2011, p. 85).

Table 5.1 An example of five theories and their propositions.

Theory	Main proposition or idea
Bronfenbrenner's theory (1979)	Individuals are affected by their environment (immediate, connections, indirect, social, and cultural values and changes over time).
Biosocial model (Engel, 1997)	An amalgamation of biological factors (e.g. genes), psychological factors (e.g. mood), and social factors (e.g. socioeconomic status).
Ecosystem health model (Levins and Lopez, 1999)	Interaction of humans with nature, e.g. how pollution or population growth impacts on individuals.
Mental health continuum model (Keyes, 2002)	Wellbeing is perceived on a continuum between mental illness and psychological functioning.
Positive psychology model (Seligman and Csikszentmihalyi, 2000)	Wellbeing is perceived as the presence of positive traits, e.g. engagement, positive relationships at individual level and civic duties and institutions moving towards citizenship at group level.

Table 5.2 Example of five frameworks and their impact on a research project relating to wellbeing.

Theory	How wellbeing relates to each theory
Bronfenbrenner's theory (1979)	Wellbeing is perceived as a construct that extends to individuals and their environment (immediate, connections, indirect, social, and cultural values and changes over time). Thus, this research project may consider the impact of the environment on individuals' wellbeing.
Biosocial model (Engel, 1997)	Wellbeing is perceived as a complex amalgamation of biological factors (e.g. impact of genes on wellbeing), psychological factors (e.g. impact of mood on wellbeing), and social factors (e.g. impact of socioeconomic status on wellbeing). Thus, this research project may consider assessing each one of the factors and identifying how they correlate with each other.
Ecosystem health model (Levins and Lopez, 1999)	Wellbeing is perceived as an outcome of the interaction of humans with nature, e.g. how pollution or population growth impacts individuals' wellbeing. Thus, this research project may consider correlating ecological data with individuals' or groups' wellbeing.
Mental health continuum model (Keyes, 2002)	Wellbeing is perceived on a continuum between mental illness and psychological functioning. Thus, this research project may consider assessing individuals' symptoms of depression, as well as psychological flourishing.
Positive psychology model (Seligman and Csikszentmihalyi, 2000)	Wellbeing is perceived as the presence of positive traits, e.g. engagement, positive relationship at an individual level and civic duties and institutions moving towards citizenship at group level. Thus, this research project may consider exploring the impact of participants positive traits on their wellbeing.

Table 5.3 Differences between theoretical framework, conceptual framework, and theory.

	Definitions	*If research is objectivist deductive*	*If the research is subjectivist inductive*
Conceptual Framework (CF)	Constructed by the researcher and provides a logical explanation for all the research decisions including methodology, methods, and why the research is important.	The CF is finalised before data collection.	The CF evolves as new research insights develop.
Theoretical Framework (TF)	Researcher constructed and used to explain the theory/s that underpins and scaffolds the research.	Theory is selected and applied to act as a framework/lens to articulate the research question and direct data analysis.	A tentative framework is proposed and then refined as the data is collected and analysed.
Theory	Description of relationships between concepts and ideas that help us understand the world.	Involves hypothesis prediction and testing and theory refinement.	Involves different ways of seeing the world and shapes all aspects of the research.

Source: Adapted from Varpio et al., 2020. A good place to start when thinking about developing your conceptual and theoretical framework is Kivunja's (2018) paper where he provides some very useful questions to ask yourself about the process.

On the other hand, you may also come across a term of "conceptual framework" which refers to the decisions you make as a researcher in relation to the literature you review, methodology you adapt, and so on. Kivunja describes a conceptual framework as "the total, logical orientation and associations of anything and everything that forms the underlying thinking, structures, plans and practices and implementation of your entire research project" (2018, p. 44). Theoretical framework on the other hand is made up of the key theories from the field you want to research that will help you make sense of your research and scaffold your thinking. Varpio et al. (2020) provide a very useful overview of how theory is linked to theoretical framework and to conceptual framework. Table 5.3 presents their thinking for you to consider.

Reflection time

What theories or models have you come across when reading about the topic of your interest? Take two of them and reflect on how different your research project would be if you took one of the other models or theories.

References

Bandura A. 1997. *Self-Efficacy: The Exercise of Control*. New York: Freeman.

Biesta, G. 2014. "Pragmatising the Curriculum: Bringing Knowledge Back into the Curriculum Conversation, but Via Pragmatism." *Curriculum Journal* 25(1): 29–49. doi: 10.1080/09585176.2013.874954.

Borman, G.D., J. Grigg, C.S. Rozek, P. Hanselman, and N.A. Dewey. 2018. "Self-Affirmation Effects Are Produced by School Context, Student Engagement with the Intervention, and Time: Lessons from a District-Wide Implementation." *Psychological Science* 29(11): 1773–1784.

Bronfenbrenner, U. 1979. *The Ecology of Human Development: Experiments by Nature and Design*. Cambridge, MA: Harvard University Press.

Cohen, L., L. Manion, and K. Morrison. 2018. *Research Methods in Education*. Abingdon, UK: Routledge.

Creswell, J.W. 2013. *Research Design: Qualitative, Quantitative, and Mixed Methods Approaches*. 4th ed. London: Sage.

Creswell, J.W., and C.N. Poth. 2018. *Qualitative Inquiry and Research Design. Choosing among Five Approaches*. London: Sage.

De Saxe, J.G. 2014. "What's Critical Feminism Doing in a Field Like Teacher Education?" *Multidisciplinary Journal of Gender Studies* 3(3): 530–555. doi: 10.4471/generos.2014.45.

Engel, G. 1997. "From Biomedical to Biopsychosocial: Being Scientific in the Human Domain." *Psychosomatic* 38(6): 521.

Hall, T., C. Connolly, S. O'Gradaigh, K. Burden, M. Kearney, S. Schuck, J. Bottema, G. Cazemier, W. Hustinx, M. Evens, T. Koenraad, E. Makridou, and P. Kosmas. 2020. "Education in Precarious Times: A Comparative Study across Six Countries to Identify Design Priorities for Mobile Learning in a Pandemic." *International Learning Sciences*. doi: 10.1108/ILS-04-2020-0089.

Imenda, S. 2014. "Is There a Conceptual Difference between Theoretical and Conceptual Frameworks?" *Journal of Social Sciences* 38(2): 185–195. doi: 10.1080/09718923.2014.11893249

Jabareen, Y. 2009. "Building a Conceptual Framework: Philosophy, Definitions, and Procedure." *International Journal of Qualitative Methods*, 50–62.

Kelly, L.M., and M. Cordeiro. 2020. "Three Principles of Pragmatism for Research on Organizational Processes." *Methodological Innovations*, 1–10. doi: 10.1177/2059799120937242

Keyes, C.L.M. 2002. "The Mental Health Continuum: From Languishing to Flourishing in Life." *Journal of Health and Social Behavior* 43(2): 207–222.

Kivunja, C. 2018. "Distinguishing between Theory, Theoretical Framework, and Conceptual Framework: A Systematic Review of Lessons from the Field." *International Journal of Higher Education* 7(6): 44–53.

Kivunja, C., and A.B. Kuyini. 2017. "Understanding and Applying Research Paradigms in Educational Contexts." *International Journal of Higher Education* 6(5): 26–41.

Kuhn, T.S. 1962. *The Structure of Scientific Revolutions*. Chicago: University of Chicago Press.

Levins, R., and C. Lopez. 1999. "Toward an Ecosocial View of Health." *International Journal of Health Services: Planning, Administration, Evaluation* 29(2): 261–293. doi: 10.2190/WLVK-D0RR-KVBV-A1DH

Lukenchuk, A. 2017. "Choosing among Paradigms and Research Designs." In *Outliving Your Dissertation: A Guide for Students and Faculty*, 57–85. Peter Lang. www.jstor.org/stable/45177753

Lukenchuk, A., and E. Kolich. 2013. "Paradigms and Educational Research: Weaving the Tapestry." In *Paradigms of Research for the 21st Century: Perspectives and Examples from Practice*, edited by A. Lukenchuk, 61–87. New York: Peter Lang.

Mertens, D.M. 2010. "Transformative Mixed Methods Research." *Qualitative Inquiry* 16(6): 469–474.

Neuman, W.L. 2011. *Social Research Methods: Qualitative and Quantitative Approaches*. 7th ed. Boston, MA: Pearson.

Perugini, M., and R. Bagozzi. 2001. "The Role of Desires and Anticipated Emotions in Goal-directed Behaivours: Broadening and Deepening the Theory of Planned Behavior." *British Journal of Social Psychology* 44: 29–45.

Popper, K.R. 1979. *Objective Knowledge: An Evolutionary Approach*. Oxford: Clarendon Press.

Prochalska, J.O., and C.C. DiClemente. 1983. "Stages and Processes of Self-change Smoking: Toward an Integrative Model of Change." *Journal of Consulting and Clinical Psychology* 51: 390–395.

Raskin, J.D., and S.K. Bridges, eds. 2002. *Studies in Meaning: Exploring Constructivist Psychology*. Washington, DC: Pace University Press.

Ravitch, S.M., and M. Riggan. 2017. *Reason and Rigor: How Conceptual Frameworks Guide Research*. 2nd ed. Thousand Oaks, CA: Sage.

Scotland, J. 2012. "Exploring the Philosophical Underpinnings of Research: Relating Ontology and Epistemology to the Methodology and Methods of the Scientific, Interpretive, and Critical Research Paradigms." *English Language Teaching* 5(9): 9–16.

Seligman, M.E.P., and M. Csikszentmihalyi. 2000. "Positive Psychology: An Introduction." *American Psychologist* 55(1): 5–14. doi: 10.1037/0003-066X.55.1.5

Shaw, R. 2019. "Interpretative Phenomenological Analysis." In *Doing Qualitative Research in Psychology*, edited by C. Sullivan and M.A. Forrester, 183–208. A Practical Guide. London: Sage.

Skinner, B.F. 1953. *Science and Human Behaviour*. New York: Free Press.

Tashakkori, A., and C. Teddie. 2003. *Handbook of Mixed Methods in the Behavioral and Social Sciences*. London, Thousand Oaks, CA: Sage.

Varpio, L., E. Paradis, S. Uijtdehaage, and M. Young. 2020. "The Distinctions Between Theory, Theoretical Framework, and Conceptual Framework." *Academy of Medicine* 95(7): 989–994. doi: 10.1097/ACM.0000000000003075. PMID: 31725464.

6   Methodology spectrum

After you decide on your research question and become aware of your positioning, your next step is to select a methodology. The methodology is a procedure you employ to address your research question. To help you do it, we have created a spectrum of methodologies (Figure 6.1), which comprises methodologies most frequently used in psychological research and includes some of the upcoming methods.

Methodologies presented at the top of the spectrum relate to empirical research projects. Empirical projects are carried out in a social environment and require human participants. They include such methodologies as action research, comparative research, or ethnography. Methodologies presented at the bottom of the spectrum are used for desk-based research projects. Despite often being practice-based, desk-based projects do not require participants. Such projects include a literature review relating to a problem you may have, a comparison of two wellbeing programmes, or secondary data analysis.

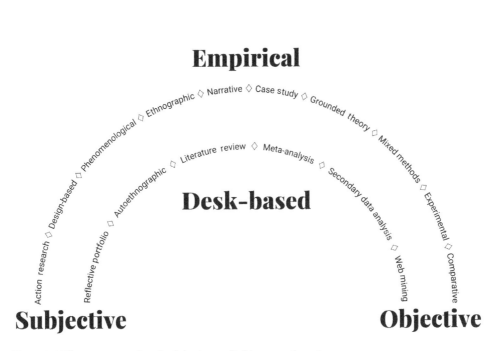

Figure 6.1 The spectrum of methodologies applied in research projects.

DOI: 10.4324/9781003262428-6

Sometimes your research question may distinctly veer you towards either empirical or desk-based projects; other times, you may have a specific research question, which can be addressed using either empirical or desk-based research. Indeed, some projects can include aspects of both. Table 6.1 provides an example of these two categories of projects in the context of a research question.

Apart from distinguishing methodologies between empirical and desk-based, we have also divided them *loosely* on a spectrum between subjective and objective approaches. We say *loosely*, as designs can be mixed, thus automatically changing their position on the spectrum. In addition to this, some methodologies can also be on a spectrum, depending on a theoretical framework used for data collection, analysis, or methods. This is why the objective-subjective spectrum is applied *loosely*. Its primary purpose is to provide a bigger picture of methodologies you can use when completing your research project. Let us now delve deeper into what subjective and objective methodologies are all about.

The subjective end of the spectrum refers to methodologies that help you focus on yourself and fully involve you as the researcher in your research project. For example, an empirical project may apply the Action Research methodology, the aim of which is to assess the effectiveness of your practice and tweak it after receiving feedback from others so that you can maximise your effectiveness. The research is subjective, i.e. focused on *you* and your changes as a practitioner. On the other hand, a desk-based project may involve you writing a reflective journal about your first year in a role and then analysing the content of your study to help you learn from your mistakes and offer suggestions for development in the future. Both research projects apply methodologies that promote a subjective perspective on practice.

On the other hand, the objective end of the spectrum refers to methodologies associated with the researcher being more detached from the participants and the data you

Table 6.1 An example of differences between empirical and desk-based project methodologies.

Research question	Empirical	Desk-based
How to help individuals overcome procrastination?	• Ethnographic research, in which you observe participants and identify the main techniques they use • Narrative research in which you interview participants and tell their stories • Experimental research in which you design intervention and test it with participants	• Literature review about the topic • Meta-analysis of experiments relating to the topic • Reflective portfolio about your experiences of the topic
What is wellbeing?	• Collectively, creating a piece of visual art depicting your participants' perception of wellbeing • Phenomenological research about the lived experiences of individuals in relation to their wellbeing • A survey assessing participants' wellbeing using psychological tests	• Systematic review of definitions of wellbeing • Secondary data analysis using a national sample • Content analysis of discussions about wellbeing in an online forum

examine. You become a mere observer of the phenomenon you study. For example, an empirical project may involve conducting a comparative analysis based on an online survey sent out to participants. A desk-based project may include analysing data from the internet. Both examples try to maximise the objectivity of the researcher.

Reflection time

Write down a list of pros and cons for carrying out an empirical and desk-based study and reflect on what approach appeals to you more and why.

6.1 Empirical research project

There are many different methodological options available to you for your empirical research project, we present ten options here (Figure 6.2). They span from subjective to objective approaches. We encourage you to briefly read all the approaches and then delve deeper into the three methodologies that can help you respond to your research question. Compare and contrast them to see what option is most suitable for you and why. This will help you select the best methodology for your research project.

We will begin by reviewing empirical subjective methodologies, such as action research and design-based research, and then move towards empirical objective methodologies, such as experimental and comparative research.

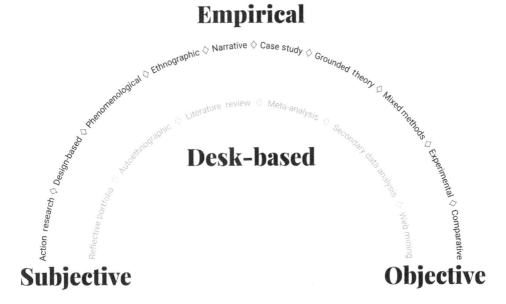

Figure 6.2 A spectrum of empirical research methodologies.

Psychological research tends to orient itself towards objective options. Recently, a systematic review of psychological methodologies revealed that 90% of psychological research published in leading peer-reviewed journals was quantitative, only 5% was qualitative, 1% was mixed methods, and the remaining 4% reviews of research, such as meta-analysis (Scholtz et al., 2020). Furthermore, this review also identified that the data was analysed predominantly using descriptive statistics, followed by correlational analysis, which identified relationships between variables, and ANOVA, which explored differences between groups. All these statistics and research designs are positioned in the objective part of the spectrum. We would like to encourage psychology students to use the broader spectrum of methodologies that would offer a more comprehensive perspective on the human psyche. We hope you will consider other options than the typical quantitative research.

6.1.1 Action research

Action research (Figure 6.3) is a well-established methodology widely used in practice-based research to solve problems and improve practice. It encourages you to make use of your own, your colleagues, and others' knowledge of practice, as well as effectively apply the theoretical literature that can help you with your research-based practice (Brookfield, 2005). Action Research is built around reflective practice, and throughout the process, you will use journaling and critical friends to help you reflect at a deeper level. A critical friend is someone you can trust to help you work on your research project, talk through your ideas and give honest feedback (Baskerville and Goldblatt, 2009). For example, if you are working on a work issue, you might ask a colleague to be your critical friend. They might meet with you every week and discuss your literature, talk through your research cycles and observe some of your work practices. Your critical friend offers another lens for you to look at your practice and enhance your reflection on it.

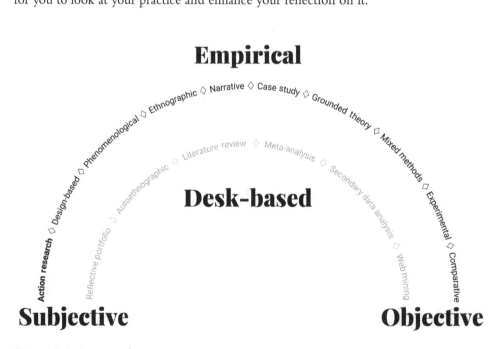

Figure 6.3 Action research.

As part of the Action Research cycle, you focus on an aspect of your practice that you want to research. Then, you reflect and collect data on your current practice, which becomes your reference point. On this basis, you plan, implement and then evaluate an action. Finally, you conclude this process and plan a further cycle(s) to work on the issue or practice (Figure 6.4).

You can apply action research in individual or group projects, and "it is founded on an active ethical commitment to improve the quality of life of others, is ethically reflective in nature and outcome, is collaborative with those affected by actions undertaken, and is made public" (Arhar et al., 2001) (p. 47). These characteristics make it applicable in any discipline and in any context to bring about change (Covenry, 2021). For example, Kidd and Kral (2005) describe how you can use it in counselling psychology, and Kelly and colleagues (2004) describe how you can use participatory action research in community research.

The following step-by-step process will walk you through the planning and reporting of an action research project:

- Step 1: Think about a problem/issue you are experiencing in your practice. Be as specific as possible. For example, you might be concerned about how to run meetings. Try to reflect on why you are interested in this topic, reflect on what it is about your leadership that you would like to improve or change. Maybe talk to another

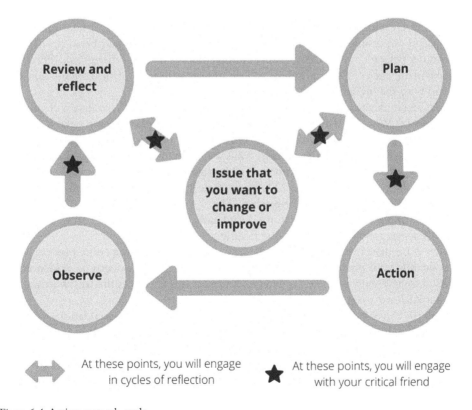

Figure 6.4 Action research cycle.

colleague and ask if they have similar concerns. Begin to map the field by looking at what the literature says about this area.

- Step 2: Is this problem just in your practice, or are others involved? A colleague may want to learn more about using time more effectively in meetings. This colleague may become your critical friend, who you can bounce ideas off, discuss issues, invite to observe your class. Your co-workers will need to be involved. You may decide that management in your workplace needs to be involved? How will you let people know about your research and get their consent/permission to join you? See Section 6.1 in this book for further information. Reflect on the issues you might encounter and the positive steps you can take to make this change.
- Step 3: What are the possible causes of the problem you are concerned about? Here you might consult the literature and discuss key findings with your critical friend. At this stage, you are narrowing down your topic and refining it to develop a research question that you can look at. You are also gathering baseline data that will give you the lay of the land ahead of the first cycle of action. This is called the recognisance stage of the research.
- Step 4: What might be the possible solution? Again you might consult the literature and your critical friend and reflect on what you are doing at the moment. Think about the ethical issues you need to consider.
- Step 5: What can you do now to solve the problem. This is your pre-implementation stage, where you map out the possible solutions to your problem and begin to develop the key supports you will need. It would help if you journaled your reflections on the process.
- Step 6: Develop a plan so that you can implement the process. Make this plan as detailed as possible to map all stages of the process. This should be so detailed that another person could take the plan and implement it with another group. This might take many cycles of development and discussion with your critical friend, consultation with the literature, and reflection on the process.
- Step 7: Think about how you will know if your plan works. What data will you need to collect? What do you need to put in place to gather data? Do you need to develop an observation schedule with your critical friend to observe your meetings? Will you survey co-workers after the process? Will you carry out interviews or focus groups? How will you do this? Will you use field notes? Your reflective journal? Conversations with your critical friend? The more time you put into this planning stage, the better the outcome for your research will be.
- Step 8: Implement your plan, journal, and gather data on working. This stage of the process may require more than one iteration.
- Step 9: Evaluate how your plan worked. Analyse the data for the entire process. When evaluating your practice, you must support all your claims concerning evidence. It is good to have evidence from different sources, as this enhances the trustworthiness of your analysis.
- Step 10: Develop conclusions, claims, explanations, and recommendations for future research. Think about how you might share your learning with others.

Action Research is a beneficial methodology to use in research projects where the focus is on changing your practice. The topic you select for Action Research should be about something that you have control over, that concerns your practice, something that you feel passionate about, and which you would like to change or improve. From the steps described earlier, you can see that you must put in the groundwork ahead of launching into changing your practice. For your research project, this change must be informed by your reflection and the literature in the area of inquiry. This makes it an informed action that you take and will strengthen your outcomes for the research.

Reflection time

Think about your research interest. Revisit the aforementioned definition of Action Research by Arhar et al. (2001) and consider what values motivate your study? Have you an ethical commitment to improve your practice? How will you do this? How will you document the process? How will you interpret the data and verify your interpretations? How will these actions make things better? How will you make your findings public?

6.1.1.1 Participatory Action Research (PAR) approach

Participatory Action Research (PAR) is similar to Action Research concerning its process but differs in that it is associated with research that seeks to bring about social transformation. It involves community members in various roles as partners in the research process. You should use methods that allow the voices of the most oppressed to be heard (Mertens, 2010) even though PAR is versatile about the contexts within which it is conducted. A wide range of research practices, and similarities are underlying this approach (McIntyre, 2007). They include the following:

1　Group commitment to resolve an issue.
2　Group and individual engagement in reflective practice.
3　A commitment of individuals and community to take beneficial action.
4　Collaborative planning, implementation, and research dissemination between researchers and the participants.

PAR is used in community psychology research (Kidd and Kral, 2005; Kelly et al., 2004).

PAR involves cycles of action and reflection and methods that encourage genuine participation, such as dialogue, storytelling, photo-ethnography, or collective action. In PAR, you aim towards a kind of participation that is a form of co-learning; participation is interactive (Kindon et al., 2007). Therefore, you a likely to take a critical position when planning this kind of research. Planning for this kind of participation requires you, the researcher, to be mindful of ethical implications throughout the process and engage with ethics-in-action (Stokes, 2020). Ethics-in-action is described as the ethical dilemmas that emerge during the research process. As your participants are co-researchers, anonymity cannot be guaranteed. At the same time, you work towards co-learning; there will always be power differences that you need to attend to. As you will be researching with your participants, you need to be mindful of your own emotional and physical safety and that of your co-researchers. Therefore, rather than addressing all your ethical dilemmas ahead of the research, you will need to keep ethics as part of your ongoing research process. In addition, researchers using PAR are often very closely connected to their co-researchers, and for this reason, you may find yourself having to confront some beneficial beliefs (Kidd and Kral, 2005).

Reflection time

Think about your research question and consider if you need to use PAR to answer it. How might you plan this research, and who could be your research participants? Now reflect on your competence to carry out this project. What support might you need?

6.1.2 Design-based research

Design-based (Figure 6.5) research is situated in authentic contexts; focusing on practice, design, and testing of interventions, it seeks to connect theory and practice. Design-based research is the term used in this book. Still, this methodology can also be referred to as design experiments, design studies, and engineering research, among others (see McKenney and Reeves, 2019, p. 18). It usually involves using mixed methods (see next section for more detail). There are multiple iterations, not unlike action research, but this methodology is different in many ways. It usually involves a partnership between researchers and practitioners who work together on designing interventions to improve practice. The work of this design team will develop design principles that can be applied in other settings, as it is concerned with an impact on practice (Anderson and Shattuck, 2012). Two primary goals of this kind of research are (1) advancing the theoretical understanding and (2) benefitting practice. Therefore, the artefact developed during the research takes on enhanced importance. Chapter 7 will delve deeper into the concept of an artefact.

Design-based research is organised around the concept of usable knowledge. It offers excellent potential in psychological research, as it can attend to experimental control

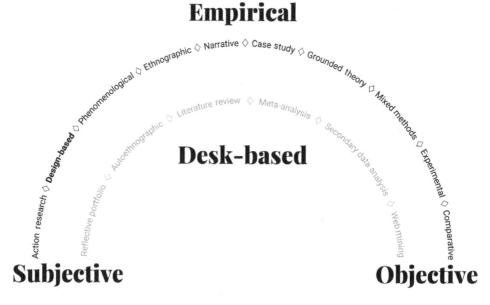

Figure 6.5 Design-based research.

and ecological validity (see, for example, McCandliss et al., 2003 for a discussion on this). Much of the thinking on design-based research stems from educational psychology. Researchers were grappling with designing complex instructional interventions and evaluating them scientifically (Sandoval and Bell, 2004). For example, you might design and develop an intervention such as a new module or teaching-learning strategy to solve a complex educational problem.

Alternatively, you might wish to design an intervention to change employee engagement with work or validate a theory. For example, you may use an approach such as positive leadership (Lucey and Burke, 2022) to change how leadership teams work in practice and identify their impact on employees' engagement. The key is to advance our knowledge about the characteristics of these interventions and the processes used to design and develop them so that others can take the work and implement it in their contexts (Plomp and Nieveen, 2013).

The guiding principles for this kind of research, like all research, are as follows:

- Pose significant question/s that can be investigated
- Link research to relevant theory so that your intervention is theory-driven
- Use methods that permit direct investigation of the question; this requires methodological creativity
- Map the process and provide a coherent and explicit chain of reasoning
- Replicate and generalise across studies if possible
- Communicate your research and encourage professional scrutiny and critique (Anderson and Shattuck, 2012; Shavelson and Towne, 2002)

Characteristics of educational design-based research:

1   It is theory-driven – The design of the research is built on theories, and the testing of the designs leads to the development of new theories.
2   It is collaborative – There is a collaboration among a range of actors connected to the problem. At the start of the process, you will consult others to establish the needs and context analysis. The development of the intervention can have communities of practice focus (Wegner, 1998). you will strengthen the design, development, and evaluation phase of the research by working with other practitioners. This will increase the chance of using the research in the context.
3   It is interventionist – The research designs an intervention for a real-world setting and watches it at work. Your research started with an important question, and the focus is on answering this question in practice in a natural work setting with others.
4   Your research is process-oriented – The research tries to explain how the design functions in real settings and why the interventions behave as they do. Your focus is on mapping the process of how the intervention works in your setting. It would help if you thought about all the different variables that can impact implementation and map these.
5   It is iterative – Not unlike action research, this research takes place through cycles of design, trialling, analysis, and redesign. You want to end up with an artefact or new theory that stands up to professional scrutiny and critique and is usable.

It is utility oriented – The quality of a design rests ultimately in how well it works, its practicality, and usefulness in the hands of the intended users (Plomp and Nieveen, 2010).

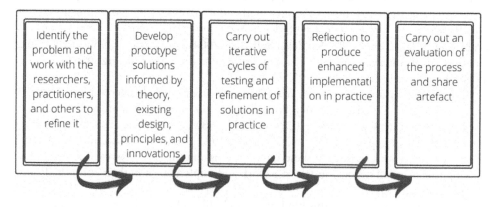

Figure 6.6 The design cycle. Adapted from Reeves (2006).

Figure 6.6 provides an overview of the process; however, it is essential to realise that there can be iterative cycles of reflection and change to your prototype at each step.

Design-based research is not without its challenges, as the researcher is a designer and often an evaluator and implementer of the intervention. Real-world settings bring real-world complications. With the iterative theory-focused design, the research needs to be adaptable. It allows for a lot of learning in the moment, which is why it is essential to capture the whole research process, including the "on the job" learning. McKenney and Reeves (2019) advise using the following guidelines for design-based research.

- Have an explicit conceptual framework (based on, for example, a review of literature, interviews of experts, studying other interventions, a mix of all three)
- Develop a congruent study design, i.e. apply a robust chain of reasoning with each cycle having its research design
- Use triangulation (of data source, data type, method, evaluator, and theory) to enhance the reliability and internal validity of the findings
- Apply both inductive and deductive data analysis
- Use full, rich descriptions of the context, design decisions, and research results
- Take data and interpretations back to the source to increase the internal validity of findings

Now take some time to reflect on what this methodology offers you.

Reflection time

Think about your research problem and consider if educational design-based research is a suitable methodology for you. Who might you invite to join your design team? What expertise do you need on the team? What theory will inform the development of your artefact?

6.1.3 *Phenomenological research*

Phenomenological research (Figure 6.7) is concerned with how individuals and collectives create and understand their own living spaces; it is concerned with perceptions and experiences. What makes phenomenological research different from other qualitative methods is that the "subjective experience is the centre of inquiry" (Mertens, 2010, p. 235). You are seeking to portray a world in which reality is socially constructed, complex, and ever-changing; you want to describe in-depth participants' subjective experiences (Patton, 2002). Phenomenology has evolved from a philosophy to a methodology (see Dowling (2007) for a good overview of the field). Phenomenological psychology refers to an approach to psychology that draws on phenomenological and hermeneutic philosophy. Hermeneutics is concerned with understanding, interpretation, and communication (Barrett et al., 2011; Finlay, 2011). See Davidsen (2013) for a good overview of the critical theorists in phenomenological philosophy. In literature, it is clear that the phenomenological approach covers many different ways to carry out research, from those that are purely descriptive to those that use more analytical approaches such as Interpretive Phenomenological Analysis (IPA) and Narrative Analysis, to name a few (Davidsen, 2013; Sullivan and Forrester, 2019). These are discussed in more detail in Chapter 8.

When carrying out a phenomenological study, your position is that of interpretivism. You provide an interpretation of others' interpretations through a lens of concepts, theories, and the literature on the phenomenon being researched (Bryman, 2008). In addition to this, you can use many different methods, including interviews, conversations, participant observation, action research, focus groups, analysis of personal histories, and other texts. You may also use a mix of methods if it helps you answer your research question.

In relation to the sampling method, you are looking for participants who have experience with the phenomenon you wish to describe. Thus, if your research is about the impact of grief on mothers, then you need to talk to mothers who have experienced

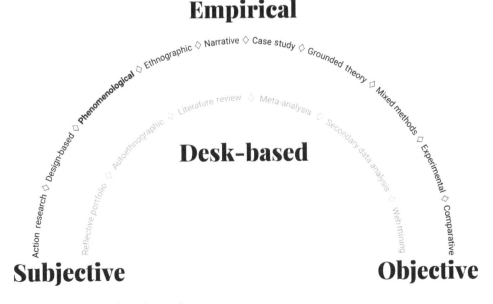

Figure 6.7 Phenomenological research.

grief. You may want to look at how grief from the loss of a child differs from that from the loss of a parent. To get this experience, you will need to carry out in-depth interviews or ask participants to keep a diary of their experience of grief. You will need to get rich descriptions. In their interviews, you are looking for depth, minimum structure, and avoiding exerting undue influence on the process. Establishing a good level of rapport and empathy is critical to gaining a depth of information, particularly when you are investigating issues where the participant has a strong personal stake; this can be difficult for novice researchers. You seek to describe the phenomena as accurately as possible rather than explain them but at all times remain true to the facts (Sloan and Bowe, 2014).

An issue with phenomenological research is that it generates a large quantity of data such as observation notes, interview transcripts, journal entries, pictures, and other materials, all of which must be analysed. An analysis is also necessarily messy, as data does not fall into neat categories. There can be many links between different parts of discussions or observations. This is where the concept of double interpretation comes into play and, indeed, in a way, triple interpretation (Bryman, 2008). You are interpreting others' interpretation of an experience and then analysing it through the lens of the concepts, theories, and literature pertaining to your research. In doing this, you need to bracket your preconceptions and remember that the object is to describe the phenomenon, not to explain it.

The phenological view of experience is complex, so it usually involves only a single or small number of participants, e.g. three. As a researcher, you reflect on the data under analysis through the following four areas: lived space – spatiality, lived body – corporeality, lived time – temporality, lived human relation – relationality; these may be seen to belong to the existential way that humans experience the world (van Manen, 1997). Form our earlier example, you may describe the experience of the mothers in their home (spatiality), what it feels like when they are doing their work (corporeality), how they experience the time when they are thinking about their loved one (temporality), and the interaction with others (relationality). This approach, therefore, focuses on describing lived experiences of participants. How these experiences are analysed varies from using rich descriptions to using IPA described in Chapter 8.

6.1.4 Ethnographic research

Ethnographic research is the study of cultural patterns and perspectives of participants in their natural settings such as schools, clubs, communities; it is about naturally occurring activities in particular settings. It is described as a way of being, seeing, thinking, and writing about experiences (Mills and Morton, 2013). In carrying out ethnography, you tell a story through narratives embedded in very particular contexts, and these contexts are described in great detail (Suzuki et al., 2005). Bryman (2008) describes ethnography as a research method in which the researcher

- is immersed in a particular social setting for an extended period;
- makes regular observations of the behaviour of members of that setting;
- listens to and engages in conversations;
- interviews informants on issues that are directly amenable to observation or that the ethnographer is unclear about or wants to know more about (see also Suzuki et al. (2007) for qualitative data collection);
- collects documents about the group;

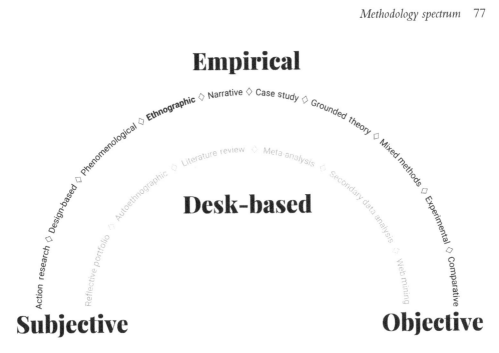

Figure 6.8 Ethnographic research.

- develops an understanding of the culture of the group and people's behaviour within the context of that culture; and
- writes up a detailed account of that setting (pp. 402 and 403).

There are several types of ethnography, including critical ethnography, autoethnography, life history, performance ethnography, feminist ethnography, portraiture, photo-ethnography, and applied ethnography (Mertens, 2010; Denzin and Lincoln, 2000).

While doing your research project, it is unlikely that you will get to carry out an ethnographic research project due to time restraints. This is because ethnography usually involves an extended period in the field. However, you can do a micro-ethnography project, studying a minor experience or very particular practice. It is focused, time-bound, and targeted. You are the "fly on the wall", so to speak, observing everything in great detail. For example, suppose you want to study how people communicate during planning meetings. In that case, you could use a micro-ethnographic approach by audio-recording (with permission) the meetings and carrying out a narrative analysis on the data to address your research aim.

You will need to deal with several issues, such as access to the site/group, decisions on whether you will carry out overt vs covert ethnography, how gatekeepers might help gain access, and will you use critical informants. Covert ethnography is when you do not tell the participants that you are carrying out the study. Key informants are the people you identify as the ones who can give you the most information about the behaviours and context of your research. Using key informants carries risks; Bryman (2008) advises the researcher to not become over-reliant on a key informer to such an extent that you begin to see the social reality through their eyes and "rather than through the eyes of members of the social setting" (p. 409).

Micro-ethnography has a lot to offer in a research project where you want to look at a phenomenon for a relatively short period, from a couple of weeks to a few months, either full time or part time. Furthermore, the ethnography approach is collaborative, meaning that you go into a community to do your research with people who live in that community; therefore, the context of your study will be determined by the sociocultural structure of a group you work with (Yanik, 2017; Pink, 2021). However, you can take it one step further and employ collaborative ethnography. The collaborators (study participants) provide the researcher with data and write the research report together (Lassiter, 2005). While this research approach is time-consuming, it can offer rich data and is worth considering.

6.1.5 Narrative research

Narrative research integrates personal and social stories and is helpful for psychologists who wish to understand the influence of social life and identity on participant's experience of everyday issues, "such as being in a family or being male, or for more specific concerns, such as life-threatening illness and traumatic experience" (Stephens and Breheny, 2013). Narrative inquiry as a methodology, however, is not just about collecting stories or telling them; it is an overarching principle where data, analysis, and representation are all narrative in form (Conle, 2000).

If you use narrative inquiry in your research, it will involve looking at how we can approach the research to hear these rich stories; it may include journals, stories, interviews, or focus groups but can also include the analysis of artefacts such as pieces of art, films, songs, memoirs, or other written words. A narrative approach to carrying out a research project acknowledges the complexities of each human being and the human centredness in research. It does not focus on synthesising participants' experiences, trying

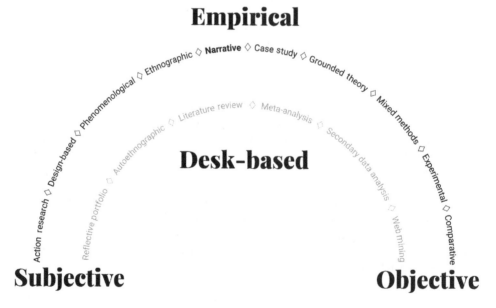

Figure 6.9 Narrative research.

to find patterns of thinking, feeling, or behaviour; instead, it focuses on telling stories, narratives about the individuals, incorporating the dynamic context within which they exist (Webster and Mertova, 2007).

You can take many approaches when selecting narrative research as a vehicle for your research project. On the most basic level, you may conduct research using a different methodology and present your findings using a narrative approach. Therefore, you tell stories about the individuals you have interviewed, e.g. narrative case study. We may also use a narrative methodology in your project, which involves designing a narrative inquiry, analysing the stories, and interpreting them by noting what is said and how it is said (Kim, 2015). Depending on our philosophical position, your analysis may be limited to just what is being said or the meaning of what is being said, rather than both. In other words, you may present the stories as critical events, or you may analyse the narrative. Josselson (2006, p. 3) contends that narrative research is always interpretive and "strives to preserve the complexity of what it means to be human".

There can be several challenges in a narrative inquiry, such as collecting extensive amounts of data and then grappling with how to analyse and present data without narrowing the story. "Focusing on critical events in narratives of experiences" can help avoid these pitfalls (Webster and Mertova, 2007, p. 115).

Reflection time

You could start your narrative inquiry by writing out the story of your educational journey to where you are today. What is your story, who were the influential people, critical events, places, and what stages of your academic path were most impactful? Are there threads you can use to link the necessary periods of your journey to reading this book? Maybe you would like to represent your journey as a picture, poem, or timeline. This might give you some ideas about capturing and presenting lived experiences.

6.1.6 *Case study*

A case study design may be a suitable option for your research project. A case study can be based on a single person, a group of people, a community, an organisation, a family, or an event. It is an approach that examines a case in-depth and where boundaries between the analysed phenomenon and its context are blurred (Yin, 2018). For instance, in a single person's case study, Freud has famously published research with Little Hans or Ona O. In a group case study, interviews were held with participants with Down syndrome and provided insights into what they did to help them thrive psychologically (Thompson et al., 2020). An example of a community-based case study included interviews with 11 general practitioners about the effect of positive health practices on their job satisfaction (Lemmen et al., 2021). If your research question requires an in-depth description of social phenomena, then more than likely, you will use a case study design. Within a case study, the context is significant to understanding the phenomenon.

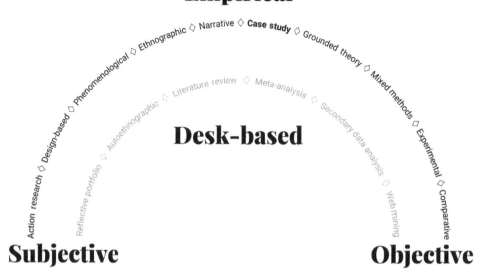

Figure 6.10 Case study research.

For example, your research project may be on trainee coaching psychologists' practice in their final year of college. Here are some of the options for research you may select:

a   You might decide to do a case study with three psychologists trained in one university (a convenience sample). In this way, your case is bound to this specific university.
b   You might also position yourself within the interpretive paradigm where you seek to understand a phenomenon, in this case, the experience of trainee coaching psychologists' practice, by interviewing 12 trainee coaching psychologists from various universities around England. You may choose to analyse their data using Braun and Clarke's Thematic Analysis (see Chapter 8 for details).
c   You may also design a cross-sectional survey as a method of data collection and send it out to the coaching psychology students in England, in which case you may collate over 300 responses and choose to analyse them using descriptive or correlational statistics.
d   Alternatively, you may apply a mixed-method design to use a survey to collect data from 200 students in England. Then, select 15 students from your survey sample and conduct focus groups with them, which will allow you to describe their experiences in more depth than a simple survey. Using this design, you could also use documents, such as participants' journal entries, feedback from their clients, or related notes that will help you understand the practice of trainee coaching psychologists.

Remember, with case study design, the purpose is not to generate generalisable findings to the total population, e.g. you will not be saying that this is the experience of all trainees across the country. Instead, even if you are carrying out a survey, you will be generalising

Table 6.2 Difference types of case studies (Yin, 2018; Bryman, 2008; Stake, 2005).

Type of case study	Purpose	Example
Intrinsic	To gain deeper understanding of a specific case	How can a teacher create and sustain a community through a district recycling project?
Explanatory	To develop and test theories	Will increased use of collaborative learning enhance student performance in examinations?
Exploratory	To develop propositions for further inquiry	Looking at our school's policy on inclusive education
Instrumental	To provide insight into a particular theory, or issue	Looking at how parent-teacher interactions happen in order to bring increase parents' agency in the curriculum making space
Collective or multiple case study	Where the study of number of cases is used to gain a bigger picture of a particular phenomenon	Looking at how homework practices impact on student engagement in five schools
Descriptive	To provide narrative accounts	Looking at the places where bullying occurs in a school

data from the survey to a specific group of people, i.e. trainee coaching psychologists in the final year of their college degree. If your data is qualitative, you may provide some rich data that will help you understand the experience of trainee coaching psychologists. Central to your research is how your results are underpinned by the theory and how your data supports your theoretical arguments; a case study can therefore be about both theory testing and theory generating (Bryman, 2008).

There are many different types of case studies (Table 6.2). Their differences depend on the research purpose, which further guides the study design and outcomes. After deciding on your study aim, you can select the approach you want to take concerning your case study that best suits your purpose.

Case studies can include qualitative and quantitative data, and from the various sources, triangulation of data can be carried out (Yin, 2018). Triangulation of data means that you will use data from different people, methods, or other sources to validate a claim, a process, or an outcome through at least two independent sources. For example, suppose my case study was looking at how I integrated technology into the curriculum in my school. In that case, I might interview teachers, observe classes, look at lesson plans, and interview students. If Teacher A tells me, "I use an online platform to mark and give feedback on homework in my class", and in an interview, a student says, "It is great that I can see the feedback on my work at home on last night's homework before I upload today's homework", you can conclude that Teacher A is using technology to mark homework. In the example in Figure 6.11, multiple data sources are used for triangulation.

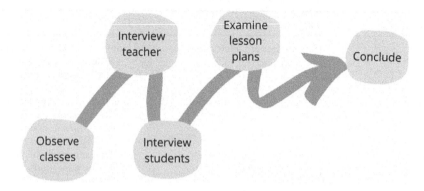

Figure 6.11 Example of triangulation.

Just as there are different types of case studies, there is no one way to design your case study. Yin (2018, p. 27) suggests that your research design must have the following five components (Table 6.3):

- The research question: case study questions are usually "how" and "why" questions. See Section 4.3 about developing a question.
- Its propositions, if any. Your propositions are theoretical and can come from your literature review or they can represent practical matters that are theoretically linked to your research question.
- Its case(s).
- The logic linking the data to the propositions.
- The criteria for interpreting the findings.

Table 6.3 shows the steps necessary when carrying out multiple case studies. Thinking about the previous example about homework practices, you might decide that you need

Table 6.3 Steps involved in case study design. Adapted from Yin (2018).

Single case	Multiple case
Determine and define the research questions	Determine and define the research questions
Define and design	Define and design
Develop theory, propositions	Develop theory, propositions
Select the case and determine data-gathering and analysis techniques	Select the cases and determine data-gathering and analysis techniques
Prepare, collect, and analyse	Prepare, collect, and analyse
Conduct case study	Conduct case studies
Evaluate and analyse the data	Write individual case reports
Prepare the report on your capstone project	Analyse and conclude
	Draw cross-case conclusions
	Write cross-case report on your capstone project

to look at homework practices on more than one site; in this case, you might decide to carry out a multi-site case study. Here, you gather data from more than one site to compare sites. For example, your case might be in a single-sex female school or a particular cultural context, and you want to see if homework practices differ or are similar in other contexts. You will gather data using identical designs in different case study sites. You must be clear on why you need multiple sites and what criteria you use in selecting sites. The criteria one might use, for example, is do you want to see if the phenomenon is present in other similar sites or if there is some factor affecting the phenomenon. In the first instance, you would choose a secondary school as similar to the first as possible, e.g. both single-sex females. In the second instance, you would select a school that is not a single-sex female school because you think that the phenomenon is linked to the gendered nature of a school. The use of more than one site in a case study can enhance your findings.

There are criteria that you can use to judge the quality of your research design for case studies. These are construct validity, internal validity, external validity, and reliability. Construct validity is concerned with the measures used in the research. You can strengthen it by pilot testing measurement instruments, replicating measures, and having key informants review your case study report. Internal validity is concerned with causal relationships and therefore is not relevant to all case studies. It would help if you showed that certain conditions lead to other conditions, as distinguished from some other unintended variable. It is essential to address rival explanations and explicate your findings using rich data to strengthen internal validity.

External validity is concerned with how the results can be generalised to other people, in different settings, at other times. Robson (2011) lists two general strategies for enhancing external validity: direct demonstration and making a case. Finally, reliability is the extent that you can replicate your findings.

You must maintain your chain of evidence and describe all steps of the research process. According to Yin (2018), applying these four lenses to your case study will increase the quality of your research design. Trustworthiness criteria can also be used to ensure quality, criteria such as credibility (prolonged, persistent triangulation, debriefing, and checks), transferability (thick descriptive data), confirmability, and dependability (external audit and audit trail) (Lincoln and Guba, 1986).

6.1.7 Grounded theory

Grounded theory (Figure 6.12) is a complex methodological approach to the generation of theory from your data; the theory emerges inductively primarily from your data. The concept was first put forward by Glaser and Strauss (1967) but has changed dramatically over the years (Bryman, 2008). The initial analysis is not based on a developed theoretical framework. In a way, you are reading your data without any "ideational baggage" (Glaser, 1978, p. 44). Grounded theory is an evolving process and is not presented as a perfect end product of your research (Chun et al., 2019). At the heart of the process is the constant comparison method, so any theory that emerges is provisional and open to falsification. Getting to the theory is not easy and requires you to be imaginative and creative in working. It is grounded in a set of procedures we propose to follow if using this methodology. Grounded theory can be seen as a methodology and a way of working with data.

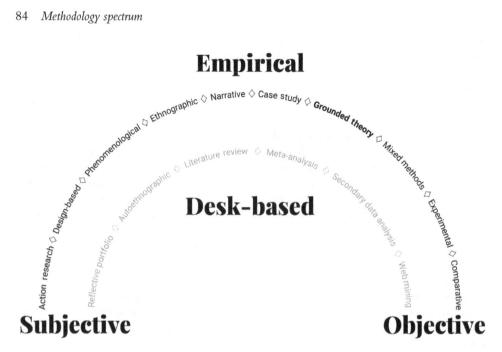

Figure 6.12 Grounded theory research.

Theoretical sampling

Theoretical sampling is a core concept of grounded theory and is concerned with how your method and data coexist in a symbiotic relationship, each one speaking to the other. This means that you begin to develop your theory through collecting, analysing, and coding data, and you see where you need more data as the theory emerges (Glaser and Strauss, 1967). In this way, the relationship is symbiotic.

The additional data may be in more interviews, observations, or conversations but could also be policy documents; it is whatever you need to make constant comparisons and further develop your theory, to answer the "why" question (Charmaz, 2008). You can use any method of qualitative data collection with grounded theory. It would help if you remained open to new possibilities both in the field and with the data at all stages. In this way, you are at all times analysing your data.

Through theoretical sampling, you can elaborate on the meaning of your categories, discover a variation within them, and define gaps between categories. Theoretical sampling relies on comparative methods for discovering these gaps and finding ways to fill them.

Coding

Line-by-line coding allows you to build your analysis from the ground up without taking off on theoretical flights of fancy. However, it is a critical stage that you cannot skip. It means naming each line on each page of your written data, even though you may not always have complete sentences.

As you read each line, ask yourself questions, such as the following:

- What is going on?
- What are people doing?
- What is the person saying?
- What do these actions and statements take for granted?
- How do structure and context support, maintain, impede, or change these actions and statements?

Try to make your codes short and specific. Try not to assume that respondents repress or deny significant "facts" about their lives. Instead, look at how they understand their situations before judging their attitudes and actions through your assumptions. There are different code levels, and the name given to the code carries its significance, and you should note the context and meaning of the code allocated.

Focused coding is the next state of the process, and it aims to synthesise and explain more significant segments of data. Focused coding means using the most significant and frequent earlier codes to sift through a large amount of data. Thus, focused coping is more directed, selective, and conceptual than line-by-line coding (Glaser, 1978). Focused coding requires decisions about which initial codes make the most analytic sense and categorise your data most accurately and completely. Yet, moving to focused coding is not entirely a linear process. Some respondents or events make explicit what was implicit in earlier statements or prior events. An "Aha! Now I understand" experience prompts you to study your earlier data afresh. Then you may return to earlier respondents and explore topics that had been glossed over or that may have been too implicit or unstated to discern. Focus coding checks your preconceptions about the topic forcing you to "act" upon the data rather than read it passively.

Constant comparisons

At a point, you will reach theoretical saturation where you have coded your data and where no new concepts or categories are emerging, and you have collected sufficient data to illuminate the category (Bryman, 2008). You may now decide to carry out more focused coding, as this moves your analysis forward in two crucial steps: It establishes the content and form of your nascent analysis and prompts you to evaluate and clarify your categories and the relationships between them. First, you need to assess which codes best capture what you see happening in your data. Raise them to conceptual categories for your developing analytic framework. Thus, going beyond using a code as a descriptive tool to view and synthesise data. A category is fully explained during the coding process.

As you raise a code to a category, you begin to write a narrative statement in memos that explicate the properties of the category

- Specify the conditions under which the category arises, is maintained, and changes
- Describe its consequences
- Show how this category relates to other categories.

Categories may consist of *in vivo* codes that you take directly from your respondents' discourse, or they may represent your theoretical or substantive definition of what is happening in the data. Novice researchers tend to rely most on in vivo and substantive codes, which results in a grounded description rather than a theory. Studying how the codes fit into categories can help you treat them more theoretically. To create categories through focused coding, you need to compare data, incidents, contexts, and concepts. Here are some of the comparisons you can make:

- Comparing different people (in terms of their beliefs, situations, actions, accounts, or experiences)
- Comparing data from the same individuals at different points in time
- Comparing specific data with the criteria for the category
- Comparing categories in the analysis with other categories

Glaser and Strauss (1967) advised writing memos about the generated categories. This memo-writing is an essential aspect of grounded theory.

Memo-writing

Memo-writing consists of taking your categories apart by breaking them into their components. It is the pivotal intermediate step between defining categories and the first draft of your completed analysis. This step spurs you to develop your ideas in narrative form and fullness early in the analytic process. Memos also help you identify which codes to treat as analytical categories if you have not already defined them. Some students find mind-mapping useful here. Then you further develop your category through more memo-writing. For example, you want to move from descriptions to reflecting on your positionality to analytical abstractions, which pave the way for you to build a theory.

Think of including as many of the following points in your memos as is possible:

- Defining each code or category by its analytic properties
- Spelling out and detaining processes subsumed by the codes or categories
- Making comparisons between data and between codes and categories
- Bringing raw data into the memo
- Providing sufficient empirical evidence to support your definitions of the category and analytic claims about it
- Offering conjectures to check through further empirical research
- Identifying gaps in the analysis

Grounded theories look for patterns, even when focusing on a single case (Strauss, 1970). Because of the stress identifying patterns, grounded theorists typically invoke respondents' stories to illustrate points rather than provide complete portrayals of their lives. Memo-writing moves your work beyond individual cases through defining patterns.

Begin with careful definitions of each category. Then, start memo-writing as soon as you have some interesting ideas and categories to pursue. Treat memos as partial, preliminary, and correctable, and direct your memo-writing to make comparisons.

Write up

After defining your theoretical categories fully, supporting them with evidence, and ordering them by sorting the memos you have written about them, you start writing the first draft of your capstone project. Writing is more than mere reporting. Instead, the analytic process proceeds through the writing of your report. Use your now developed categories to form sections of the project. Show the relationships between categories. The analytical focus encourages making theoretical relationships explicit and using verbatim material to explicate these (Glaser, 1978). After you have developed your conceptual analysis of the data, go to the literature in your field and compare how and where your work fits in with it – be specific. At this point, you must cover the literature thoroughly and weave it into your work explicitly.

Grounded theory is a systematic methodology involving iterative comparative analysis and data-gathering cycles. It is complex and should be considered cautiously (Chun et al., 2019). Therefore, if it is your first research project, we recommend you select an alternative methodology.

6.1.8 Mixed methods

Mixed-methods research (Figure 6.13) intentionally combines or integrates quantitative and qualitative approaches as research components. If using several different qualitative approaches, such as observation, interview, and some arts-based methodologies, your study is better described as a multimethod design rather than mixed methods. These approaches can occur at different points in the research process (Hall, 2020; Caruth, 2013; Creswell and Plano, 2011; Teddlie and Tashakkori, 2009). To describe a study as a mixed-methods, you would need to have a quantitative component, e.g. an experiment using a survey before intervention and after, and a qualitative component, such as an in-depth interview afterwards to delve deeper into the experiences of participants undergoing an experiment.

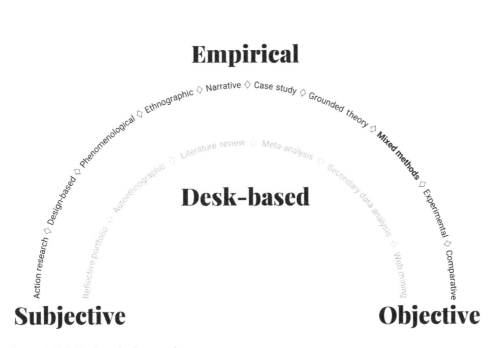

Figure 6.13 Mixed-methods research.

In the planning phase, where the research plan is developed, you choose to use this methodology when it becomes clear that you cannot address the research problem from the unique perspective of a quantitative or qualitative study. Your research requires a mix of data to be collected for you to answer the question. The research questions of the study are the focus of all methodological decisions. The research question guides the study and determines which quantitative and qualitative methods components are used and at what points in the research process. It is an excellent idea to develop a matrix with your research question broken down and linked to what data you need to collect and how you will do this.

You will be using quantitative measurement instruments with qualitative research techniques to generate quantitative and qualitative data to address the research problem. These can be combined in different ways, depending on your position. You may adopt various positions, including straddling two positions, including, for example, a post-positivist, interpretive, or pragmatic position. Once the study is in place, any decisions on how to combine or integrate quantitative and qualitative approaches are based on how these provide an insight into the complexity of the problem and answer the study's research questions to achieve the research objectives. You will intentionally integrate quantitative and qualitative data analysis, and each method will inform the other within the process. You will incorporate quantitative and qualitative data in presenting the study findings. You will use the strengths from one research method to offset methodological shortcomings from the other to reach more robust conclusions. (Hall, 2020; Caruth, 2013; Creswell and Plano, 2011; Teddlie and Tashakkori, 2009; Green, 2007).

The basic structure of the mixed methods study

There are several different typologies for mixed methods (Hall et al., 2020; Creswell and Plano, 2011; Teddlie and Tashakkori, 2009). When selecting a mixed-methods design, you must use your research question to drive the design you choose to use.

- Research in sequential phases (sequential phases design). This signifies that the researcher begins their study with a research approach (Phase I) and uses findings to design a second phase (Phase II) but using another research approach. For example, you might survey coaching psychologists specialising in health coaching and inquire into what type of coaching approaches they use. On analysis of these data, you will realise that some use specific approaches and models of coaching, while others use an eclectic approach to health coaching. To find out what motivates them to select their approach, you might interview them. Alternatively, you may start your research by gathering a few coaching psychologists in a focus group to discuss their approach to health coaching. You will then carry out a thematic analysis of the collected data. To determine if their experience is similar to most coaching psychologists specialising in health coaching, you might design a survey, the aim of which is to generalise your data.
- Research in parallel phases (convergent parallel design). This means that the researcher simultaneously uses quantitative and qualitative approaches to develop their study. Generally, parallel phase studies study the problem integrated from the quantitative and qualitative approaches.

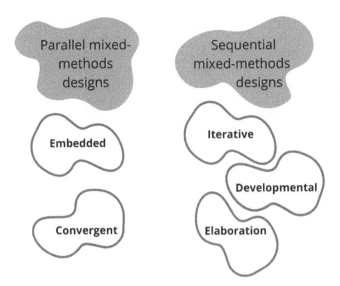

Figure 6.14 Mixed-methods design. Source: Adapted from Hall (2020).

See Figure 6.14 for a pictorial representation of other sequential and parallel options for mixed-methods design.

Following on from Figure 6.14, the five types of mixed-methods design are as follows:

1   Convergent parallel design – the qualitative and quantitative methods are of equal status and are implemented independently, with integration occurring at the interpretation phase of the research.
2   Embedded parallel design – one method (e.g. the qualitative) is embedded in the other (e.g. the quantitative). Usually, the embedded component plays a minor role.
3   Elaboration sequential design – the quantitative method precedes the qualitative method. Usually, the qualitative is designed to follow up some of the findings in the quantitative to provide further understanding.
4   Developmental sequential design – the qualitative method precedes the quantitative method. Usually, the quant method is designed to examine the generalisability of the findings of the qualitative method or to develop concepts identified at the qualitative stage.
5   Iterative sequential design – more than two methods are implemented sequentially, with subsequent methods designed to explore findings in preceding methods.

Mixed methods as a research methodology offer many affordances in answering research questions. Remember that it is your research question that drives the methods used.

Reflection time

Use the following headings to sketch out how your research questions will link with the quantitative and qualitative methods you will use. Then think about how you will sequence the research; this will help you design the research project.

Research question	*Qualitative/s and quantitative/s methods you might use*	*Stage in the process*

6.1.9 *Experimental*

In the same way, as we have distinguished between quantitative and qualitative methodologies in research, some researchers also differentiate between experimental (Figure 6.15) and non-experimental research (Hoy and Adams, 2016). These categories help us make sense of and identify uniqueness about the approach we select. Experimental research is research in which you manipulate one variable (factor) to determine the effect of this manipulation on other variable/s. It is often used when evaluating the effectiveness of an intervention. Let us provide you with an example.

Empirical

Phenomenological ◇ Ethnographic ◇ Narrative ◇ Case study ◇ Grounded theory ◇ Mixed methods ◇ Experimental

Action research ◇ Design-based ◇ ... ◇ Autoethnographic ◇ Literature review ◇ Meta-analysis ◇ Secondary data analysis ◇ Web mining ◇ Comparative

Reflective portfolio

Desk-based

Subjective   Objective

Figure 6.15 Experimental research.

Say that you are interested in identifying to what extent switching off a phone one hour before going to bed impacts participants' overall wellbeing. You, therefore, divide participants into two groups. You will ask your experimental group to switch off all their computing devices one hour before going to sleep, while the control group will continue to do what they have been doing without any change. You will then assess all participants' (experimental and control group) wellbeing before the intervention and one week later. You will see that the wellbeing of the experimental group is significantly higher than the control group; therefore, you may conclude that the intervention of switching off a phone one hour before going to bed enhances participants' wellbeing (Hughes and Burke, 2018). This is how an experiment is conducted.

If you were to design a non-experimental study, you would assess all participants' wellbeing and phone use before bed. Suppose your data showed you that those who do not use their phones before going to bed have higher levels of wellbeing. In that case, you might conclude that not using phones is associated with higher wellbeing. Still, you would not attribute their wellbeing to phone use without experimenting directly. This is why experimental studies claim they can demonstrate causality, i.e. switching off the phone before bed enhances wellbeing. In contrast, other non-experimental methods cannot make such claims. They can only maintain that there is indeed an association between two variables (phone use and wellbeing), but we don't know whether it is directly related to each other.

An important point to note is that while most of the experimental research is quantitative, there are also examples of qualitative experimental studies whereby qualitative instead of quantitative methods are selected for data collection (e.g. interviews, focus groups) and analysis (e.g. Phenomenological, Thematic Analysis) within true experimental conditions (e.g. Robinson and Mendelson, 2012; Round and Burke, 2018). Therefore, we can have a quantitative experimental design and a qualitative experimental design. However, please note that an experimental design is not the only one you can select when evaluating the efficacy of a programme, curriculum, or workshop. To do this, we can also use qualitative approaches, such as action research or design-based research.

There are, however, many challenges associated with experimentation. Firstly, many of the experimental studies use a small sample of participants. For example, meta-analyses of studies about the impact of positive psychology interventions on wellbeing showed that, on average, there were approximately 50–80 participants per experimental study, with some published research having as few as 13 participants (White et al., 2019). Say that your study has 30 participants in the control group and 30 in an experimental group. This is not a large sample, given the overall population. This is why replication in research, especially given the small sample size, is of utmost importance (Travers et al., 2016). Replication means that the same study is carried out with another group of participants.

Let us give you an example of the usefulness of replication in research. Ego depletion is an outcome of a process of suppressing thoughts over a prolonged period, which results in the depletion of mental resources that control our urges (Baumeister et al., 1998). When our thoughts are suppressed for too long, we may start acting out a character, become aggressive, say things we later regret, or when dieting, we start binge eating. All the suppressing of our thoughts comes out as an uncontrolled outburst due to our ego depletion. It also happens to you as a student, and when it does, it leads to a decline in their performance and school-related burnout (Price and Yates, 2010; Seibert et al., 2016).

Since the concept of ego depletion was first introduced, over 300 experimental studies were carried out to assess the efficacy of this concept (Dang, 2018). Some of these studies were a direct replication of previous studies. Other studies introduced different variables. There have also been a few meta-analyses introduced, which was to assess the collective efficacy of the interventions. Unfortunately, the results of small studies are often inflated compared to larger samples, which creates a small-study effect that researchers attempt to address in meta-analyses (Sterne and Egger, 2001). This is why it is important to replicate a study to ensure that the results are similar with a different sample.

Secondly, all studies are influenced by the publication bias, whereby findings showing that a concept does not work or studies that do not fully follow the experimental protocol are rarely published, therefore, skewing the results further. Taking all into consideration, as in all research, there are challenges with using experimental studies that need to be considered when designing it for your capstone project.

Let us now look at various types of experimental studies. Table 6.4 provides a list of the experimental study designs and an example of how you can use them in a research project. The theme we will select for all of them is a pedagogical intervention, such as an Appreciative Inquiry (AI) facilitation (Cooperrider et al., 2018), which we assess concerning its impact on students' wellbeing.

Control groups

One of the biggest challenges of experimenting is the natural changes occurring in our lives. For example, we have carried out an experiment in a school, the objective of which was to enhance pupils' sense of school belonging (Dunleavy and Burke, 2019). The experiment took place after the midterm and lasted a month. Both experimental and control groups were asked to complete the survey before and after the intervention. When the experiment began, the school was quiet. By the time it finished, all students were right in the middle of their year, they had tests every week, and the school was buzzing with activities. The school's circumstances were very different at the beginning

Table 6.4 Three main experimental designs. Adapted from Denscombe (2014).

Experimental design	Example
Controlled experiment in a lab	You invite your participants into a lab (a room at the educational institution) where they are being guided through the AI process. You are trying to reduce the influence of other variables and make the conditions of your experiment similar for all participants.
The randomised controlled trial	You select your participants (students) randomly from various schools and assign them randomly into two groups (1) a control and (2) an experimental group (see the following for details). You assess (e.g. survey) both groups at the same time before the experiment begins. Then, the experimental group goes through the AI process, while the control group does not. Finally, you ask both groups to complete an assessment (e.g. a survey) afterwards and compare the results for both groups before and after.
The quasi-experiment	You are teaching two classes. You assign one of your classes as a control group and another one as your experimental group. You assess them before and after the experiment but only the experimental group goes through the AI process.

and the end of the experiment, meaning that they may have affected pupils regardless of whether they took part in the experiment or not. This is why, apart from comparing pupils' survey results before and after the experiment, we had to compare them with other pupils' results who had not participated in the experiment (control group) and were affected by different circumstances associated with the school's natural changes. Having a control group is essential, as it will indicate the actual impact of your experiment, controlling for the natural differences in the environment.

Random selection

A few practical things to remember when designing an experimental research project. Firstly, be mindful of your access to participants. You may have designed a complex study on the effect of a programme amalgamating lifestyle medicine and positive psychology with patients waiting for a liver transplant. If you already work in a liver transplant unit, your chances of accessing patients are more likely than if you are a trainee psychologist not associated with a hospital. At the same time, if you decide to access your patients and recruit them to an experimental trial of a programme amalgamating lifestyle medicine and positive psychology, you need to bear in mind the ethical issues associated with power relations between psychologists and their patients (see the ethics chapter), as well as the limits associated with the specific experimental design you selected, i.e. quasi-experiment. On the other hand, if you choose to choose your participants from a random pool in a random manner, you need to think of how you can access a larger pool of participants. Ease of access is a crucial consideration when designing such a study.

Another thing that needs to be considered in an experimental design study is the follow-up time. The longer the study, the higher the attrition rate. For example, if participants are asked to complete a task for a week, and then a follow-up survey is sent to them a week later, their likelihood of doing it is higher than when they are asked to complete a task for a month. Similarly, according to the research design, participants are asked to complete three surveys (one before the experiment, one shortly after, and the last one three months later). In that case, we need to consider that some people may not complete the test at time three and will need to be excluded from the study. This is why, if you are planning to follow up with the participants, you need to consider how many weeks or months pass by, as the longer you leave it, the less likely they are to respond. That said, the long-term effect of an intervention is always a welcome addition to research results. Many of my students who selected a random sample had as many as 20%–30% of participants either not completing their intervention or not completing the follow-up survey. It is easier with a quasi-experimental study delivered in a school, workplace, or another organisation. The participants are known to the researcher and less likely to drop out of the study. That said, the attrition rate, although smaller, still exists.

Another thing to consider is the time of the year. For example, it may suit you to research during the summer months; however, your participants may not be available to engage with the experiment during this time fully. Also, it would help if you considered the weather at specific times of the year and its impact on participation, or national holidays, which may also get in the way of your research. So the timing is crucial when designing your study.

Experimental research involves using the scientific method to test a hypothesis or prove a known fact (Shadish et al., 2002). Experiments are theory-driven in that the researcher must specify the variables to be included in the research and the exact procedure to be followed. To do this, you will need to have a well-developed theory of the phenomenon being researched (Robson, 2002). A variable is defined as a property or characteristic of a person, thing, group, or situation that you can measure somehow. The independent variable is the variable you change or manipulate; the dependent variable is the variable that is shown to change because of the intervention/manipulation. Other variables that are controlled during the intervention are control variables. As we will see later in the discussion on causality, it is not always this clear cut in social science to measure and control variables.

In experimental research, there are many difficulties due to what Campbell refers to as the "intransigencies of the research setting and to the presence of recurrent seductive pitfalls of interpretation" (1969, p. 1). Over 40 years after Campbell's work, researchers are still grappling with the messy and complex world in which we live. However, this does not mean that you cannot complete experimental research. Instead, this means that this research needs to be attentive to context and process.

In a randomised experiment, groups are assigned to either the experimental or control groups randomly, such as a coin toss or computer-generated random numbers. Borman (2002) contends that if the random assignment is carried out correctly and the sample is large enough, then the two groups should be essentially the same or as different. For example, if the experimental group gets an intervention in learning algebra, the control group receives no intervention. However, if the intervention has been adequately implemented over time, any differences between the groups at the end of the experiment period can reasonably be attributed to the intervention. This is the simplest version of the randomised experiment; there are other versions, including two or more interventions or versions of interventions.

In quasi-experimental research, the researcher studies the effect of an intervention on intact groups rather than randomly assigning participants to experimental or control groups (Cook, 2002). You can use many different designs in quasi-experimental research (Bryman, 2008). However, matching an experimental group with a control group is central to the success of a quasi-experiment.

To some extent, the groups being compared are non-equivalent. To compensate for this weakness, it is important to have explicit controls for threats to validity. The researcher has the task of differentiating between differences due to variables of interest and differences that are the product of the initial group variation. Breaugh and Arnold (2007) advise asking the following questions:

- On which variables should the participants be matched?
- What is the theoretical rationale for the choice of matching variables?
- On how many variables should the groups be compared?
- How close does the match have to be?
- Is matching based on a one-to-one match or group similarities? (p. 525)

It is essential that the intervention is implemented consistently in the research and that the underlying theory is clearly articulated before the intervention and the process of implementation mapped (Bryman, 2008). For example, it is of limited use to find out at the end of a process that an intervention works in a particular setting if you cannot say what it was about the intervention that worked. Equally, this additional information is essential where an intervention is not successful. To get at these nuances of an intervention's effects requires evidence on how you developed the intervention, how you implemented it, the formative evaluation of the intervention, assessment of the impact of the intervention, and so on, not unlike the design-based cycles described in Section 6.1.2 of this chapter.

6.1.10 Comparative

Comparative research (Figure 6.16) refers to research approaches that involve comparing cases and variables. While it is used mainly in quantitative research, you can also apply comparative research in qualitative methodologies. An example of quantitative comparative research includes assessing the wellbeing of final year students during COVID-19 lockdown and comparing it with an equivalent group of students five years earlier (Quinn et al., 2021). Data were collected using a survey and a validated scale. An example of a qualitative comparative study includes the analysis of quality of life across participants with three subtypes of multiple sclerosis, i.e. (1) primary progressives, (2) secondary progressive, or (3) relapsing-remitting (Ando et al., 2021). The researchers used a semi-structured method to elicit participants' responses and analysed them using thematic analysis. Their results identified similarities and differences in quality of life across all three participants. Thus, comparative research can be both quantitative and qualitative research.

All the methods used by social scientists, including surveys, historical analysis, fieldwork, different forms of data analysis, can be used in comparative studies; it depends on your research question. In addition, comparative research can be used by many other actors, parents, practitioners, policymakers, international agencies, and academics for various purposes (Bray et al., 2014). First, however, in comparative research, you must develop an analytical framework to support your comparison (Bray et al., 2014). For example, if you wanted to compare suicide supports in two different countries. Your analytical framework would describe the statistics you would use in describing suicide in both countries, the types of support you would look at and how you would categorise these. If

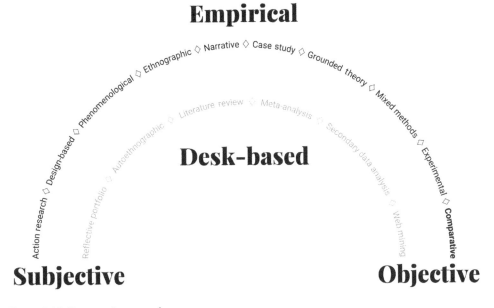

Figure 6.16 Comparative research.

you were interviewing people it would provide guidelines on the questions asked linked to your theoretical and conceptual framework and on analysis of data. This is to ensure that the data from both places are treated the same for the comparison.

The two types of comparisons we can carry out in quantitative research are (1) contrasting and (2) exploring relationships. Contrasting identifies statistically significant differences between two or more variables. When a statistically significant difference occurs, the difference between variables did not happen by chance. Exploring relationships refers to identifying correlations between two or more variables. If the relationship is statistically significant, it means it did not happen by chance. Your research question will inform what type of comparison you carry out in your research.

You can select many different methods for carrying out comparisons. The most frequently used is a survey that you can administer either as a pen-and-paper or an online format. However, some comparisons can be carried out using other methods, such as observing participants and systematically noting their results. You can use them separately or combine them. For example, your research may be associated with identifying the difference in perception between participants who score high on optimism and wellbeing compared with others. In step 1 of your research, you can ask all participants to complete a survey measuring their optimism and wellbeing. In step 2, you can ask participants to spot 20 differences between two pictures, and you estimate the amount of time it took them to complete the activity. You can then assess whether there is a relationship between their optimism, wellbeing, and the time it took them to spot the differences. To move it up a level, you may even identify how much of the variance in their speed of test completion can be explained by different optimism and wellbeing. These are just some examples of your outcomes when you combine your methods for collecting data.

To perform either of the comparisons, you will need to make a few critical decisions:

1   What is my hypothesis? Go to Section 4.3.1 to help you construct it.
2   What are the variables I am trying to compare? For example, if my null hypothesis states no statistically significant relationship between students' GRIT and their test results, my two variables are GRIT and test results.
3   Which one of the variables is dependent, and which one is independent? You will need this information to construct your research question and run your statistical test. The independent variable is not related to the other variables; therefore, it is not changed by them. For example, your independent variable can be gender or age. A dependent variable depends on other variables; therefore, you can change it. For example, your dependent variable can be wisdom. Your null hypothesis would thus state that there is no relationship between age and wisdom. In this example, your independent variable is age, and the dependent variable is wisdom, as we try to assess how it differs over time.
4   What statistical test do I need to use? The statistical tests you require will differ depending on the purpose of your study. Section 4.3.1 will provide you with some examples.

If you are considering doing comparative research, you need to ensure that the basis on which you compare things is the same. This means the definitions you use to create the data categories are the same. In all research, careful research design and planning are essential when using the comparative methodology.

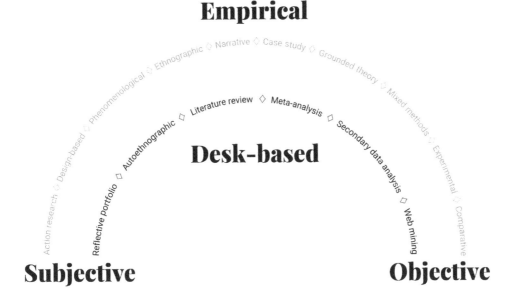

Figure 6.17 Spectrum of desk-based methodologies.

6.2 Desk-based

You can complete a desk-based research (Figure 6.17) project entirely from the comfort of your home. You do not need participants, and you don't need any ethical approvals to do it. All you need is to decide which approach you take, and you can do it in your own time and at your own pace, with a deadline for the completion of your project as the only restriction to consider. This section will discuss research projects you can do ranging from subjective, such as a reflective portfolio and autoethnography, to meta-analytical and web-mining approaches.

6.2.1 *Reflective portfolio*

Experience is not enough to learn a profession (Gibbs, 1988). Our reflection on that experience allows us to know how to do our job in various circumstances best. The ability to reflect on past actions is a springboard for growth (Wolffe et al., 2013). This is why a reflective portfolio is helpful for a research project, which aims to enrich professional practice. A reflective portfolio (Figure 6.18) is a collection of students' work that includes reflective practice (Klenowski et al., 2006). It can be viewed as either a (1) product portfolio, which refers to an assessed piece of work, or a (2) process portfolio, which documents students' non-assessed earning journey during a programme (Orland-Barak, 2005). In the context of a research project, a product portfolio can become an outcome of the project. Alternatively, the process portfolio can be used as an artefact of the capstone project and a data source, further analysed using narrative or thematic analysis.

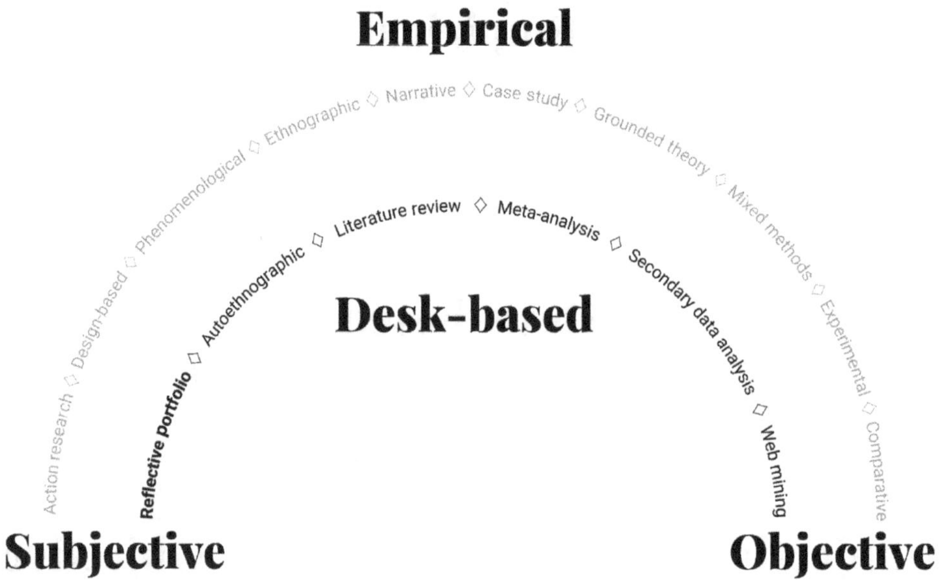

Empirical

Figure 6.18 Reflective portfolio.

There are different approaches to creating portfolios (Smith and Tillema, 2001). When the purpose of a portfolio is developmental, and practitioners engage with it voluntarily, it can help them improve their practice long-term. When the purpose is developmental, but an organisation mandates it, it becomes a training portfolio that helps practitioners exhibit what they have learned in their studies. Apart from the developmental processes, a portfolio can also become a tool for assessment and selection, in which case it can be referred to as a selective purpose portfolio. A selective portfolio can be voluntary, whereby it provides a collection of the work relating to personal goals, practice, and reflections demonstrating practitioners' professional growth, or it can be mandatory, in which case, it becomes a dossier portfolio, which is a record, or evidence of the work you have carried out concerning your practice. All these approaches will influence the perspective you take on your practice. It is, therefore, worthwhile for you to decide what your approach is concerning writing your portfolio and clarify what type of content you want to include in it.

A reflective portfolio includes a range of formats (Osteneck, 2020; Woodward, 1998). You may collate your reflections about your own or observations of other educators' practices through a series of video or audio recordings. You may incorporate art-based formats, such as prose or poetry writing, drawing, painting, music-making, and much more. Within a traditional journal writing context, you may practice free-writing techniques or more structured writing, scaffolded by a model of reflection you select. See Chapter 2 for a list of models you can apply to guide you through reflection. Some of you may choose to use prompts instead of a reflective model, such as pictures that inspire you to write or sentences that stimulate your imagination (e.g. *What I like about my practice is . . .*). Alternatively, you can also create mind maps, lists (e.g. what works vs what doesn't), clusters and other pictorial forms of organising thoughts. All these formats allow you to widen the scope of the investigation into your practice.

The benefits of a reflective portfolio include advancement of critical thinking, developing a teaching philosophy, building professional confidence, improving lifelong learning, and developing higher-order thinking and self-directed learning (van Wyk, 2017; Al-karasneh, 2014; Rahgozaran and Gholami, 2014), all of which are beneficial at all stages of an educational career. However, given that a capstone project is focused on research-based practice, it is vital to strike a balance between reflecting on your practice and learning from your educational programme content and the research you have read during your studies. This means that your reflections are based not only on your experiences and deeper analysis of them but also on your engagement with evidence-based concepts that you are trying to apply in your practice or observe others applying in theirs. This reflection may relate to the books, academic journal papers you have read, or conversations with an expert in the field, which you try to incorporate into your practice.

For example, say you have experienced a conflict situation at work. You reflect on the situation and how you handled it. You then review the literature about conflict resolution and come across the Inventory of Personal Conflict Management Styles (Thomas and Kilmann, 1974). You read a few articles about it, complete a questionnaire that assesses your conflict style, and reflect in your journal on your results. Now that you have assimilated your knowledge, it is good to bring your thinking into a semi-private space by discussing it with a knowledgeable other; this may be a mentor, a colleague, or an expert in the area (professional consultation). It will allow you to open up your thinking to critical feedback. This feedback may help you adjust your practice. As your learning process continues, you may try to implement what you have learnt in real-life situations, reflect on your experience of putting theory in practice, and tweak your style further until you are happy enough with it.

As you continue to change your perspective, you may realise that you have not used your listening skills to their full potential. You then read more of the literature about listening skills and come across more models you continue to reflect on. This allows you to enter the next cycle as your evidence-based practice continues. This circular process of reading literature, reflecting on it, and implementing it (Figure 6.19) deepens your critical thinking, improves your practice, and allows you to create an evidence-based reflective portfolio, which can become part of your capstone project.

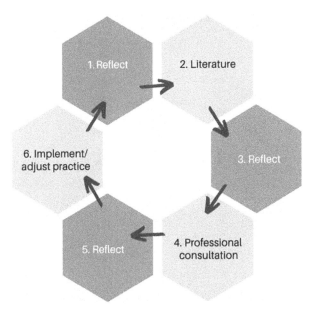

Figure 6.19 The cycle of reflection on the evidence-based practice.

6.2.2 Autoethnography

Autoethnographic research (Figure 6.20) derives from sociology and refers to a systematic description of personal experiences in the social context so that your cultural background can be better understood (Ellis et al., 2011). Yet, it is increasingly used in psychology and psychotherapy and referred to with sentiment as a "methodological chat with self" (Egeli, 2017). The cultural context differentiates the reflective portfolio, which is focused on the self, from autoethnography. Although autoethnography can be viewed from a collective perspective as the experiences of a group in a culture (Denshire, 2014), in which case it will become empirical research that requires ethical approval (see the ethnographic research section earlier on in this chapter), in this section, we will focus on applying autoethnography to self, as desk-based research.

As it stands, autoethnographic research views the researcher as a mirror-reflection of the culture, subculture, or a group within which they exist, while at the same time being focused on the researcher and their experiences of the culture (Walford, 2009). It, therefore, offers reflections on the interaction that goes from the researcher to the group, and then back again in circles, as opposed to focusing on the self and their experiences devoid of the context within which they exist.

Autoethnographic research applies many strategies to study self in the social context (Cohen et al., 2018). They include self-observation, observation of others, dialogues and reflections, notes, documents, and other artefacts that may help engage in reflexivity. Data analysis may comprise thick descriptions used previously and grounded theory. When carrying out this type of study, some of the questions that you would ask yourself are as follows: *What is my experience of the school where I teach? What is my experience of the school community values? How do events in the school affect me? What are the turning points in my experience as a teacher in my school?* and similar.

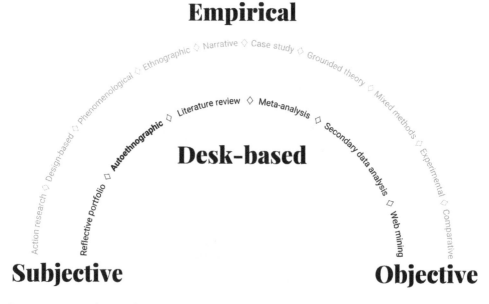

Figure 6.20 Autoethnographic research.

For example, one of our students carried out an autoethnographic inquiry into his first year as a sports team coach. In his project, he discussed his critical reflections concerning what it was like for him, but he provided rich context associated with his reflections. The outcomes of his research were presented in an analytical form, even though the research concerned his views and reflections related to his experience. This is just one of two ways you can present autoethnographic research (Cohen et al., 2018). Another way is via evocative style, whereby the researchers' perspective is celebrated. Using autoethnography in sport psychology is scarce and encouraged (Sae-Mi et al., 2020), as it provides an opportunity for researchers who are also practitioners to engage in critical reflection that can alter their future practice.

Autoethnographic research is usually carried out by researchers who have gained critical reflective skills and have gone through a meaningful experience they reflect on. It includes a short story of an experience of mental breakdown by a PhD student, who was subsequently involuntarily detained (Clarke, 2018), an experience of coming out as a member of LGBTQ community (Leung, 2021), or an experience of studying fine art and the actualisation of the theory of transpersonal and coaching psychology (Clegg and Law, 2017). Autoethnographic research may also apply to a group of researchers who study the self, referred to as community autoethnography. For example, three trainees completing a counselling psychology doctoral degree used this approach to analyse and discuss their experience of an internship, and from that, they provided recommendations for change (Wang et al., 2020). Often, researchers try to remove themselves from their research, even though their experiences may have motivated them to conduct a study. In this community autoethnographic approach, the three researchers undergoing similar experiences drew upon them to inform future research and practice.

There is some controversy associated with this approach, around it not meeting the minimum standards required for social science objectives (Delamont, 2009) and representing a lazy approach to research (Delamont, 2007). Even though these researchers continue to encourage its use as it contributes to knowledge, which is one of the main objectives of the research (Walford, 2021). Autoethnography seeks to develop evocative and thick descriptions, and texts can be presented in many ways, such as short stories, poetry, fiction, photographic essays, personal essays, journals, and plays. What we need to remember is that it is about the process and the product (Ellis et al., 2011), and it adds tremendous value to research. Therefore, it is yet another methodology that can be considered for a final research project.

6.2.3 Literature review

Research projects can also be based on reviewing the existing literature (Figure 6.21) about a topic of your interest. Often when we initially introduce this idea, some students wonder how a literature review can be perceived as practice, yet there is a way to do it. The traditional final year approaches to reviewing the literature focus on creating a background to a study, identifying a gap in research, or reviewing variables relevant to a topic of interest (Hart, 2018). They do not usually focus on practice. If you tweak the literature review to inform your practice, it can become the sole outcome of your capstone project.

There is a range of capstone or final projects you can carry out that involve conducting only the literature review. Let us review some of the examples.

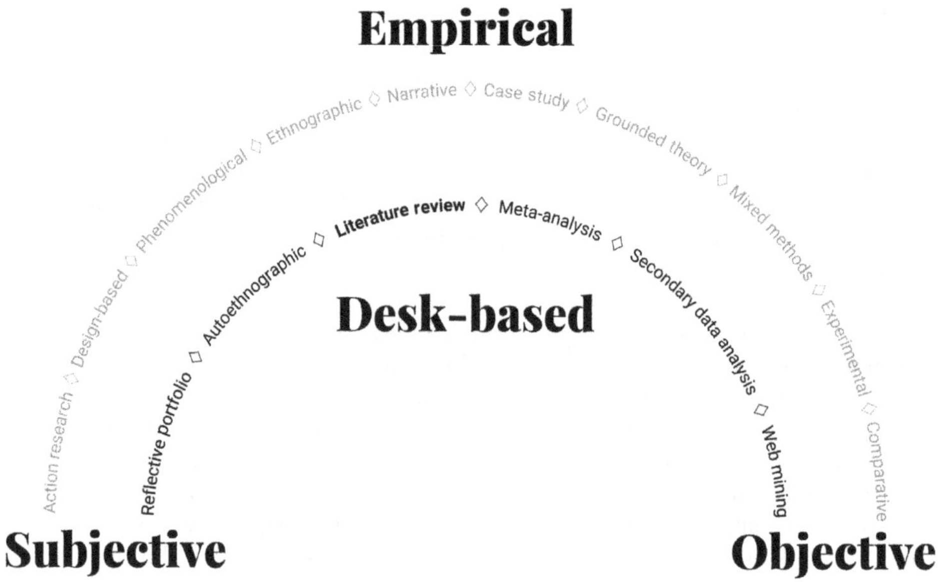

Empirical

Desk-based

Subjective   **Objective**

Figure 6.21 Literature review.

1 Synthesising literature relating to praxis

This is the most common literature review used for a capstone project. You begin your inquiry by posing a practice-related issue, and your objective is to find the answer to your question by synthesising the existing literature. Here are some questions you may have: How do I motivate students halfway through the semester? What are the best approaches to enhancing wellbeing? How can I improve my confidence as a leader?

2 Rationalise the practical significance of a problem using evidence-based theory

Instead of resolving an issue about your psychological practice, you can also pose a problem in your practice, which is not usually discussed by others, and provide a rationale for it becoming a problem by reviewing related literature.

3 Critique of an existing theory and its adaptation for practice

This literature review is based on the theories you have read about, or theory-based practice you have observed. It aims to de-construct the existing theory in the context of its usefulness in practice and offer alternatives. For example, one of our students presented research on AI and critiqued the quality of studies applying AI in education. He identified limitations and offered solutions on how to improve both research into this area and practice while exercising caution.

4 Understand the origins and structure of a subject that can inform practice

You can use this approach to the literature review when you attempt to get to the bottom of a topic of your interest and understand how to do it. For example, you have been using the SMART goal-setting technique (S = specific, M = measurable, A = achievable, R = realistic, T = timely) as part of your coaching practice. This is the most frequently used model for goal-setting. However, you wonder about the model's origin and why this structure came about. Your literature review draws on research based on which it was created and critiqued the model by adding additional structures to it that can enrich your teaching practice.

5 Repositioning of existing theory in practice

Some theoretical models have been extensively used in practice, and some have not yet been applied. If you come across such a model, you may review the existing literature about it and draw from other used models, suggesting how you can apply it in your psychological practice. For example, one such model that has not yet been fully applied in psychology is the dualistic model of passion (Vallerand, 2015), which one of our students repositioned to use in education.

6 Review of a psychological issue from various discipline perspectives

This type of literature review relates to considering a psychological issue that you frequently grapple with, or a topic that has been recently discussed in psychology, and trying to view it from a range of disciplinary perspectives, such as sociological, philosophical, economics and others. For example, if you are interested in wellbeing, you may come across research showing that it is beneficial in school to create a multidisciplinary approach to wellbeing (Burke, 2021). Therefore, you may try to view it from the typical psychological perspective, through to medical, philosophical, and, finally, educational perspectives, to create a series of wellbeing initiatives for your school.

7 Theory-driven artefact design

Another way in which you can construct your literature to help you with your psychological practice is by starting with a theory/ies and carrying out a literature review on the theories as they pertain to your psychological context and using this to design an artefact. For example, you may be concerned about your team's motivation for working in the online environment. You could carry out a literature review on the main theories of motivation and use this to design an artefact to support your team in learning in the online space. The artefact could be a short film explicating how they can enhance their motivation.

These types of literature reviews are not exhaustive. Instead, they serve as examples of tweaking a theoretical project to help psychological practice. Doing a literature review as a sole focus of a capstone and final year project seems like an easy task, but it is not at all. Some even claim it to be more challenging than carrying out an empirical study, which is easier to present. After all, a literature review needs to be comprehensive, clear, and coherent to add value. It is difficult to do when it is just a part of a project and even harder when it is the sole focus. Please see Chapter 7 for techniques you can employ to write a literature review.

6.2.4 Meta-analysis and systematic review

Every year, tens of thousands of research articles are published in psychology. Researchers conduct empirical qualitative and quantitative studies that provide the research world with unique findings. At times, researchers replicate past studies to identify the efficacy of the original results in a different context, such as geographical location or a specific participant group. Regardless of their approach, we might have several articles about a particular topic, such as "kindness". Some findings may provide similar results; for example, the research may show that performing acts of kindness in various forms, e.g. planned or spontaneous kindness, is suitable for individuals and their community. Other findings, however, may indicate contrasting results. To understand the bigger picture of a multitude of findings across various studies, we need to synthesise the existing literature in a structured manner, which is what this approach to a research project is about (Figure 6.22).

There are many types of approaches to synthesising data. Table 6.5 provides examples of some of the main approaches and a brief explanation of them. These approaches vary from reviewing specific quantitative or qualitative studies to reviewing mixed methods studies and even reviewing all the reviews. There is a keen interest in meta-analytical research in psychology, offering substantial benefits to both researchers and practitioners.

For example, imagine you would like to introduce a wellbeing initiative in a workplace. You have reviewed a range of individual programmes, but you wonder which one provides you with the best results concerning building children's resilience. A meta-analytical study carried out worldwide can help you find this information. Table 6.5 provides a list of approaches you can use to synthesise research.

You can view research synthesis from varied epistemological and ontological positions (Suri, 2013). It can be introduced as a purely positivist or a post-positivist approach, applying a range of variables, objectively describing and predicting findings, and quality-insuring them through validity and reliability reports. Alternatively, it can be viewed from an interpretative perspective, providing more profound and comprehensive narrative findings that include thick descriptions. Finally, it can also be perceived from a critical paradigm perspective, whereby predominant narratives are deconstructed and transformed.

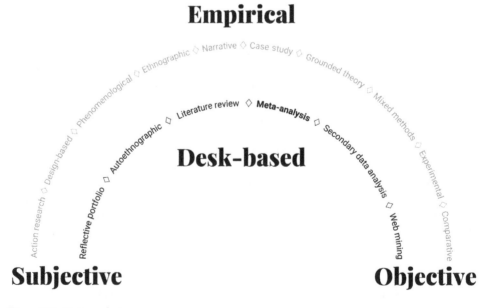

Figure 6.22 Meta-analysis.

Table 6.5 Types of research synthesis approaches.

Research synthesis approach	Description
Systematic reviews	A methodological approach to a literature review about a specific topic
A systematic review of systematic reviews	A methodological approach to synthesising findings from several systematic reviews carried out about a specific topic
Meta-analysis	A statistical analysis of empirical research findings from several quantitative studies, usually associated with interventions
Meta-synthesis	An analysis of findings across several qualitative studies, which involve a new interpretation of the qualitative data
Mixed-methods research synthesis	An analysis of the results from quantitative, qualitative, and mixed-methods studies
Review of reviews	An analysis of findings from several meta-analyses and/or meta-syntheses

Therefore, synthesising data is yet another capstone project idea that students can explore regardless of their interest to enhance educational practice.

While these reviews seem easy to conduct at first, they are often performed by experienced researchers. Furthermore, they follow a detailed process to ensure accuracy and minimise bias (Buecker et al., 2021). Moreover, they take a lot of time and effort to conduct, which is why we recommend that while it is an option for a research project, you should use it with caution. However, there is one synthesis that can be relatively easily carried out by students and offer a lot of practical benefits to practitioners, and it is a systematic review.

6.2.4.1 Systematic review

A systematic review integrates studies to provide findings that can inform policymaking (Gough et al., 2012) and practice in psychology (Newman and Gough, 2019). There are two main approaches in carrying out systematic reviews, one that relates to randomised controlled trials and another one that incorporates mixed-method designs and qualitative research (Cohen et al., 2018). What differentiates a standard literature review from a systematic review of the literature is that the latter applies a rigorous technique to minimise bias concerning the content of the literature and the strategies used to obtain it. In addition, it is a comprehensive review of all the published material about the topic in question. These topics are similar to those discussed in the literature review section; however, the procedure for carrying them out is not ad hoc as in a literature review.

There are five steps for carrying out a systematic literature review (Khan et al., 2003):

1   Framing the questions for a review
2   Identifying relevant work
3   Assessing the quality of studies
4   Summarising the evidence
5   Interpreting the findings

In the first step, you need to clarify your research question; what are you looking to achieve through a systematic review.

In the second step, unambiguous criteria for inclusion and exclusion of research should be stated. For example, if you are interested in the impact of gratitude in reducing nurses' burnout, your inclusion criteria may include synonyms for "burnout", e.g. burn-out, burn out, or burnout; synonyms for "gratitude", e.g. gratitude, gratefulness, three good things; and synonyms for "nurses", e.g. nurses, nursing. Furthermore, you may be interested in nurses in a specific country or with a particular specialism. Therefore, before you begin your systematic review, you need to specify your criteria and the exact keywords you will be searching for. The limitations of your study may be dependent on the keywords you selected. In addition to the criteria relating to the content, you also are required to specify a list of online and offline resources you are planning to use in your inquiry. Step two is an important step that requires a lot of work.

Once your criteria are set, you are ready to begin your review. In step 3, you assess the quality of the studies you selected. Quality assessment is partially related to the criteria you have previously set up. Therefore, you reject the papers that do not meet your criteria, thus reducing the number of papers to review. Also, say you are reviewing interventions for relieving depression; your quality review relates to whether the research included in your review had control groups or whether they measured depression before and after an intervention. As a researcher, it is up to you to make these decisions based on a specific rationale. The reduced literature needs to be further interrogated with a critical thinking hat on to ensure that all the criteria you set up before carrying out your review are met. This will allow you to create a heterogeneous sample of studies that you can compare with each other.

In step 4, you need to summarise the research. You can do it by triangulating all the results and providing a narrative summary of your findings. Finally, step 5 includes data interpretation, which offers new meaning across all the studies.

6.2.5 Secondary data analysis

Earlier in this book, when discussing the design of research questions, we mentioned the importance of reviewing the literature and deciding on a research question before selecting a research methodology and method of data collection and subsequent analysis. Even though this is usually the process of carrying out research, there are some exceptions to this rule, one of them being secondary data analysis (SDA: Figure 6.23), which reverses this process.

SDA refers to a process of using existing data to respond to a new research question (Doolan and Froelicher, 2009). Therefore, after data is collected for a different purpose, you review it, construct another research question and analyse it accordingly. Another purpose for using an existing data set is to apply a new technique to analyse it or a different theoretical model (Smith, 2008a). For example, you may have previously used data to determine the psychological impact of bullying. Then, an SDA would be carried out to determine the correlations between bullying and victimisation.

An SDA can be carried out by researchers who have collected data or other researchers who have access to it, such as students completing their capstone project. You may be engaged in an SDA of a research project carried out by someone else for your capstone project. That person could be your supervisor, a researcher in the educational institution you are associated with who has given you access to their data, or an external body.

Many external bodies provide access to secondary data. For example, in Ireland, *Growing up in Ireland* is a government-funded longitudinal research, which follows children

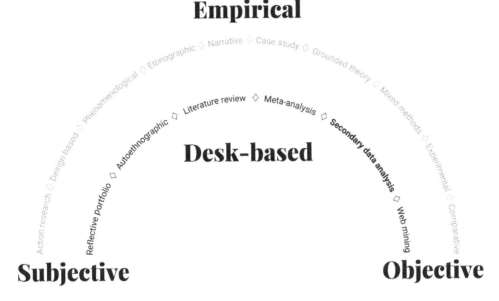

Figure 6.23 Secondary data analysis.

born in 2006 throughout their lives. While regular publications are shared with the public by the official researchers, other researchers have access to the data set upon request. One of our students accessed data from the *Growing up in Ireland* study and made it part of her dissertation. She has searched for correlations and links that other researchers have not considered to date, thus contributing to science and practice with her SDA. You can do something similar with data available in your geographical area.

Many international organisations provide data for SDA. They can be your local government statistics offices, some universities, and organisations carrying out longitudinal studies, for example, international databases, surveys, assessment programmes, such as the Programme for International Student Assessment. You may also search for secondary data in your institutional library and various international organisations such as the Organisation for Economic Co-operation and Development, UNESCO, or the World Bank, all of which provide you with worldwide data that may include your country-related information. On a more localised level, perhaps a study was carried out in your school, which you can now reanalyse as part of your capstone project to come up with additional findings. As long as they contribute to the psychological practice, any such approaches are part of a research project.

In addition to this, SDA can be carried out using other resources (data) available in the public domain, such as policy documents, communication statements, online blogs, online forums, and podcasts, to mention but a few. As a researcher, you use data generated by participants for a different purpose. For example, as part of your research, you may choose to review online forum entries from individuals who have recently separated from their partners, analyse data and provide a unique perspective on their challenges associated with separation. In addition, you can analyse online data, such as this one, using one of the approaches to content analysis or thematic analysis, which will help you derive new meaning from data available in the public domain. This is what the new research area of cyberpsychology delves into. It is a study of the impact of technology on human behaviour (Aiken, 2016) that is gaining traction and providing fascinating insights into the differences in the human psyche in a digital vs non-digital environment. Some of the SDA gathered online can enrich research in this area.

There are several benefits to SDA (Chow and Kennedy, 2014; Devine, 2003). Firstly, more research findings can derive from collected data. From the pragmatic viewpoint, no additional data collection is required, thus saving the costs and the burden of participant effort. Moreover, when data is reused, it sometimes provides a larger sample of participants, thus offering more diverse views, otherwise challenging to obtain. Finally, experienced researchers usually carry out large-scale studies; therefore, the transparency and data quality is high. These are just some of the benefits that SDA may offer.

SDA is well established in the field of quantitative research. However, it is more challenging to carry out an SDA of qualitative research. Two main criticisms are related to ethical considerations and research rigour (Ruggiano and Perry, 2019). The ethical concern is that you gave ethics approval and subsequent consent to researchers for the first analysis. Regarding the research rigour, qualitative research is highly subjective and context-sensitive. Therefore, when data are analysed at a different point in time, the contextual matters are diluted, thus potentially making the research less valid. Although the criticisms of SDA are applied to qualitative research, there are plenty of studies incorporating this approach, and some even provide a mixed secondary analysis of both qualitative and quantitative data (e.g. Hampden-Thompson et al., 2011).

There are various approaches to reanalysing data. The frameworks for data analysis range from provision of a simple step-by-step process, e.g. Brewer (2007), through to reflective questions on the research purpose, quality of data selected for SDA, and implications for the practitioners (educators) of conducting an SDA (Smith, 2008b). For example, Logan (2020) has adapted a Knowledge Discovery in Data Framework to an SDA process, which includes the following five steps: (1) Selection, (2) Pre-processing, (3) Transformation, (4) Data analysis, (5) Interpretation/evaluation. Therefore, when analysing secondary data, we first need to select the database in question and then assess the data's suitability and validity. Once this was carried out, we needed to reduce the data set to the variables of interest to us, analyse it, and offer an alternative explanation. This is just one of many frameworks you can use in an SDA process in education.

As it stands, the SDA approach is underutilised in psychology, yet it offers potentially great opportunities for psychologists. Some argue that this type of data can be advantageous in education to help inform policymakers about evidence-based changes that can be made in schooling (Chudagr and Luschei, 2016), as many international institutions have data-rich resources, some of which are analysed using only descriptive statistics without going further into the analysis that can potentially serve as a springboard for policymaking.

6.2.6 Web mining

Online content is ever-increasing, and we often use it in education when creating websites and databases, promoting knowledge, and learning skills via the web. Nowadays, everything that is worth sharing with others usually ends up online. This means that every 20 months, web content doubles (Witten et al., 2017), making it overwhelming for many and beneficial for research. Data mining is a process of identifying patterns in extensive

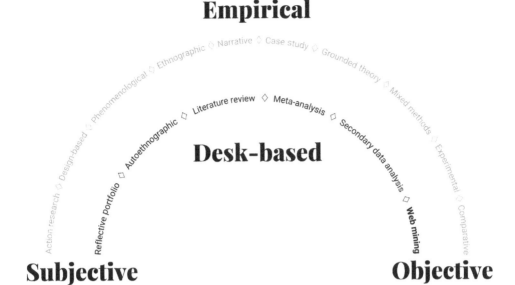

Figure 6.24 Web mining.

data (Witten et al., 2011). There are three types of web data-mining (Figure 6.24) research (Singh and Singh, 2010):

1   Web-content mining
2   Web structure mining
3   Web uses mining

All three types of research can be used in psychology. Given that worldwide there is a lot of big data available that can be gathered by governments, organisations, groups of institutions, and individuals, all this information can be used to analyse trends and answer questions. All this can be studied as part of the research project.

Here are some examples of psychology-related data-mining research carried out over the last few years:

•   Twitter mining identified almost 69,963 posts from 139 accounts of psychology professors to identify "hot spots" in psychology (Bittermann et al., 2021). Their findings extended as far as recommending this method of data collection to predict conference topics.
•   Social media were analysed and discovered underlying sensations of human emotions (Lee et al., 2021).
•   Social media posts of 3,853 influencers were analysed to discover what techniques they use to persuade their followers (Lahuerta-Otero and Cordero-Gutiérrez, 2016)

Even though data mining is a new approach to data analysis in psychology, we are already aware of many advantages to it (Iwatani, 2018). From the statistical perspective, it is often easier to analyse data using data-mining techniques than the traditional approaches, which are sensitive to various statistical assumptions. From a practical viewpoint, it is useful, as it often provides some surprising patterns that would not be otherwise available to practitioners. Also, data mining not only includes numbers but also non-traditional forms of data that can be included in your analysis, such as images, audio, video, and even social interactions. This is why it offers a great opportunity to analyse thousands of available online sources to create a new meaning that would prove useful in psychology.

The software that can be used for educational data mining is constantly evolving.

Therefore, it is best to check the latest available software and familiarise yourself with it before you choose to use it in your capstone project. Some of the software is user-friendly, and the approaches to data mining are straightforward. All you need to do is enter a question, in a similar way as you would when searching for something on the internet, and the software provides you with a detailed analysis of web trends applicable to your question. You can then analyse your data and use it to inform your educational practice.

The disadvantage of data mining is the algorithms that are used, which are often difficult to understand or critique. In order to carry out big data research, you need to be familiar with software programming (Chen and Wojcik, 2016). There are also ethical issues associated with it, whereby care needs to be taken to ensure that only data available in the public domain is used, otherwise ethical approval will be needed for your research.

Reflection time

Select two to three methodologies from the spectrum that can help you address your research question. List the pros and cons of each methodology. Decide which one best suits your project and why.

References

Aiken, M. 2016. *The Cyber Effect: A Pioneering Cyberpsychologist Explains How Human Behaviour Changes Online*. London: John Murray Press.

Al-karasneh, S.M. 2014. "Reflective Journal Writing as a Tool to Teach Aspects of Social Studies." *European Journal of Education* 49(3): 395–408. doi: 10.1111/ejed.12084.

Anderson, T., and J. Shattuck. 2012. "Design-Based Research: A Decade of Progress in Education Research?" *Educational Researcher* 41(1): 16–25.

Ando, H., Cousins, R. & Young, C.A. Understanding quality of life across different clinical subtypes of multiple sclerosis: a thematic analysis. Qual Life Res (2021). https://doi.org/10.1007/s11136-021-03041-7

Arhar, J.M., M.L. Holly, and W.C. Kasten. 2001. *Action Research for Teachers: Traveling the Yellow Brick Road*. Columbus, OH: Merrill Prentice Hall.

Barrett, F.J., E.H. Powley, and B, Pearce. 2011. "Hermeneutic Philosophy and Organizational Theory." *Research in the Sociology of Organizations* 32: 181–213

Baskerville, D., and H. Goldblatt. 2009. "Learning to Be a Critical Friend: From Professional Indifference Through Challenge to Unguarded Conversations." *Cambridge Journal of Education* 39(2): 205–221.

Baumeister, R.F., E. Bratslavsky, M. Muraven, and D.M. Tice. 1998. "Ego Depletion: Is the Active Self a Limited Resource?" *Journal of Personality and Social Psychology* 74(5): 1252–1265. doi: 10.1037/0022-3514.74.5.1252.

Bittermann, A., V. Batzdorfer, S.M. Müller, and H. Steinmetz. 2021. "Mining Twitter to Detect Hotspots in Psychology." *Zeitschrift Fur Psychologie* 229(1): 3–14. doi: 10.1027/2151-2604/a000437

Borman, G.D. 2002. "Experiments for Educational Evaluation and Improvement." *Peabody Journal of Education* 77(4): 7–27.

Bray, M., B. Adamson, and M. Mason. 2014. *Comparative Education Research: Approaches and Methods.* Hong Kong: Springer.

Breaugh, J.A, and J. Arnold. 2007. "Controlling Nuisance Variables by Using a Matched-Groups Design." *Organizational Research Methods* 10(3): 523–541.

Brewer, E.W. 2007. "Secondary Data Analysis." In *Encyclopedia of Measurement and Statistics*, edited by N.J. Salkind and K. Rasmussen, 870–877. Thousand Oaks, CA: Sage.

Brookfield, S. 2005. *Becoming a Critically Reflective Teacher.* San Francisco: Jossey-Bass.

Bryman, A. 2008. *Social Research Methods.* 3rd ed. New York: Oxford University Press.

Buecker, S., J. Stricker, snd M. Schneider. 2021. "Central Questions about Meta-analyses in Psychological Research: An Annotated Reading List." *Current Psychology: A Journal for Diverse Perspectives on Diverse Psychological Issues.* doi: 10.1007/s12144-021-01957-4

Burke, J. 2021. *The Ultimate Guide to Implementing Wellbeing Programmes for School.* London: Routledge.

Campbell, D.T. 1969. "Reforms as Experiments." *American Psychologists* 24: 409–429.

Caruth, G.D. 2013. "Demystifying Mixed Methods Research Design: A Review of the Literature." *Mevlana International Journal of Education* 3: 112–122.

Charmaz, K. 2008. "Grounded Theory as an Emergent Method." In *Handbook of Emergent Methods*, edited by S.N. Hesse-Biber and P. Leavy, 155–170. Guilford: The Guilford Press.

Chen, E.E., and S.P. Wojcik. 2016. "A Practical Guide to Big Data Research in Psychology." *Psychological Methods* 21(4): 458–474. doi: 10.1037/met0000111.supp (Supplemental)

Chow, K.F., and K.J. Kennedy. 2014. "Secondary Analysis of Large-scale Assessment Data: An Alternative to Variable-centred Analysis." *Educational Research and Evaluation: An International Journal on Theory and Practice* 20(6): 469–493.

Chudagr, A., and T.F. Luschei. 2016. "The Untapped Promise of Secondary Data Sets in International and Comparative Education Policy Research." *La promesa no aprovechada del uso de datos secundarios en la investigación y comparativa de las políticas educativas* 24(113/114): 1–16.

Chun, T.Y., M. Birks, and K. Francis. 2019. "Grounded Theory Research: A Design Framework for Novice Researchers." *SAGE Open Medicine* 7. doi: 10.1177/2050312118822927.

Clarke, S.P. 2018. "Madhouse and the Whole Thing There." *Qualitative Research in Psychology* 15(2/3): 247–259. doi: 10.1080/14780887.2018.1429989

Clegg, N., and H. Law. 2017. "The Art of the Transpersonal: Its Psychology and Coaching Application." *Transpersonal Psychology Review* 19(1): 24–44.

Cohen, L., L. Manion, and K. Morrison. 2018. *Research Methods in Education.* Abingdon, UK: Routledge.

Conle, C. 2000. "Thesis as Narrative or 'What Is the Inquiry in Narrative Enquiry?'." *Curriculum Inquiry* 30(2): 189–214.

Cook, D.T. 2002. "Randomized Experiments in Educational Policy Research: A Critical Examination of the Reasons the Educational Evaluation Community Has Offered for Not Doing Them." *Educational Evaluation and Policy Analysis* 24(3): 175–199.

Cooperrider, D.L., M. McQuaid, and L.N. Godwin. 2018. "A Positive Revolution in Education: Uniting Appreciative Inquiry with the Science of Human Flourishing to 'Power Up Positive Education'." *AI Practitioner* 20(4): 3–19. doi: 10.12781/978-1-907549-37-3-1.

Covenry, A. 2021. "Connecting Research and Practice for Professionals and Communities." *Educational Action Research* 29(1): 1–4. doi: 10.1080/09650792.2021.1883824.

Creswell, J., and C.V. Plano. 2011. *Designing and Conducting Mixed Methods Research.* 2nd ed. Thousand Oaks, CA: Sage.

Dang, J. 2018. "An Updated Meta-analysis of the Ego Depletion Effect." *Psychological Research* 82(4): 645–651. doi: 10.1007/s00426-017-0862-x.

Davidsen, A.S. 2013. "Phenomenological Approaches in Psychology and Health Sciences." *Qualitative Research in Psychology* 10(3): 318–339. doi: 10.1080/14780887.2011.608466

Delamont, S. 2007. "Arguments against Auto-Ethnography." *British Educational Research Association Annual Conference*, London.

Delamont, S. 2009. "The Only Honest Thing: Autoethnography, Reflexivity and Small Crises in Fieldwork." *Ethnography and Education* 4(1): 51–63.

Denscombe, M. 2014. *The Good Research Guide*. 4th ed. Maidenhead, UK: Open University Press.

Denshire, S. 2014. "On Auto-ethnography." *Current Sociology* 62(6): 831–850. doi: 10.1177%2F0011392114533339.

Denzin, N.K., and Y.S. Lincoln, eds. 2000. *Handbook of Qualitative Research*. 2nd ed. Thousand Oaks, CA: Sage.

Devine, P. 2003. "Secondary Data Analysis." In *The A-Z of Social Research*, edited by R.L. Miller and J.D. Brewer. Thousand Oaks, CA: Sage.

Doolan, D.M., and E.S. Froelicher. 2009. "Using an Existing Data Set to Answer New Research Questions: A Methodological Review." *Research and Theory for Nursing Practice* 23(3): 203–215.

Dowling, M. 2007. "From Husserl to van Manen. A Review of Different Phenomenological Approaches." *International Journal of Nursing Studies* 44(1): 131–142. doi: 10.1016/j.ijnurstu.2005.11.026.

Dunleavy, G., and J. Burke. 2019. "Fostering a Sense of Belonging at an International School in France: An Experimental Study." *Educational & Child Psychology* 36(4): 34–45.

Egeli, C. 2017. "Autoethnography: A Methodological Chat with Self." *Counselling Psychology Review* 32(1): 5–15.

Ellis, C., T.E. Adams, and A.P. Bochner. 2011. "Autoethnography: An Overview." *Forum: Qualitative Social Research* 12(1): 1–18.

Finlay, L. 2011. *Phenomenology for Therapists: Researching the Lived World*. Chichester, UK: Wiley-Blackwell.

Gibbs, G. 1988. *Learning by Doing: A Guide to Teaching Learning Methods*. Oxford: Oxford Brookes University.

Glaser, B.G. 1978. *Theoretical Sensitivity*. Mill Valley: Sociology Press.

Glaser, B.G., and A.L. Strauss. 1967. *The Discovery of Grounded Theory: Strategies for Qualitative Research*. London: Routledge.

Gough, D., J. Thomas, and S. Oliver. 2012. "Clarifying Differences between Review Designs and Methods. *Systematic Reviews* 1(28).

Green, J.C. 2007. *Mixed Methods in Social Inquiry*. San Francisco: Jossey-Bass.

Hall, R. 2020. *Mixing Methods in Social Research*. London: Sage.

Hall, T., C. Connolly, S. O'Gradaigh, K. Burden, M. Kearney, S. Schuck, J. Bottema, G. Cazemier, W. Hustinx, M. Evens, T. Koenraad, E. Makridou, and P. Kosmas. 2020. "Education in Precarious Times: A Comparative Study across Six Countries to Identify Design Priorities for Mobile Learning in a Pandemic." *International Learning Sciences*. doi: 10.1108/ILS-04-2020-0089.

Hampden-Thompson, G., F. Lubben, and J. Bennett. 2011. "Post-16 Physics and Chemistry Uptake: Combining Large-scale Secondary Analysis with In-depth Qualitative Methods." *International Journal of Research & Method in Education* 34(3): 289–307. doi: 10.1080/1743727X.2011.609550.

Hart, C. 2018. *Doing a Literature Review: Releasing the Social Science Research Imagination*. London: Sage.

Hoy, W.K., and C.M. Adams. 2016. *Quantitative Research in Education: A Primer*. 2nd ed. Thousand Oaks, CA: Sage.

Hughes, N., and J. Burke. 2018. "Sleeping with the Frenemy: How Restricting 'Bedroom Use' of Smartphones Impacts Happiness and Wellbeing." *Computers in Human Behavior* 85: 236–244. doi: 10.1016/j.chb.2018.03.047

Iwatani, E. 2018. "Overview of Data Mining's Potential Benefits and Limitations in Education Research." *Practical Assessment, Research & Evaluation* 23(15): 1–8.

Josselson, R. 2006. "Narratives in action." *Narrative Inquiry* 16(1): 3–10.

Kelly, J.G., L.S. Azelton, C. Lardon, L.O. Mock, S.D. Tandon, and M. Thomas. 2004. "On Community Leadership: Stories about Collaboration in Action Research." *American Journal of Community Psychology* 33(3–4): 205–216. doi: 10.1023/b:ajcp.0000027006.48815.5a. PMID: 15212179.

Khan, K.S., R. Kunz, J Kleijnen, and G. Antes. 2003. "Five Steps to Conducting a Systematic Review." *Journal of the Royal Society of Medicine* 96: 118–121.

Kidd, S.A., and M.J. Kral. 2005. "Practicing Participatory Action Research." *Journal of Counseling Psychology* 52(2): 187–195. doi: 10.1037/0022-0167.52.2.187

Kim, J-H. 2015. *Understanding Narrative Inquiry: The Crafting and Analysis of Stories as Research*. London: Sage.

Kindon, S., R. Pain, and M. Kesby, eds. 2007. *Participatory Action Research Approaches and Methods. Connecting People, Participation and Place*. London: Routledge.

Klenowski, V., S. Askew, and E. Carnell. 2006. "Portfolios for Learning, Assessment and Professional Development in Higher Education." *Assessment & Evaluation in Higher Education* 31(3): 267–286. doi: 10.1080/02602930500352816.

Lahuerta-Otero, E., and R. Cordero-Gutiérrez. 2016. "Looking for the Perfect Tweet. The Use of Data Mining Techniques to Find Influencers on Twitter." *Computers in Human Behavior* 64: 575–583. doi: 10.1016/j.chb.2016.07.035

Lassiter, L.E. 2005. *The Chicago Guide to Collaborative Ethnography*. Chicago, IL: University of Chicago Press.

Lee, J., A. Jatowt, and K. Kim. 2021. "Discovering Underlying Sensations of Human Emotions Based on Social Media." *Journal of the Association for Information Science & Technology* 72(4): 417–432. doi: 10.1002/asi.24414

Lemmen, C.H.C., G. Yaron, R. Gifford, and M.D. Spreeuwenberg. 2021. "Positive Health and the Happy Professional: A Qualitative Case Study." *BMC Family Practice* 22(1): 1–12. doi: 10.1186/s12875-021-01509-6

Leung, E. 2021. "Thematic Analysis of My 'Coming Out' Experiences Through an Intersectional Lens: An Autoethnographic Study." *Frontiers in Psychology* 12: 654946. doi: 10.3389/fpsyg.2021.654946

Lincoln, Y.S., and E.G. Guba. 1986. "But Is It Rigorous? Trustworthiness and Authenticity in Naturalistic Evaluation." *New Directions for Program Evaluation* (30): 73–84. doi: 10.1002/ev.1427.

Logan, T. 2020. "A Practical, Iterative Framework for Secondary Data Analysis in Educational Research." *Australian Educational Researcher* 47(1): 129–148. doi: 10.1007/s13384-019-00329-z.

Lucey, C., and J. Burke. 2022. *Positive Leadership in Practice*. London: Routledge.

McCandliss, B.D., M. Kalchman, and P. Bryant. 2003. "Design Experiments and Laboratory Approaches to Learning: Steps toward Collaborative Exchange." *Educational Researcher* 32(1): 14–16. doi: 10.3102/0013189X032001014

McIntyre, A. 2007. *Participatory Action Research (Qualitative Research Methods Series 52)*. London: Sage.

McKenney, S., and T. Reeves. 2019. *Conducting Educational Design Research*. 2nd ed. Abingdon: Routledge.

Mertens, D.M. 2010. "Transformative Mixed Methods Research." *Qualitative Inquiry* 16(6): 469–474.

Mills, D., and M. Morton. 2013. *Ethnography in Education. Research Methods for Education*. London: Sage.

Newman, M., and D. Gough. 2019. "Systematic Reviews in Educational Research: Methodology, Perspectives and Application." In *Systematic Reviews in Educational Research*, edited by O. Zawacki-Richter, M. Kerres, S. Bedenlier, M. Bond, and K. Buntins, 3–22. Wiesbaden: Springer.

Orland-Barak, L. 2005. "Portfolios as Evidence of Reflective Practice: What Remains 'Untold'." *Educational Research* 47(1): 25–44. doi: 10.1080/0013188042000337541.

Osteneck, U. 2020. "Adult Journalling: A Method of Learning and of Assessment." *Journal of Higher Education Theory & Practice* 20(4): 123–131. doi: 10.33423/jhetp.v20i4.2991.

Patton, M.Q. 2002. *Qualitative Research and Evaluation Methods*. 3rd. ed. London: Sage.

Pink, S. 2021. *Doing Visual Ethnography*. 4th ed. London: Sage.

Plomp, T., and N. Nieveen. 2010. *An Introduction to Educational Design Research*. Netherlands: Netherlands Institute for Curriculum Development.

Plomp, T., and N. Nieveen. 2013. *Educational Design Research Part A: An Introduction*. Enschede: Netherlands Institute for Curriculum Development (SLO).

Price, D.A., and G.C.R. Yates. 2010. "Ego Depletion Effects on Mathematics Performance in Primary School Students: Why Take the Hard Road?" *Educational Psychology* 30(3): 269–281.

Quinn, P., S. McGilloway, and J. Burke. 2021. "COVID-19 and the Class of 2020: A National Study of the Mental Health and Wellbeing of Leaving Certificate Students in Ireland." *Irish Educational Studies* 40(2): 375–384. doi: 10.1080/03323315.2021.1916564

Rahgozaran, H., and H. Gholami. 2014. "The Impact of Teachers' Reflective Journal Writing on Their Self-Efficacy." *Modern Journal of Language Teaching Methods* 4(2): 65–74.

Reeves, T.C. 2006. "Design Research from a Technology Perspective." In *Educational Design Research*, edited by J. van den Akker, K. Gravemeijer, S. McKenney, and N. Nieeven, 86–109. London: Routledge.

Robinson, S., and A.L. Mendelson. 2012. "A Qualitative Experiment: Research on Mediated Meaning Construction Using a Hybrid Approach." *Journal of Mixed Methods Research* 6(4): 332–347.

Robson, C. 2002. *Real World Research: A Resource for Social Scientists and Practitioner-Researchers*. Oxford: Blackwell Publishers Ltd.

Robson, C. 2011. *Real World Research: A Resource for Social-scientists and Practitioner-Researchers*. 3rd ed. Oxford: Blackwell Publishing.

Round, J., and J. Burke. 2018. "A Dream of a Retirement: The Longitudinal Experiences and Perceived Retirement Wellbeing of Recent Retirees Following a Tailored Intervention Linking Best Possible Self-expressive Writing with Goal-setting." *International Coaching Psychology Review* 13(2): 27–45.

Ruggiano, N., and T.E. Perry. 2019. "Conducting Secondary Analysis of Qualitative Data: Should We, Can We, and How?" *Qualitative Social Work* 18(1): 81–97. doi: 10.1177/1473325017700701.

Sae-Mi L., J. Fogaça, and M. Harrison. 2020. "Can Writing Be Wrong? Collaborative Autoethnography as Critical Reflective Practice in Sport, Exercise, and Performance Psychology." *Qualitative Report* 25(10): 3562–3582.

Sandoval, W.A., and P. Bell. 2004. "Design-Based Research Methods for Studying Learning in Context: Introduction." *Educational Psychologist* 39(4): 199–201.

Scholtz, S.E., W. de Klerk, and L.T. de Beer. 2020. "The Use of Research Methods in Psychological Research: A Systematised Review." *Frontiers in Research Metrics and Analytics* 5: 1.

Seibert, G.S., R.W. May, M.C. Fitzgerald, and F.D. Fincham. 2016. "Understanding School Burnout: Does Self-control Matter?" *Learning and Individual Differences* 49: 120–127. doi: 10.1016/j.lindif.2016.05.024.

Shadish, W.R., T.D. Cook, and D.T. Campbell. 2002. *Experimental and Quasi-experimental Designs for Generalized Causal Inference*. Boston, MA: Houghton, Mifflin and Company.

Shavelson, R.J., and L. Towne. 2002. *Scientific Research in Education*. Washington, DC: National Research Council, National Academy Press.

Singh, B., and H.K. Singh. 2010. "Web Data Mining Research: A Survey." Paper presented at the 2010 IEEE International Conference on Computational Intelligence and Computing Research.

Sloan, A., and B. Bowe. 2014. "Phenomenology and Hermeneutic Phenomenology: The Philosophy, the Methodologies, and Using Hermeneutic Phenomenology to Investigate Lecturers' Experiences of Curriculum Design." *Quality & Quantity: International Journal of Methodology* 48(3): 1291–1303. doi: 10.1007/s11135-013-9835-3.

Smith, E. 2008a. "Pitfalls and Promises: The Use of Secondary Data Analysis in Educational Research." *British Journal of Educational Studies* 56(3): 323–339.

Smith, E. 2008b. *Using Secondary Data in Educational and Social Research*. Maidenhead: McGraw Hill/Open University Press.

Smith, K., and H. Tillema. 2001. "Long-term Influences of Portfolios on Professional Development." *Scandinavian Journal of Educational Research* 45(2): 183–203. doi: 10.1080/00313830120052750.

Stake, R.E. 2005. "Qualitative Case Studies." In *The Sage Handbook of Qualitative Research*, edited by N.K. Denzin and Y.S. Lincoln, 443–466. London: Sage.

Stephens, C., and M. Breheny. 2013. "Narrative Analysis in Psychological Research: An Integrated Approach to Interpreting Stories." *Qualitative Research in Psychology* 10(1): 14–27. doi: 10.1080/1478 0887.2011.586103

Sterne, J.A.C., and M. Egger. 2001. "Funnel Plots for Detecting Bias in Meta-analysis: Guidelines on Choice of Axis." *Journal of Clinical Epidemiology* 54: 1046–1055.

Stokes, T. 2020. "Using Participatory Methods with Young Children; Reflections on Emergent 'Ethically Important Moments' in School-Based Research." *Irish Educational Studies* 39(3): 375–387.

Strauss, A.L. 1970. "Discovering New Theory from Previous Theory." In *Human Nature and Collective Behavior: Papers in Honor of Herbert Blumer*, edited by T. Shibutani. Englewood Cliffs, NJ: Prentice-Hall.

Sullivan, C. and M.A. Forrester. 2019. *Doing Qualitative Research in Psychology: A Practical Guide*. 2nd ed. London: Sage.

Suri, H. 2013. "Epistemological Pluralism in Research Synthesis Methods." *International Journal of Qualitative Studies in Education (QSE)* 26(7): 889–911. doi: 10.1080/09518398.2012.691565.

Suzuki, L.A., M.K. Ahluwalia, A.K. Arora, and J.S. Mattis. 2007. "The Pond You Fish in Determines the Fish You Catch: Exploring Strategies for Qualitative Data Collection." *The Counseling Psychologist* 35(2): 295–327. doi: 10.1177/0011000006290983

Suzuki, L.A., M.K. Ahluwalia, J.S. Mattis, and C.A. Quizon. 2005. "Ethnography in Counseling Psychology Research: Possibilities for Application." *Journal of Counseling Psychology* 52: 206–214.

Teddlie, C., and A. Tashakkori. 2009. *Foundations of Mixed Methods Research: Integrating Quantitative and Qualitative Approaches in the Social and Behavioral Sciences*. Los Angeles: Sage.

Thompson, T., D. Talapatra, C.E. Hazel, J. Coleman, and N. Cutforth. 2020. "Thriving with Down Syndrome: A Qualitative Multiple Case Study." *Journal of Applied Research in Intellectual Disabilities* 33(6): 1390–1404. doi: 10.1111/jar.12767

Thomas, K.W., and R.H. Kilmann. 1974. *The Thomas-Kilmann Conflict Mode Instrument*. Mountain View, CA: CPP.

Travers, J.C., B.G. Cook, W.J. Therrien, and M.D. Coyne. 2016. "Replication Research and Special Education." *Remedial & Special Education* 37(4): 195–204. doi: 10.1177/0741932516648462.

Vallerand, R.J. 2015. *The Psychology of Passion: A Dualistic Model, Series in Positive Psychology*. New York, NY: Oxford University Press.

van Manen, M. 1997. *Researching Lived Experience: Human Science for an Action Sensitive Pedagogy*. 2nd ed. Ontario: The Althouse Press.

van Wyk, M.M. 2017. "Student Teachers' Views Regarding the Usefulness of Reflective Journal Writing as an Eportfolio Alternative Assessment Strategy: An Interpretive Phenomenological Analysis." *Gender & Behaviour* 15(4): 10208–102219.

Walford, G. 2009. "The Practice of Writing Ethnographic Fieldnotes." *Ethnography and Education* 4(2): 117–130.

Walford, G. 2021. "What Is Worthwhile Auto-ethnography? Research in the Age of the Selfie." *Ethnography & Education* 16(1): 31–43. doi: 10.1080/17457823.2020.1716263.

Wang, S.C., R.R. Hubbard, and C. Dorazio. 2020. "Overcoming Racial Battle Fatigue through Dialogue: Voices of Three Counseling Psychologist Trainees." *Training and Education in Professional Psychology* 14(4): 285–292. doi: 10.1037/tep0000283

Webster, L., and P. Mertova. 2007. *Using Narrative Inquiry as a Research Method*. Abingdon: Routledge.

Wegner, E. 1998. *Communities of Practice: Learning, Meaning, and Identity*. New York: Cambridge University Press.

White, C.A., B. Uttl, and M.D. Holder. 2019. "Meta-analyses of Positive Psychology Interventions: The Effects are Much Smaller Than Previously Reported." *PLoS ONE* 14(5). doi: 10.1371/journal.pone.0216588

Witten, I.H., F. Eibe, and M.A. Hall, eds. 2011. *Data Mining: Practical Machine Learning Tools and Techniques*. 3rd ed. Burlington, MA: Morgan Kaufman Publishers.

Witten, I.H., F. Eibe, M.A. Hall, and C.J. Pal. 2017. *Data Mining: Practical Machine Learning Tools and Techniques*. 4th ed. The Netherlands: Elsevier.

Wolffe, R., H.A. Crowe, W. Evens, and K. McConnaughay. 2013. "Portfolio as a Teaching Method: A Capstone Project to Promote Recognition of Professional Growth." *Journal of College Teaching & Learning* 10(1): 1–6.

Woodward, H. 1998. "Reflective Journals and Portfolios: Learning Through Assessment." *Assessment & Evaluation in Higher Education* 23(4): 415. doi: 10.1080/0260293980230408.

Yanik, B. 2017. "An Ethnographic Approach to Education: What Are You Doing in This Village?" *Online Submission* 8(26): 113–118.

Yin, R.K. 2018. *Case Study Research and Applications. Design and Methods.* 6th ed. London: Sage.

7   Methods

Methods refer to the techniques or tools you use for data collection and sourcing. For your empirical research project, you can use various methods to collect your data, ranging from questionnaires, interviews, observation, and others. Some methods are distinct features of a research methodology you selected; you can use other methods in multiple methodologies. Figure 7.1 provides the most frequently used methods in empirical research projects. We will delve deeper into each of them to help you apply them effectively in your project.

For your desk-based research projects, you can use a variety of methods for data sourcing depending on your methodology, such as journaling (portfolio and autoethnographic), web or document screening (e.g. web mining), literature review techniques (literature review and meta-analysis). The journaling method is described in Section 7.7. The remaining desk-based methods are described as processes in the methodology in Section 6.2.

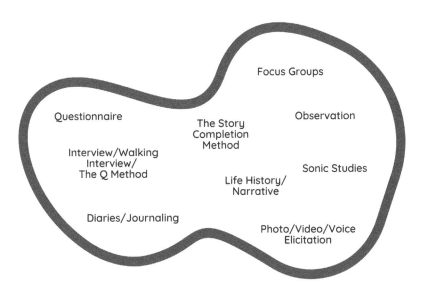

Figure 7.1 Frequently used methods in empirical research projects.

DOI: 10.4324/9781003262428-7

7.1 Questionnaires

Questionnaires are one of the most popular methods for data collection. They can be self-administered in pen-and-paper or online formats. Alternatively, they can be completed to evaluate other people's behaviours and attitudes. Some questionnaires are designed for the researcher to use when observing participants' behaviours. In this section, we will focus mainly on creating a self-administered questionnaire.

7.1.1 Questionnaire structure

Whenever we design a survey, we need to ensure that we have all the relevant types of questions asked. Firstly, we identify the demographic of our participants. The three core questions we ask most participants relate to their (1) age, (2) gender, and (3) location. You can supplement the core questions with additional questions relating to your specific sample. For example, suppose your project refers to coaching psychologists. In that case, you can ask them about their length of service, level of education, number of coachees they work with weekly, number of hours they work, the coaching approach they practice, and other relevant information. Your demographic questions are essential, as they allow you to create a profile of your sample and identify the limitations of your project. For example, if too many participants from a specific group responded to your survey, or you have a small representation from a significant group, it may impact your results.

The remainder of the questionnaire focuses on addressing your research questions. You can do it by constructing a questionnaire that consists of your (1) self-constructed questions and/or relevant (2) tests. Self-constructed questions are questions and statements you create that are relevant to your research topic. Tests relate to reliable and validated knowledge-based or person-based questionnaires, including behaviours, attitudes, beliefs, values, motivations, interests, personalities, and others (Rust et al., 2021).

Reliability refers to the consistency of the measure. For example, if your participant is completing an IQ test today and redoing it next week, their results should be the same or at least similar. If they are not, the test may not be reliable. Validity refers to whether the test you use measures what it is supposed to measure. For example, if your participant is completing an IQ test, but in it, some questions belong to Emotional Intelligence assessment, then the test is not a valid assessment of IQ. Tests or scales previously created by researchers are more likely to be valid and reliable than questionnaires you make yourself; this is why it is good to use them for your research project.

If there is a test available for a topic of your interest, it is recommended that you use it instead of creating your questionnaire. For example, there are over 100 validated tests measuring wellbeing. If your research aims to assess your students' wellbeing, there is little point in you creating your questionnaire to apply one of the validated tests. Your biggest challenge will be discerning which theoretical model of wellbeing you choose for your project, as each test is associated with a different model. Some projects, however, will require you to create your questionnaire. For example, if your research question states, *What is the coachee's experience of using a DISCO health coaching model?* You will need to skilfully design a series of questions to establish participants' experience. This is what the next section is about.

7.1.2 Constructing questions

You can ask many types of questions to elicit participants' responses. They range from alternate-choice and multiple-choice rating scales (Rust et al., 2021) to open-ended questions, which you can analyse qualitatively or quantitatively. See Section 8.3.1 for further detail on the analysis of open-ended questions. Each type of question has its advantages and disadvantages. They are listed in Table 7.1.

It is essential to consider each question carefully. A valuable technique to decide on the question type is to begin with an end in mind. Then, ask yourself what data each question will elicit and whether your findings will address your research question. For example, suppose your research question states, *What are the differences between patients who experienced a stroke and myocardial infarction in the last six months in relation to their optimism?* to address this question. In that case, you will need to identify two groups of participants, the group that (1) experienced stroke and (2) experienced myocardial infarction. An alternate-choice question will allow you to do it.

On the other hand, if your research question states, *What is the association between the support patients with stroke and myocardial infarction experienced and optimism?* then you will need to ask them a rating-scale question to address your research question because it

Table 7.1 Advantages and disadvantages of question types.

Question type	Example	Advantages	Disadvantages
Alternate-choice	Do you feel supported by your partner? Yes – No	It is fast for respondents to answer and provides a definite response. Allows you to carry out statistical comparisons profiling the participants who responded yes vs no to your question.	Responses are extreme, and some participants may feel undecided or might not know the answer. Not effective with personality, attitude, ability, and similar person-related assessments. Limits some of the statistical tests you can use.
Multiple-choice	What supports are most important to you? a. Partner support b. Friends support c. Family support	Options make it easier for participants to respond. Good for knowledge-based questions.	May not be exhaustive, and if not well constructed, important questions may be ignored. Should not be used with person-based questions.
Rating scale	Rate your agreement with the following statements: I feel supported by my partner. Strongly agree – agree – disagree – strongly disagree	Most frequently used in person-based questions. Provides many options that allow respondents to adequately express themselves.	The meaning of scale may differ for individuals. It is not precise. While it is popular in social science, medical researchers avoid it and replace it with percentages.
Open-ended	What support does your partner provide?	Provides responses that the researcher didn't consider. Adds quality data that can explain some of the quantitative findings.	More challenging and time-consuming to analyse.

implies correlations, which require a rating-scale question. This is why beginning with an end in mind can prove helpful when deciding on the types of questions you ask.

Sometimes, an excellent way to learn how to construct good questions is by reviewing the problematic questions, such as leading, double-barrelled, or vague questions (Sullivan and Artino, 2017). Here are some examples of poorly designed questions and their alternatives.

Leading questions

EXAMPLE: "WHY IS IT GOOD FOR A THERAPIST TO BE CLIENT-FOCUSED?"

It is a bad practice to ask leading questions. They will not elicit honest answers, as the participants cannot share their opinions. To improve this question, you can rate their agreement about the importance of being student-focused (rating scale); you can ask them to rate the importance of several practices, including being student-focused (multiple-choice); you can explore with them the reasons for and against being student-focused (open-ended). These questions would provide you with richer data than the leading question they replaced.

Double-barrelled questions

EXAMPLE: "DO YOU GO OUT FOR A WALK EVERY DAY; IF SO, HOW LONG IS YOUR WALK, AND IF NOT, WHY NOT?"

This is a typical double-barrelled question that consists of at least three questions in one. Most people reading it will probably need to do a second take on it before they respond. This is why it is more beneficial to break it down into parts. Also, if your online survey tool allows it, you can set up an automatic follow-on question. For example, if your question is, *Do you go for a walk every day?*, when your respondents say "*no*", they will be re-directed to a question: "*Why not?*" If they say "*yes*", they will be asked, *On average, how long is your walk?* This structure makes it easier for participants to respond to your survey. When they get confused, you may lose them halfway through the survey, thus reducing your number of respondents.

Vague questions

EXAMPLE: "HOW WAS YOUR EXPERIENCE OF WORKING WITH CLIENTS DURING THE FINANCIAL CRISIS?"

Vague questions, such as this one, often confuse participants or make them respond to them in ways you did not expect. Some respondents will be left uninspired by this question and leave you a one-word answer: *Okay.* Others may describe an experience that does not relate to your study. So here is how you can rephrase this question to make it more straightforward: *How have you changed your practice during the financial crisis?* and *What were your main challenges during the financial crisis?*

Negatively worded questions

EXAMPLE: "WHICH PARTS OF THE PRESENTATION DID YOU NOT FIND DISENGAGING?"

Many negative questions require extra concentration from readers to understand. But, again, simplicity when designing questions wins over complexity. To rephrase this confusing question, we need to turn it positive: *Which parts of the presentation did you find engaging?*

Overlapping or incomplete range

EXAMPLE: HOW LONG HAVE YOU BEEN A PSYCHOLOGIST?

(a) Less than 1 year; (b) 1–2 years; (c) 2–5 years; (d) 5+ years   While the question is not incorrect, the responses to it are confusing. For example, if I had two years' experience, which option should I choose, option b or c? Therefore, care needs to be taken when offering respondents options and ensuring that all options are present. The missing option may be *I don't know* or *Other* in some cases. For example, some respondents take offence if there are no *Prefer not to say* options available for gender. This is why when constructing a questionnaire, make sure you consider all possible options.

Consistency of choices

EXAMPLE: "HOW STRESSFUL DO YOU FIND DISABILITY ASSESSMENTS?"

(a) Very stressful; (b) stressful; (c) coping well; (d) coping very well   The rating scale for this question changes halfway through. A question that aims to measure stress becomes a question that measures coping. It is essential to ensure that the responses we provide match the questions and that there is a consistency of responses throughout. These responses could include a range between *very stressful* to *not stressful at all*. Alternatively, the question should focus on how well they coped with disability assessment. The rating scale, in this case, should range from *coping very badly* to *coping very well*. Table 7.2 provides examples of consistent five-item, rating-scale responses.

Absolutes

EXAMPLE: "ARE YOU ALWAYS ENGAGED IN A CLASSROOM?"

Absolutes relate to words, such as *never, always, forever, all, none, nobody, every*. Questions that include absolutes are hard for participants to respond to, as an average person can usually think of exceptions to the rule; the one time when they did not behave in that way, which makes it harder to respond. Therefore, it is better to rephrase it by asking about the *average* behaviour or the frequency of behaving in a certain way. These types of questions will provide a more genuine response.

Provide examples

EXAMPLE: "HOW MANY COMPUTING DEVICES DO YOU HAVE AT HOME?"

This question seems relatively innocent; however, its responses may vary depending on participants' definitions of computing devices. To improve this question and ensure the consistency of response, you can ask the question and provide examples in brackets (e.g. PC, tablet, smartphone).

When constructing a survey, you need to be mindful of the order of the questions and tests you use. For everything we ask our participants to write about, they will experience various emotions. If the questionnaire is long and repetitive, they may feel bored and stop completing it halfway through. If the questionnaire is challenging, they may experience fatigue. If the questionnaire is filled with leading questions, it may irritate participants. If the questions bring back unpleasant memories, the survey can make them feel anxious or depressed. Whatever emotions they experience as they engage with a survey will impact their responses. Therefore, the order of the questions you ask matters.

For example, we once asked participants to complete a lengthy survey. We divided participants into two groups, and each group received the same survey, but the order of questions we asked differed. When participants completed a scale assessing their depression before optimism, their results showed higher levels of pessimism, which may have

Table 7.2 Example of consistent five-item, rating-scale responses.

1	2	3	4	5
Strongly disagree	Disagree	Neither agree nor disagree	Agree	Strongly agree
Strongly dissatisfied	Dissatisfied	Neither satisfied nor dissatisfied	Satisfied	Strongly satisfied
Dislike a great deal	Dislike somewhat	Neither like nor dislike	Like somewhat	Like a great deal
Extremely slow	Somewhat slow	Average	Somewhat fast	Extremely fast
Extremely unlikely	Somewhat unlikely	Neither likely nor unlikely	Somewhat unlikely	Extremely unlikely
Not at all important	Slightly important	Moderately important	Very important	Extremely important
Does not describe me	Describes me slightly	Describes me moderately well	Describes me very well	Describes me extremely well
Do not prefer	Prefer slightly	Prefer a moderate amount	Prefer a lot	Prefer a great deal
Extremely bad	Somewhat bad	Neither good nor bad	Somewhat good	Extremely good
Never	Once a week	Two to three times a week	Four to six times a week	Daily
Never	Once or twice	Once a month	Once a week	Daily
Never	Sometimes	About half the time	Most of the time	Always
Much less	Somewhat less	About the same	Somewhat more	Much more
None at all	A little	A moderate amount	A lot	A great deal
Not challenging at all	Slightly challenging	Moderately challenging	Very challenging	Extremely challenging

been due to the lower mood that assessing depression put them into. Also, when a complicated optimism test was completed as the last set of questions, the reliability of the test was reduced, which may have been due to the participants' fatigue. Therefore, care needs to be taken when deciding on the order of questions.

7.1.3 Piloting a survey

It is good practice to pilot a questionnaire before it goes out with participants similar to those for whom the survey is designed. Therefore, if your sample is made up of psychologists, try to pilot it with some of your friends who are psychologists. If your pilot is with young people, try to pilot it with young people. There are many different reasons for piloting a questionnaire. They range from assessing the time it takes participants to complete a survey to checking for the clarity of questions, asking participants about their experiences, or providing preliminary analysis to see if they got the questions right.

7.2 Interviews

Interviews are used predominantly to collect qualitative data. Some interviews can be highly structured to include quantitative data or semi-structured or unstructured and can be conducted with individuals or groups. If the purpose of the interview is to collect information, then a structured interview may be the choice. We often see interviews used like this in market research or opinion polls. In research, it could be that you want to know if pre-screening is widespread in mental health services. To get the answer to this, you may conduct phone/internet interviews with several mental health services in a cross-section of the country and ask the same five questions around pre-screening practices. If you want to explore issues more deeply, semi-structured or unstructured interviews would be more desirable.

Depending on your positioning, an interview can serve many functions in your research. For example, if you are conducting quasi-experimental design research within the post-positivist paradigm, you may want to use standardised open-ended interviews. This kind of interview is where a set of carefully designed questions are asked of all participants in the same sequence. The interview schedule is vital. You could include some ranking exercises as part of the interview. For example, as part of a quasi-experimental research project, a researcher asked students in interviews to rank 1–4 the time spent in class on a list of different activities. In this way, you can collect qualitative and quantitative data in interviews.

On the other hand, if you are carrying out an ethnography design within the interpretivist paradigm, you may have some questions prepared to open the interview and then let the interviewee's responses lead your questions. In addition, you may carry out multiple interview sessions with the same person over some time. Here you are focused on the participant's experience of a phenomenon, and therefore you need to let the interviewee have the scope to bring you to topics not planned for.

Suppose you are carrying out a PAR project within the critical paradigm. In that case, the interview might take the form of a walk and an informal chat about what issues are essential to the researcher and the co-researcher. Table 7.3 provides a planning framework that can help you think about what data you want to collect from interviewing.

Table 7.3 Planning for interviews.

Prompts	Notes
General area you are interested in	
Your research question	
What do you want to learn from the interview/s?	
What will participants need to discuss in order for you to learn this?	
What kind of questions will you need to ask to get participants to talk about this? [list questions]	
Are there language issues you need to think about?	
Check back to see if the interview questions will help you answer your research question	
Are there any ethical implications you need to consider?	
Identify suitable candidates to trial the interview with ahead of finalising your interview schedule	

In interviews, it is essential to bracket your own experience and presuppositions and be open to what the interviewee says. Think about the following ahead of the interview:

1 **Interview schedule** – Have you trialled the interview schedule? Is your language appropriate to the age and language level of the participant? How do you know this?
2 **Physical setting** – Where will the interview take place? Can you ensure that it is in a private environment? For example, if interviewing on the internet, can you ensure the participant is in a space where others cannot hear the responses? Are you in a private room? Do you feel safe in the setting for the interview? How can you enhance your safety if this is an issue? How will you set up the room? Where will you sit concerning the interviewee?
3 **Recording the interview** – How will you capture consent for the recording? Does the device used for recording meet all General Data Protection Regulation (GDPR) guidelines and the safety of data needed? Have you a backup plan in case a device doesn't work?
4 **Timing the interview** – Have you considered the length of the interview? Will you need to take a break? Will you need to provide refreshments ahead or after the interview? What time of the day/week suits the interviewee?
5 **During the interview** – How will you observe and note body language? How will you deal with silences? Have you a backup plan if the interviewee gets upset discussing any issue? Have you rehearsed your body language? Have you considered your tone of voice and facial expressions? Have you made yourself familiar with prompts you can use?
6 **After the interview** – How will you debrief with the participant? Have you considered how you can share the transcript and timing around that? Does the interviewee know they can ethically exit the research at any stage of the process, even after the interview? How will you record your field notes on the interview? At what stage will you anonymise the data from the interview?

7.2.1 *Trialling your interview*

To prepare for interviews, we strongly suggest that you trial your interview with a few participants who are as close as possible to the demographics you will be interviewing in your research. This trialling provides several advantages for your research and allows you to think about the questions posed in the six points mentioned earlier. After the trial, you can adjust your interview schedule to suit the language of the participants; you will know approximately how long your interview will take; you will be able to identify data gaps in the information; if you can video the process, it will help you work on your body language and interview technique. It is good to have a frank conversation with the participants in the trial and learn from their constructive criticism of the process. We suggest you use this to practice reflection. Table 7.4 provides some valuable prompts that you can use during the interview.

7.3 The Q method of interviewing

The psychologist and physicist William Stephenson (1935) introduced this mixed-methods approach to research as a systematic way to explore human subjectivity where the researcher gathers information on participants' views, opinions, and beliefs about a chosen topic through a card sorting activity usually accompanied by a semi-structured interview. It is used in a variety of disciplines (Churruca et al., 2021)It is described as a methodology and a method. In this book, we decided to put it in the methods section. It is a very good method to use with young people when trying to elicit their views on a

Table 7.4 Interview prompts.

Process	Prompt questions
Asking for clarification	I'm not sure I am following you.
	What difference did that make?
	Can you explain what you mean by . . . ?
Asking the respondent to be specific	Could you give me an example of that?
	Can you tell me a day that . . . ?
	Can you tell me how that made you feel at that moment?
Summarising and searching for connections	I think this is what you are saying.
	Do you think there is a link between?
	Is this the same as the time . . . ?
Asking for elaboration	Could you tell me more about that?
	What do you mean by that?
	Was there more to this experience?
Searching for opinions	Do you have any ideas why?
	What would you give as the main reasons?
	Why would that happen?
Looking for comparisons	Is this the same as the time . . . ?
	Some students would say . . . would you agree?
	Would you have a similar experience?
Asking for prioritisation	What is the most significant?
	What is the most important?
	What is your favourite?
Searching for feelings	How did you feel when . . . ?
	Can you describe how you felt when . . . ?
	How might they have felt?

topic (O'Connell et al., 2019). Participants may not always be certain about their feelings about a specific topic (e.g. belonging, learning, attachment). The Q methodology helps to add statistical significance to a phenomenon being researched. A benefit of this mixed method is that it utilises statistics to obtain and/or expand on qualitative findings (Franz et al., 2013; Killam et al., 2013). Another benefit of conducting this method of data collection in place of a standard interview and/or questionnaire is that it offers you an ability to talk the participant through the process as it is conducted face-to-face with participants and allows you to explain any text that the participant may not understand (Killam et al., 2013; Franz et al., 2013).

According to McKeown and Thomas (2013, pp. 5–6), there are five main steps in a Q method study:

1 Creating the Q statements or samples
2 Selecting the research participants
3 The Q sort activity
4 Factor analysis
5 Factor interpretation

The first important step in this method is the development of the statements for the Q sort. The creation of the Q concourse is the beginning point of any Q study. In general, a set of between 40 and 80 statements are considered satisfactory during a Q sort activity (Shinebourne, 2009; Brown, 1993). This process is based on your literature review, may be based on questions from a questionnaire or through working with key concepts that you are researching.

In the process of the Q sort, participants complete the Q sort activity on an individual basis with the interviewer asking the questions about their view on the topic being researched as they sort their statements and after their final sorting. At the beginning of the interviews, participants are asked to arrange the 48 statements into two groups: statements they agreed with and statements they disagreed with. At any stage, participants can ask the interviewer about any statements they were unclear about or needed relevant examples of. They then rank the statements in a quasi-normal distribution by arranging them from strongly agree to strongly disagree, this is known as the condition of instruction (Brown, 1993) in a Q method activity (Figure 7.2). While this is happening the researcher can question and encourage participants to comment on statements and their rankings, which help in the interpretation of the sorting configurations (Shinebourne, 2009). After the activity, a picture can be taken of each Q sort placemat for later analysis. The activity can also be audio recorded and transcribed for data analysis.

Quantitative factor analysis of the completed Q sorts is carried out. PQ method software (Schmolck and Atkinson, 2002) can be used for this stage of analysis. This can be followed by principal components analysis (PCA) followed by a varimax rotation with eigenvalues greater than 1.00 to determine what factors emerge. PCA is a determinant form of factor analysis (Brown, 1993) and commonly used within a Q study (Akhtar-Danesh, 2016). Varimax rotation is a simple and reliable method of analysis and maximises the amount of variance explained by the extracted factors (Watts and Stenner, 2005, p. 81). The analysis is used to identify groups or clusters with similar ranking patterns. The rankings of participants within a cluster are then combined to form a representative sort (or factor exemplar) for the viewpoint related to that factor (McKeown and Thomas,

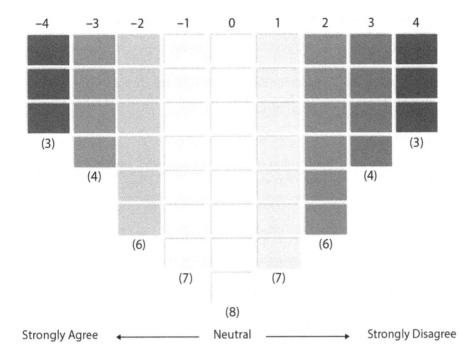

Figure 7.2 Placemat in fixed- and quasi-normal distribution. Ranking values range from −4 to +4. The numbers in brackets indicate the number of items that can be assigned to any particular rank. A total of 48 items can be sorted in the distribution illustrated (O'Connell et al., 2019). For an alternative example, see Watts and Stenner (2005).

2013). These data are then described with the supporting qualitative data from the interview during the process. If you are considering using this method, a good place to start is with McKeown and Thomas (2013). This provides a very good introduction to the Q sort methodology.

7.4 Walking interviews

Walking interviews are an innovative qualitative research method that recently gained popularity among cross-disciplinary researchers (Pink et al., 2010). Walking interviews entail researchers and participants talking while walking together; it is a kind of walking inquiry with links to narrative and storytelling (Finnegan and O'Neill, 2020). This method has been employed in various settings and with participants of all ages. Adekoya et al. (2020) used walking interviews as a way to explore the perspectives of older adults living with dementia. Walking interviews are a valuable means of deepening understandings of lived everyday experiences in particular places. The rich, detailed, and multisensory data generated by walking interviews demonstrate that they are a valuable, valid, feasible, and empowering means of conducting a qualitative inquiry. They can also be employed concurrently with other qualitative methods, such as ethnographic observation and arts-based research. For example, O'Neill (2018) uses walking to do participatory arts-based research with women seeking asylum. She concludes that this method provides a means for intercultural and transcultural communication.

> Arts-based walking methods are embodied, relational, sensory, multi-modal and can often help access the unsayable or things that might not have emerged in a standard research interview. They involve the imaginary, imagination and politics – a radical democratic imaginary.
>
> (2018, p. 92)

The affordances of this method within research methodologies, such as PAR, arts-based research, and ethnography, are numerous.

7.5 Focus groups

A focus group is where you have a small group of people, typically between five and ten, discuss a topic of interest. Focus groups are used a lot in market research, as they encourage participants to question each other and build on others' observations; the interaction between the participants is essential. In addition, they are good if you focus on a particular topic with participants. For example, in a research project looking at the experience of first-year undergraduate students on the transition into the third level, researchers used focus groups to discuss key findings from a student questionnaire. They sought a diversity of experiences for this research, and the focus group provided the context where through interaction between the participants, they explored their experiences. However, as focus groups require mutual disclosure, they are not suitable for all topics.

The following are some key considerations ahead of organising your focus groups:

- Decide on how many you want in your group. All must have time to contribute and group transcription should be possible.
- Sampling needs careful consideration; a good sample is central to the success of the focus group. For example, will each focus group member bring a particular characteristic that is required to answer some of your questions?
- Give thought to where you will host the focus group and if this is convenient for all your participants. The room's set-up is vital, with all group members able to face and see and hear each other.
- Consider if you need to use an icebreaker to get people talking and give time for people to settle into the group situation.
- Think about how you will chair the meeting so that you are not too directive and keep the conversation on the topic you are interested in.
- Consider the time of day you will hold the group and how this might impact your findings; if it is during the day, do you exclude some of your samples?
- You might use prompts in your focus groups such as pictures, videos, or activities. When working with young children, getting them to draw or make models can open up space to talk. Researchers working with young children have been known to use puppets to ask questions so that the children are put at ease.
- Some researchers like to start the group with refreshments to settle into the meeting. However, this can also cause background noise if you record and can be distracting.

- Consider using a note-taker and/or audio and video recording of the group. At a minimum, it is advised to use an audio recorder for the group.

The following are some key considerations ahead of working with your focus group:

- Think about who will greet the participants as they arrive and show them to the room where the focus group will take place.
- Decide where you will sit and where others will sit.

Check that your audio and or video recording devices are working. If using a note-taker rather than recording the event, decide where they will sit and how they will take notes.

- Agree on group rules for the session and timing. For example, group rules could be that everyone gets to speak, we listen to contributions, and what is discussed is not shared outside the group. Also, agree on how a person will indicate that they want to talk.
- Your role as moderator is vital, as you need to manage the situation and encourage participation while being neutral and allowing all opinions to be expressed.

Focus groups are social and, therefore, can be complicated to manage. This is why you need to put ample time into planning and thinking about facilitation before embarking on using them in your research.

7.6 Photo/video/voice elicitation

This method involves asking research participants to use a camera or voice recording app (often on their smartphones) to take photos or make videos or voice memos about their everyday practices and interactions that they can then share with the researcher. The artefact, picture, can be used as a prompt for an interview (see also Pink, 2021 on visual ethnography). Torre and Murphy (2015) carried out a systematic review on the use of photoelicitation interviews in educational research, and they concluded that they provide a practical way to put the participant at the centre of the research process and to gain insights into the less visible dimensions of the participants lived reality. This lived reality can come "alive" in the participants' choice of what they share with you, the researcher. Pain (2012) warns that you must take extra care to make sure it is the participants' reality that is represented in the analysis and presentation of findings.

7.7 Observational methods

Observational research often referred to as field research, involves observing events or situations as they occur. The events observed may be natural as they appear in the real world, such as children interacting in the playground, or occurrences set up by the researcher, such as a group discussion. Observations can be structured, semi-structured, or unstructured (Bryman, 2008). In any observation research, you will be writing field notes either in tandem with observation or after it has occurred. Writing field notes is a craft you need to practice, as it is a critical strategy in research (Walford,

2009). How this is done depends on the context, there will be times you are sitting observing a situation, a meeting, or children playing, and you can write copious notes; at other times, you may need to jot down a few thoughts. It is essential to revisit your field notes and add details where needed while the observation is fresh in your mind in both cases.

Using observation can give you access to social situations that other methods cannot capture, such as interviews or surveys. You can use it in combination with other methods. For example, you could follow up by observing children in a playground with an interview with parents. Here you rely less on memory, and your discussion can focus on crucial moments in the playground. You can ask the parents, *What did you think when your child did x today in the playground?* If you video children playing, it can provide a record of an unfolding situation that you can analyse from various perspectives later. The transcript of the playground play can be time-stamped and used for data analysis. In this way, observational data can be supplemented by other research techniques to understand the research context from different perspectives and highlight matches and mismatches in your data.

By observing and looking at something from different perspectives, you can see the familiar as strange. To avoid falling into the trap of seeking confirmation for what you want to know, it is good in some cases to develop an observation schedule. An observation schedule can also be called a coding scheme. For example, in one research project on questioning, the researcher coded how often the teacher asked questions in the class and if the questions could be classified as higher-order thinking questions or lower-order thinking questions. Then, using video of the class, she further coded the length of time given for students to answer questions. When observing it is important that you observe and make note of the following:

- The setting – for example, if observing behaviour in the workplace, describe the physical environment.
- The people – who are the people in the environment, and how do they interact?
- The behaviours – depending on your research question, observe and make very detailed notes on all the relevant behaviours.
- Note informal and unplanned activities – here you are looking for body language and nonverbal cues.
- Note language use – what kind of verbal communication is happening?
- Note what is not happening – is there a focus on one gender in the setting, is there a lack of inclusive behaviour? (See Mertens, 2010)

For example, the student looking at questioning could develop an observation schedule with some of the following content: description of the classroom environment (e.g. room layout, displays, seating plan, resources available to students), lesson outline/distribution of learning (e.g. time taken for marking homework, introduction, group work, individual work, class recap), key features of the lesson (e.g. whole class, peer-to-peer, teacher-student), teacher instructions (e.g. outlining tasks, adjusting instruction, learning intentions, setting success criteria for an activity), group work, student engagement, and feedback practices (e.g. acknowledging success, guiding future thinking, teacher and/or students).

You should develop an observation schedule from your research question and your literature review. It helps to keep you focused on what you will observe.

Reflection time

Think about how you might use observation in your research project. For example, will you be using filed notes or an observation schedule? Using an observation schedule, begin to draw up a draft based on your research question and literature review.

7.8 Diaries/journaling

You can also combine diaries with interviews and other methods, where sometimes the diary can act as a prompt for further discussion. Diaries can be structured (with prompt questions) or unstructured (asking for more free-flowing reflection). The length of time you allow for diary entries depends on your research; you could use it at the end of a session or over several weeks. For example, in a research project with smokers attempting to quit smoking, the researcher asked participants to fill in a journal at the end of each day and describe their experience of trying to cease smoking during that day over a month. The entries were free-flowing; some participants wrote only a few lines, whereas others wrote pages and included drawings and pictures. The analysis of the journals was complex and supported by interviews with the writers. While diaries or journaling can take many forms, it is essential to consider the participants. What they would find easy to use and what you will be able to analyse within the analytical approach you have chosen.

7.9 The story completion method

The story completion method offers a very different approach to data collection than traditional self-report techniques, such as interviews, focus groups, and diaries, and their introduction to the *Qualitative Research in Psychology* special issue on the topic is a great place to start exploring this method (Braun et al., 2019). It is particularly useful as a means of comparing and exploring the views of different social groups (Clarke et al., 2017).

Story completion comes from a psychoanalytical, personality assessment technique of "projective technique" (projecting beliefs and attitudes onto other people) and was initially used in clinical settings (Lansky, 1968). In research, it is a writing method that can take place in face-to-face situations using pen and paper but can also be conducted online where you can send prompts to participants, and they can complete them in their own time. This method involves the use of story "stems" or "cues", in which a fictional character is introduced to an ambiguous story, and, commonly, they face a dilemma they need to resolve. Participants are asked to complete the story. The constructed narratives are then analysed for what they reveal about understandings, meaning-making, discourses, or imaginaries concerning the topic of the story stems (Gravett, 2019).

For example, a group of therapists and psychology undergraduate students participated in data completion research relating to sexual refusal in heterosexual relationships (Shah and Clarke, 2021). The data collected identified significant differences in the way therapists and students perceived the issue of refusal. Namely, therapists included less problematisation and presented more opportunities for change. These findings led the researchers to question the nature of psychology students' training and the need to understand sex-related issues better.

In another example, participants were presented with four-story stems online (Watson and Lupton, 2021). Each story introduced a fictional character grappling with a consumer digital privacy issue. Participants were asked to respond to open-ended questions, such as "What happened next?" And, "How does the character feel?" The study demonstrated the complexity between the appropriate use of online data and its relational impact.

You will need to consider design issues ahead of using this method. These include the design of the story stem and what instructions you will give your participants for completing the story (Clarke et al., 2019; Gravett, 2019). As with all methods, you need to consider sample size and selection decisions. You will also need to consider how you will analyse the data (see the section on data analysis). Gravett (2019) contends that this method is underutilised in research and can be used in combination with other methods. We believe it can offer great possibilities for students doing research projects.

7.10 Using sonic studies to gather data

Sonic studies describe research that uses sound. It is an interdisciplinary and international field. Sonic studies have included work on sound histories, sound philosophies, sound culture, sound and race, and sound methodologies (Gershon and Appelbaum, 2018). There has also been increasing attention to sound scholarship in education, "regardless of their origin or interpretation, sounds are theoretically and practically foundational to educational experiences" (Gershon and Appelbaum, 2020, p. 1). Recently, sonic studies have been used in psychology to assess emotional impact or interaction using sound from media (e.g. Cuadrado et al., 2020).

There are many ways to use sonic studies in your research. For example, you can use music to give voice to those who often do not have a say in the system; this method is thus used with phenomenology (Gershon, 2018). In one research project working with urban youth, the researcher used the music and lyrics of their music to understand their culture. Wozolek (2020) reports on how schooling can bring some students to the breaking point in how inequalities are perpetuated or ignored; here, the researcher is listening to "the classroom, the corridor, to the curriculum" and how these everyday reverberations contribute to this breaking (p. 26). If considering this method, the work of Gershon and Appelbaum (2020) is a great place to start.

Reflection time

Select two to three methods that you may consider for your project design. List the pros and cons of applying each method to your project. Then, decide which one best suits your project and why.

Recap time

In this chapter, we discussed your research project design. We began by identifying your positioning concerning how you view the world and the knowledge you acquire. Next, we asked you to reflect on your own set of beliefs and keep it in mind as you progress through your project. Remember that you can choose a different positioning to the one you hold if it better suits your research. We then reviewed a spectrum of methodologies you can choose for your research project. We asked you to select two to three that are most suitable for addressing your research question, decide on the advantages and disadvantages of each one of them, and pick the one that can best respond to your question. Finally, we reviewed an array of methods you can apply in your research and encouraged you to select one best suited for your project.

References

Adekoya, A.A., and L. Guse. 2020. "Walking Interviews and Wandering Behavior. Ethical Insights and Methodological Outcomes while Exploring the Perspectives of Older Adults Living with Dementia." *International Journal of Qualitative Methods*. January 2020. doi: 10.1177/1609406920920135

Akhtar-Danesh, N. 2016. "An Overview of the Statistical Techniques in Q Methodology." *Operant Subjectivity: International Society for the Scientific Study of Subjectivity* 38(3–4): 29–36.

Braun, V., V. Clarke, N. Hayfield, H. Frith, H. Malson, N. Moller, and I. Shah-Beckley. 2019. "Qualitative Story Completion: Possibilities and Potential Pitfalls." *Qualitative Research in Psychology* 16(1): 136–155. doi: 10.1080/14780887.2018.1536395

Brown, S. 1993. "A Primer on Q Methodology." *Operant Subjectivity* 16(3/4): 91–138.

Bryman, A. 2008. *Social Research Methods*. 3rd ed. New York: Oxford University Press.

Churruca, K., K. Ludlow, W. Wu et al. 2021. "A Scoping Review of Q-methodology in Healthcare Research." *BMC Medical Research Methodology* 21: 125. doi: 10.1186/s12874-021-01309-7

Clarke, V., Braun, V., Frith, H., & Moller, N. (2019). Editorial introduction to the special issue: Using story completion methods in qualitative research. Qualitative Research in Psychology, 16(1), 1–20. https://doi.org/10.1080/14780887.2018.1536378

Clarke, V., N. Hayfield, N. Moller, I. Tischner and The Story Completion Research Group. 2017. "Once Upon a Time . . . Qualitative Story Completion Methods." In *Collecting Qualitative Data: A Practical Guide to Textual, Media and Virtual Techniques*, edited by V. Braun, V. Clarke, and D. Gray, 45–70. Cambridge University Press. doi: 10.1017/9781107295094

Cuadrado, F., I. Lopez-Cobo, T. Mateos-Blanco, and A. Tajadura-Jimenez. 2020. "Arousing the Sound: A Field Study on the Emotional Impact on Children of Arousing Sound Design and 3D Audio Spatialization in an Audio Story." *Frontiers in Psychology*. doi: 10.3389/fpsyg.2020.00737

Finnegan, F., and J. O'Neill. 2020. "Spalpeens on the Isle of Wonder: Reflections on Work, Power and Collective Resistance in Irish Further Education." In *Caliban's Dance: FE after the Tempest*, edited by M. Daley, K. Orr, and J. Petrie, 148–159. London: Institute of Education Press.

Franz, A., M. Worrell, and C. Vögele. 2013. "Integrating Mixed Method Data in Psychological Research: Combining Q Methodology and Questionnaires in a Study Investigating Cultural and Psychological Influences on Adolescent Sexual Behavior." *Journal of Mixed Methods Research* 7(4): 370–389. ISSN 1558-6898.

Gershon, W.S. 2018. *Sound Curriculum Sonic Studies in Educational Theory, Method, & Practice*. New York: Routledge.

Gershon, W.S., and P. Appelbaum. 2018. "Resounding Education: Sonic Instigations, Reverberating Foundations." *Educational Studies: A Journal of the American Educational Association* 54(4): 357–366.

Gershon, W.S., and P. Appelbaum. 2020. *Sonic Studies in Educational Foundations. Echoes, Reverberations, Silences, Noise*. London: Routledge.

Gravett, K. 2019. "Story Completion: Storying as a Method of Meaning-Making and Discursive Discovery." *International Journal of Qualitative Methods* 18. doi: 10.1177/1609406919893155.

Killam, L., K.E. Timmermans, and J.M. Raymond. 2013. "The Barriers to and Benefits of Conducting Q-sorts in the Classroom." *Nursing Research* 21(2) (November): 24–29. doi: 10.7748/nr2013.11.21.2.24.e1210. PMID: 24171634.

Lansky, L.M. 1968. "Story Completion Methods." In *Projective Techniques in Personality Assessment*, edited by A.I. Rabin, 290–324. New York, US: Springer.

McKeown, B., and D.B. Thomas. 2013. *Q Methodology*. 2nd ed. Thousand Oaks, CA: Sage.

Mertens, D.M. 2010. *Research and Evaluation in Education and Psychology*. 3rd ed. London: Sage.

O'Connell, N.B., M. Dempsey, and A. O'Shea. 2019. "An Investigation of Students' Attitudes to Science, Mathematics and the Use of Technology in Lower Secondary Education." *International Journal of Education in Mathematics, Science and Technology* 7(4): 319–334.

O'Neill, M. 2018. "Walking, Well-being and Community: Racialized Mothers Building Cultural Citizenship Using Participatory Arts and Participatory Action Research." *Ethnic and Racial Studies* 41(1): 73–97. doi: 10.1080/01419870.2017.1313439.

Pain H.A. 2012. "Literature Review to Evaluate the Choice and Use of Visual Methods." *International Journal of Qualitative Methods* 303–319. doi: 10.1177/160940691201100401

Pink, S. 2021. *Doing Visual Ethnography.* 4th ed. London: Sage.

Pink, S., P. Hubbard, M. O'Neill, and A. Radley. 2010. "Walking Across Disciplines: From Ethnography to Arts Practice." *Visual Studies* 25(1): 1–7.

Rust, J., M. Kosinski, and D. Stillwell. 2021. *Modern Psychometrics: The Science of Psychological Assessment.* 4th ed. New York: Routledge/Taylor & Francis Group.

Schmolck, P., and J. Atkinson. 2002. "PQMethod (version 2.35)." Web published. http://schmolck.userweb.mwn.de/qmethod/downpqmac.htm

Shah, B.I., and V. Clarke. 2021. "Exploring Therapists' and Psychology Students' Constructions of Sexual Refusal in Heterosexual Relationships: A Qualitative Story Completion Study." *Counselling & Psychotherapy Research* 21(4): 946–956. doi: 10.1002/capr.12388

Shinebourne, P. 2009. "Using Q Method in Qualitative Research." *International Journal of Qualitative Methods* 8(1): 93–97.

Stephenson, W. 1935. "Technique of Factor Analysis." *Nature* 136: 297. doi: 10.1038/136297b0

Sullivan, G.M., and A.R. Artino. 2017. "How to Create a Bad Survey Instrument." *Journal of Graduate Medical Education* 9(4): 411–415. doi: 10.4300/JGME-D-17-00375.1

Torre, D., and J. Murphy. 2015. "A Different Lens: Changing Perspectives Using PhotoElicitation Interviews." *Education Policy Analysis Archives* 23(111): 1–23. doi: 10.14507/epaa.v23.2051

Walford, G. 2009. "The Practice of Writing Ethnographic Fieldnotes." *Ethnography and Education* 4(2): 117–130.

Watson, A., and D. Lupton. 2021. "Tactics, Affects and Agencies in Digital Privacy Narratives: A Story Completion Study." *Online Information Review* 45(1): 138–156. doi: 10.1108/OIR-05-2020-0174

Watts, S., and P. Stenner. 2005. "Doing Q Methodology: Theory, Method and Interpretation." *Qualitative Research in Psychology* 2: 67–91.

Wozolek, B. 2020. "In 8100 Again: The Sounds of Students Breaking." In *Sonic Studies in Educational Foundations: Echoes, Reverberations, Silences, Nose*, edited by W.S. Gershon and P. Appelbaum. London: Routledge.

8 The analysis (empirical only)

8.1 Ethics

As described in Chapter 3, your research project can be either empirical or desk-based. Empirical projects are carried out in an educational environment with participants; thus, you must get ethical approval in your institution before you engage with your participants.

All social research has an ethical dimension and can be fraught with challenges for the researcher. Researching in social settings presents issues in data collection, such as participant recruitment, informed consent, data management, storage, and balancing burdens and benefits. Therefore, research ethics should be at the forefront of every project undertaken. This means that you must consider issues such as "conformity and resistance, context, power, emotion, and the role of social norms, organisational pressures and group/self-identity" (The British Psychological Society (BPS), 2018, p. 3). This assessment and reassessing can be done in consultation with your research project supervisor and involve conversations with your participants. You must engage in active deliberation on critical issues of concern. Ethical issues are present throughout the research project. They do not end once approval by an ethics board has been granted, and you need to keep them in the forefront while interpreting, analysing, and reporting your findings.

Social Research Ethics Committees review research projects that involve human participants and personally identifiable information about human beings to ensure that the proposed research is ethically sound and does not present any risk of harm to research participants. You should conduct all research within an ethic of respect for the person, knowledge, democratic values, the quality of educational research, and academic freedom (BERA, 2018). The American Psychological Association (APA)

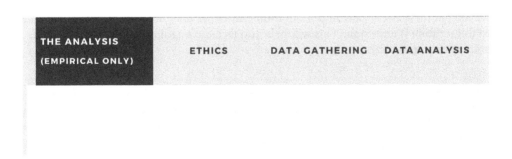

Figure 8.1 The Analysis

DOI: 10.4324/9781003262428-8

provides guidelines on psychologists' activities that are part of their scientific, educational, or professional roles. Areas covered include but are not limited to the clinical, counselling, and school practice of psychology; research; teaching; supervision of trainees; public service; policy development; social intervention; development of assessment instruments; conducting assessments; educational counselling; organisational consulting; forensic activities; program design and evaluation; and administration (APA, 2017).

Applying for ethical approval can differ from one institution to another. However, in general, you will need to complete an ethical review protocol, which details your project topic, design, and ethical considerations. It will usually be reviewed by a board composed of academics from different departments. The committee members will individually review the protocol and then meet as a group to discuss their evaluations. They may ask for more information or for you to change the original application if they feel the treatment of participants is not clear or acceptable. When the ethics board is satisfied that participants will not be placed at risk or that the potential risk will be minimal compared to the research benefits, they will issue approval in writing. As a first step, we recommend you familiarise yourself with the procedure in your educational institution and obtain the guidelines for the procedure.

The British Psychological Society's code of ethics is based on four ethical principles of (1) Respect, (2) Competence, (3) Responsibility, and (4) Integrity (BPS, 2018). In addition to the Code of Ethics and Conduct documents, the BPS has a Code of Human Research Ethics (BPS, 2021). This is an excellent resource for any student researching psychology. It provides clear information on many of the ethical dilemmas you may face. They remind us that ethical researchers "prioritise respect for the rights and dignity of participants in their research and also consider legitimate interests of stakeholders such as funders, institutions, sponsors and publics" (BPS, 2021, p. 4).

Professional organisations developed other codes of ethics, such as the British Educational Research Association (BERA, 2018) and the American Educational Research Association (AERA, 2011). You must familiarise yourself with one code of ethics and follow its guidelines. All research is vulnerable to abuse, especially social research, as it seeks to interpret meanings and implications of human practices; good ethical reflection guards against this (Pendlebury and Enslin, 2001). Ongoing critical reflection is essential at all research cycle stages (see Section 2.1.1 for our reflection framework). Guillemin and Gillam (2004) call this ethics in practice, and we see this as particularly important in social research, as practice lies at the centre of all projects. This ethics in practice concerns the day-to-day ethical issues that arise while researching. The reflection framework helps you navigate these issues and confront them as they arise. Guillemin and Gillam (2004) suggest we look at these as ethically important moments rather than dilemmas or issues. The key to this scrutiny is reflection. This will help you face the ongoing ethical vital moments as you encounter them.

Applying for ethical approval

When applying for ethical approval for your empirical research project, you must write your ethics application in clear, plain English (or equivalent), avoiding discipline-specific jargon. This is because the ethics committee will be composed of individuals from different disciplines across the social sciences. Regardless of their specialities, they need to understand your research application.

The headings in a typical protocol for ethical review of a research project involving the participation of humans are as follows:

a   Title of the research project
b   Research objectives
c   Methodology
d   Participants
e   Risk-benefit analysis
f   Informed consent
g   Data management and storage
h   Follow up

We will now delve deeper into each of these headings to assist you with completing the application.

a. Title of the research project

The title of your research should give a clear indication of the kind of research you intend to carry out.

b. Research objectives

In this section, you present your research question and objectives.

c. Methodology

This section provides a succinct description of your methodology under the following headings.

Where will the research be carried out?

Be clear where your research will take place. If you are visiting multiple settings, you will need to list them.

Briefly describe the overall methodology of the project

In this section, give a brief overview of the research design. This includes details on methods, research context, issues to be explored, potential questions to be used, and details on data collection and analysis, as appropriate. For example, you might include the following:

- An observation schedule if conducting classroom observation
- Any questionnaires you intend to use
- Sample focus group or interview protocol

However, if you intend to use participant-led research, you cannot include the questions that will be asked, as these will only become apparent during the research. It would be best to make every effort to make the ethics board aware of how you will research in as much detail as possible.

If your participants are located in the European Union (EU), check if your research is compliant with the GDPR. The GDPR is a regulation on data protection and privacy in the EU and the European Economic Area (EEA). It also addresses the transfer of personal data outside the EU and EEA (European Commission, 2019). Your educational institution will have GDPR guidelines that you can consult.

d. Participants

In this section, you want to clarify who the participants in your research are. Give exact information about your sample and outline the recruitment process, considering any criteria for inclusion/exclusion. Consider if there are gatekeepers concerning accessing your participants. These are people who can help you gain access to the research site and may help you recruit participants. If gatekeepers exist, you need to obtain a letter or email showing that consent to carry out the research has been granted. These can be included as an appendix in your ethics application.

For example, if researching a care setting, you will need the Management Board to grant access to the setting. If you work in this setting, you may have access to specific data, as a professional, such as minutes of meetings and policy documents, but this does not permit you automatic access for research purposes. Make sure you distinguish between your professional role and that of your researcher role for your protection and the protection of your participants. If you are a practitioner engaging in insider research, consider what would be required by an outsider to carry out this research in your place of work. You need to apply the same standards to your access. As a professional, you should show that you have reflected on your role, both in terms of participants' recruitment and the nature of the research. It would be best to give a clear rationale for researching within your workplace. A well-developed information sheet about your research is an excellent place to start. The BPS (2021, p. 12) advise that "sufficient information about the research in an understandable form is crucial to giving them an adequate basis for deciding whether or not to participate". See the section on developing your information sheet later in this chapter.

It would be best if you gave a clear rationale for your criteria for the inclusion and exclusion of participants. For example, if you want to research with all-female clients between the ages of 138 and 30, you must present your rationale for choosing one gender and the specific age category. In addition, you will need to be clear about communicating exclusion criteria with the participants.

Working with vulnerable persons

The EU describes a vulnerable person as

> minors, unaccompanied minors, disabled people, elderly people, pregnant women, single parents with minor children, victims of trafficking in human beings, persons with serious illnesses, persons with mental disorders and persons who have been subjected to torture, rape or other serious forms of psychological, physical or sexual violence, such as victims of female genital mutilation.
>
> (Union, Official Journal of the European, 2013)

Situational vulnerability can be due to timing, theme, questions, history, and/or power. If you argue that a population is not vulnerable, explain why. The participant(s) could be vulnerable because of the topic, of the questions asked, of the data-gathering location, or any number of other reasons. If working with children under 18, consider how you might get their consent to the research. Consider their stage of development and what is possible for them as participants. Children might feel safer being interviewed in a focus group rather than on their own. You might ask a parent or caregiver to sit in on the interview. If you intend to do this, details of how it will be organised will need to be included in the ethics form and confidentiality issues discussed with the adult co-researcher or observer.

What will the research participants be asked to do for this research?

This section needs to present precise details on what participants will be asked to do. For example, participants will be asked to complete an online questionnaire, taking approximately 20 minutes. Participants will be asked to attend a focus group. The focus groups will last no more than one hour.

Will the participants be reimbursed, and if so, in what form?

This is important as it links to research integrity. It is not an issue to reimburse people for their time; however, you must consider how this might impact your data.

Conflict of interest

This section will consider any conflict of interest you may have. You should be familiar with it when carrying out empirical research project research. In the area of study, conflict of interest usually involves researchers being able to benefit from certain information generated in the research personally or personally benefitting directly or indirectly due to engaging in the research. Typically, although not exclusively, conflict of interest involves financial gain for oneself, family or friends, or business associates. To avoid conflicts of interest, it is essential to be clear on how your research is being funded and ethically communicate the research findings.

Will the research involve power relationships (e.g. student/employee, employer/colleagues)?

If you answer yes to this question, then you need to outline the basis of the potential power relationship and describe the steps you will take to address this should it arise. For example, if you are researching in your place of work, your colleagues may feel vulnerable. How have you addressed this in your research design? Your employer may be concerned if your findings reflect adversely on them. You will need to discuss any issue of power with your supervisor.

e. Risk/benefit analysis

Considering the potential risks and benefits, you will need to justify proceeding with the research as outlined in your project design. Identify and describe any potential risks arising from the research techniques, procedures, or outputs (physical stress/reactions, psychological-emotional distress, or responses). For each one, please explain how you will address or minimise them. You can cause some risks if the methodology of a project is not suitable or a researcher lacks essential skills. For example, an inexperienced researcher may ask questions that make the respondent feel uncomfortable; they may cause stress by asking or responding to questions. After identifying the risk, list all the potential benefits of the research and ensure that the benefits outweigh the dangers before applying for ethical approval.

f. Informed consent

This section of your ethics application focuses on what and how you tell participants about your research and obtain their informed consent. It is arguably the most crucial section of the ethics application. It is typically expected that participants' voluntary informed consent is received at the start of the study. However, researchers will remain sensitive and open to the possibility that participants may wish to withdraw their consent for any reason and at any time. The "principle of proportionality should apply" where the procedures for consent are in line with the risks involved (BPS, 2021, p. 12). These principles of consent apply to children and young people, as well as to adults. For example, data that could identify a student must not be made available to researchers without parental or legal guardian consent. It is essential to consider the multiple layers of consent that you might need – e.g. parental/caregiver consent and young people's permission – and a potential gatekeeping role for the Management Board in providing access to participants if the research is in a social setting.

Confidentiality refers to separating or modifying any personal, identifying information provided by participants from the data; for example, you may know the names of all your participants, but in your research, you will assign them pseudonyms and keep the list of names separate from the data. Anonymity refers to collecting data without obtaining any personal, identifying information; for example, when using an anonymous survey, neither you nor anyone reading the data knows the identity of the participants (Walford, 2005; Saunders et al., 2015).

Anonymity is related to identity protection; confidentiality is related to information and who has access to it. The concept of confidentiality is closely connected to anonymity; in social research, anonymity is how confidentiality is maintained. However, anonymisation of data does not cover all issues of confidentiality. Confidentiality also includes not deliberately or accidentally disclosing what has been said in the process of data collection. For example, the person may be identified by telling someone what a participant said in an interview without giving a name. In addition, when interviewing online, another person not involved in the research may hear the interview; these breaches of confidentiality must be guarded against.

Explicit confidentiality is openly negotiated between the researcher and the participant. This is usually achieved through an information sheet and consent form. Expectations and guarantees are elaborated to the respondent before the research takes place and are honoured throughout the research and any subsequent publication of results. Anonymity is impossible in focus group interviews, as participants will be together and may already know each other. However, participants must be aware that what is discussed in the group is not discussed outside of the group.

Deception

It would help if you avoided deception at all stages of your research. It should only be used when it is essential to achieve the research results required (BPS, 2021). Observing in a public place is only acceptable if the participants expect to be observed by strangers. In one research project, a student attended a specific political event and observed participants' engagements. They did not disclose that they were conducting research. Their observations included coffee breaks with people and so on. BPS advise that "If the reaction of participants when deception is revealed later in their participation is likely to lead to discomfort, anger or objections from the participants then the deception is inappropriate" (2021, p. 23).

Interviews, observations, and focus groups bring the researcher in close contact with their participants. This closeness is part of the data collection and can provide rich data and insights and create unintended influences. For example, if you observe or are told about physical or psychological abuse of any kind, you must report it. In cases such as this, consult your academic advisor for support in doing so; see Guillemin and Gillam (2004) for a discussion on ethically crucial moments.

Dealing with photographic images and artefacts

If you are collecting photographs or video images and intend to use them in your research project or conference presentation, you need to get written permission. Their use might also be time-bound to one year after the project.

Information sheet and consent forms

you must write the information sheet and consent forms for your research in plain English and age-appropriate language. It would help if you tried to ensure that all participants understand, as well as they can, what is involved in a study. They should be told why their participation is necessary, what they will be asked to do, what will happen to the information they provide, how it will be used, and how and to whom it will be reported. It would help if you also informed them about the research data's retention, sharing, and possible secondary uses. Equally, from an ethical perspective, you need to consider if participants might experience any distress from their participation – giving potential participants an indication of the sorts of questions they might be asked can help them decide if they want to participate. Consider if you need to provide an appropriate referral point in case of distress.

Prompt questions to use in designing your research information sheet (see also the list provided by BPS, 2021, p. 13).

• What is the purpose of the study?
• What will the study involve?
• Who has approved this study?
• Why have you been asked to take part?
• What kind of information will you collect?
• Will your participation in the study be kept confidential? Include a statement on limits to confidentiality.
• What will happen to the information which you give?
• What will happen to the results of the research?
• What are the possible disadvantages of taking part?
• Any further queries? Here you include your contact details.

Please note that if you are using a transcription service or another individual to transcribe your interviews, you must seek consent. You should be able to guarantee anonymity and confidentiality. This will entail you ensuring all data are cleaned of any identifiers before transcription.

Verbal consent form

It is also possible to record verbal consent. The researcher talks through the consent form with the participant, and then the participant states that they consent.

Receiving consent from vulnerable participants

When working with participants from vulnerable populations, it is vital to balance the protection principles of vulnerable groups and their rights to self-determination (Iacono and Murray, 2003). Bracken-Roche and colleagues (2017), in their in-depth analysis of policies and guidelines in the United States, listed the following groups as most frequently identified as vulnerable: children; minors or young people; prisoners, as well as persons with mental health issues; patients in emergency settings; and certain ethnocultural, racial, or ethnic minority groups (2017). All issues about vulnerability are around harm and consent. If considering researching a vulnerable population, we suggest you consult some papers from health research (see, for example, (Boxall and Ralph, 2009; Iacono, 2006; Iacono and Murray, 2003). For example, Iacono shows in her paper that the "issue of who can give consent or permission on behalf of a person with intellectual disability – i.e. proxy consent – is also fraught with complexities" (2006, p. 175). However, it is vital that we as researchers do not neglect the voice of vulnerable participants and that we face and address the complex ethical decisions in our research.

g. Data storage

You must store all data in a secure location. Any paper copies of consent forms must be scanned and uploaded to a secure location. you should then destroy paper copies. If you are recording interviews or focus groups, data must be transferred from the recording device to a secure location as soon as possible after the participants have been recorded. It is essential to check if the device is GDPR compliant. Also, note that the participant is entitled to reject the use of devices in recording their responses, which is tied to their right to withdraw from the research.

h. Follow up

Consider the social implications of your research and how you will communicate the research findings. Researchers have a responsibility to consider the most relevant and valuable ways of informing participants about the research outcomes in which they were or are involved. In the spirit of openness, this means that we need to think about reporting our research through the channels people use, including online media, virtual convening, and academic papers.

Other considerations

The ethics of fieldwork in the online environment

During the COVID-19 pandemic, some research moved from being face-to-face to online. This section will look at the particular challenges this presented to researchers. Figure 8.2 presents some options researchers used in place of face-to-face interviews and observation.

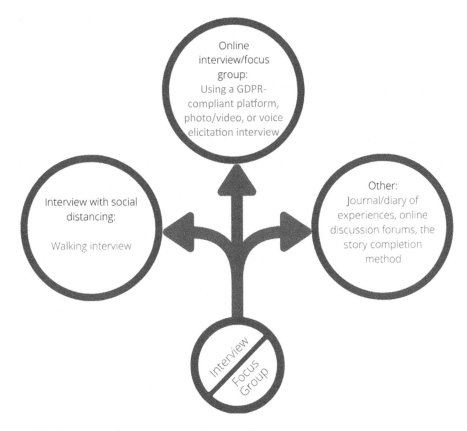

Figure 8.2 Alternative to face-to-face interviews and focus groups.

Some educational researchers who could not visit on-site due to COVID-19 restrictions opted to use video recording. However, the same confidentiality issues exist in the online space, with additional issues around storing the videos and using personal images.

Another method used in online research involved asking research participants to use a camera or voice recording app (often on their smartphones) to take photos, make videos, or voice memos about their everyday practices and interactions that they can then share with the researchers in response to questions or prompts. In this instance, one must guard against taking any images or sound files that include participants who have not consented to be in the research. It is important to password protect all data and transfer it to an encrypted device. If conducting interviews on platforms such as Teams or Zoom, both the researcher and participant must ensure that they are in a private room where a third-party listening in cannot compromise their interview.

In addition to all the ethical considerations discussed, there are other points you may choose to mention in your ethics form, such as the following:

- Acknowledging the contributions of others
- Copyright issues in research
- Ethical dilemmas

Good planning and a well-designed and carefully constructed study are vital to ethical approval. Therefore, take good care when reflecting on the ethics of your research project.

Reflection time

What is the main ethical consideration you will need to reflect on when designing your research project?

8.2 Data gathering

Your data gathering approach depends on the methods you plan to use. We have reviewed some of the main methods in Chapter 5 related to planning your data collection. This section, however, is about actioning your plans, which is an exciting part of a research project journey. Following on from your project design, your research may involve a single method or multiple data collection methods. Whatever approach you select, you must execute it in the intended order, giving careful consideration to the process and its impact on both you and the participants. When necessary, you intervene, as per ethical principles that guide your research.

8.2.1 Sampling method

When you embark on data collection, the participants you work with must be correctly selected. There are two types of sampling: a non-probability and probability sampling method. Qualitative research, such as action research, ethnography, or phenomenological research, uses non-probability sampling, meaning that the participants are not representative of the general population. Qualitative research usually goes more profound in its analysis than quantitative (e.g. thick descriptions), and it includes a smaller number of participants. In some cases, as few as one to three participants are recommended

Table 8.1 Non-probability sampling methods.

Sampling method	Description	Example
Purposive sampling	Sampling of a specific group of participants that are of interest to the researcher.	You may select care assistants if your project relates to exploring their views about inclusion.
Convenience sampling	Choosing participants you can access easily.	You may choose to carry out a project with your colleagues, who you interact with every day.
Snowball sampling	Selecting participants from a group that you wish to target and asking for a recommendation of other participants you can approach.	As a psychologist, you may be interested in the views of homeless mothers about a topic of your choice. After interviewing one mother you ask her if she can put you in touch with others in similar circumstances.
Quota sampling	Selecting a specific number of participants who represent a strata/group so that you have representatives of all levels you are interested in.	You may be interested in exploring how students at all levels understand meaning in life. You, therefore, interview two students from each year from one to six.

Table 8.2 Probability sampling methods.

Sampling method	Description	Example
Simple random sampling	A lottery method is applied whereby everyone has a chance to be selected.	From a list of the entire population, participants are randomly selected and asked if they wish to participate in a study about their experience of online learning during the COVID-19 pandemic.
Stratified random sampling	The population is divided into strata/groups to ensure that all parties are represented equally. Then from each group, a random sampling method is applied.	You may be interested in support for homeless mothers and how this differs in different regions. From the entire population in each region, you divide numbers by region and then send them randomly an invitation to complete a survey.
Multistage sampling	You employ a number of sampling methods one after another.	You start by selecting random organisations to participate in your research, then select random departments to participate in your study, and from each department, select a random sample of employees to participate in a survey.

to participate in research (e.g. interpretative phenomenological analysis); therefore, you cannot make inferences about the general public. Table 8.1 provides examples of non-probability sampling methods you can use in your data gathering. While they are not exhaustive, they represent the most frequently used non-probability sampling methods.

Quantitative research uses probability sampling methods, as it is more repetitive of the general population. Probability sampling is also referred to as representative sampling, and it uses larger groups of participants in the research. However, some quantitative studies apply non-probability sampling methods, especially student-led research. This includes convenience sampling, snowball sampling, and sometimes quota sampling. Table 8.2 provides descriptions and examples of probability sampling methods.

8.3 Qualitative analysis

8.3.1 Narrative analysis

When your data is presented in a narrative form, you tell stories about your participants using one of the five lenses as per Table 8.3 (Chase, 2005). These lenses refer to multidisciplinary perspectives you can take when analysing data, such as psychological, sociological, anthropological, and autoethnographic and various epistemological and ontological positions. A specific lens is applied in some research through which participants' stories are narrated. In other research, a mix of lenses is used to do it. What option you select depends on your research question.

Table 8.3 Examples of most frequently used statistical tests in research projects.

Spectrum	Purpose	Example	Variable types	Statistical test (parametric)	Statistical test (non-parametric)
Experimental	Contrast	You compare students' levels of school belonging before (time 1) and after a class (time 2), the aim of which is to help them get to know each other better.	One categorical at two times (before and after), one continuous (school belonging)	Paired-samples t-test	Wilcoxon signed-rank test
Experimental	Contrast	The same example as presented earlier, except you identify changes in school belonging before the class (time 1), after the class (time 2), and a month later (time 3).	One categorical at three times (before, after, and a month later), one continuous (school belonging)	One-way repeated ANOVA	Friedman test
Comparative	Contrast	You try to identify the difference in motivation between boys and girls in your school.	One categorical with two options (male and female), one continuous (motivation)	Independent samples t-test	Mann-Whitney U test
Comparative	Contrast	You try to identify the difference in motivation between class 1, class 2, and class 3.	One categorical with three options (class 1, 2, 3), one continuous (motivation)	One-way between groups ANOVA	Kruskal-Wallis
Comparative	Contrast	You try to identify the difference between boys and girls in the number of times (groups: 0–1, 2–5, 6+) they helped their friends with their homework in the last month.	Two categorical (gender and the number of times they helped)	No test available	Chi-square

Spectrum	Purpose	Example	Variable types	Statistical test (parametric)	Statistical test (non-parametric)
Comparative	Relationship	You try to identify the relationship between employees' job satisfaction and their length of service.	Two continuous (job satisfaction, length of service)	Pearson product-moment correlation coefficient	Spearman's rank-order correlation
Comparative	Relationship	You wish to identify how much of the variance in employees' job satisfaction can be explained by their length of service.	Two continuous (job satisfaction, length of service)	Multiple regression	No test available

In your narrative, you may introduce participants' stories one by one, or you may synthesise their stories by producing taxonomies and categories (Polkinghorne, 2006). When you choose to synthesise their data, you can follow the synthesis route described in Section 8.3.2.

8.3.2 Synthesis

When you synthesise data, your objective is to identify taxonomies and categories in your data by searching what all their responses have in common. Depending on what approach you take, you either search for themes (thematic analysis), theories (grounded theory), or descriptions (content analysis). Given that grounded theory is a complex methodology with complicated analysis, we suggest you use it judiciously in a final year project. Consult Glaser and Strauss (1967) for further information. We will delve deeper into identifying themes and descriptions from your data in the following sections.

8.3.3 Thematic analysis

Themes are patterns of shared meaning that are united by a central organising concept (Braun and Clarke, 2013, 2021). Thematic analysis is a popular method for analysing qualitative data and can be completed in various ways, with many different kinds of data. For example, we have had students transcribe their qualitative data and use a simple technique of colour coding to identify themes; others cut out quotes and arrange them on a storyboard to develop themes. Many use software programmes that allow them to work in more sophisticated ways with their data, and others advocate using a combination of both (Maher et al., 2018). What is of most importance is your familiarity with the data and that you work in a systematic way. Assumptions and positionings are always part of qualitative research (Braun and Clarke, 2019). Using our PAUSE model to reflect throughout the process is vital for understanding and unpacking thematic analysis.

One of the most widely used thematic analysis methods was developed by Braun and Clarke (2006) and added to later in their publications (for example, Clarke and Braun, 2014; Braun and Clarke, 2019, 2021). They have, in later work, put the researcher's subjectivity and reflexivity as central to thematic analysis (Braun and Clarke, 2019, 2021). Their method is theoretically flexible and focused on you, the researcher, and identifying patterns in your data to answer your research question. This does not mean it is not theoretically solid or easy to complete. It requires you to be deeply familiar with your data through reading and re-reading, carrying out systematic coding cycles until you develop your themes; you are interpreting and creating rather than on a voyage of discovery (ibid., 2019). Using a reflective journal of the whole process will provide you with an audit trail and help you revisit different stages.

The phases of thematic analysis developed by Braun and Clarke (2006, 2019, 2021) are as follows:

Familiarisation with the data The best way to know your data is to read it, re-read it, and begin to get a feel for it. You may have some observations from your reflections noted when you gathered these data; it is worth adding these as a notation to the data file (Xu and Zammit, 2020). If you transcribed the data yourself, this helps you gain familiarity. It is good to read the transcript, then, while you listen to the audio file to be sure you have captured all the nuances of the data.

Coding At this stage, you begin to develop codes assigned to specific quotes. It is best to do this systematically across your entire data set and look at how it relates to your research question or the phenomenon under scrutiny. Xu and Zammit (2020) provide an excellent example of how you can use codebooks at this stage of the process. There is no right or wrong way to do this coding stage, but it is good to be reflexive throughout the process and keep good notes on your thinking as you code. Freeman and Sullivan (2018) suggest asking the following questions as you code. (1) Have you coded all the relevant data? Being systematic in the process helps you be sure of this. (2) Have you coded each extract as many times as needed? Some extracts may have more than one code assigned to them. (3) Have you kept the meaning of the data? Here you want your coded extracts to make sense to the reader.

Generating initial themes At this stage, you are to collate codes into themes. You want to see patterns in your data where you will end up with a collection of codes with relevant extracts representing a theme (Freeman and Sullivan, 2018). Themes in thematic analysis relate to the concepts that participants discuss most frequently or in-depth. You may have some a priori themes from your literature review that you expect to see in your data. This is deductive analysis. This stage of analysis can take a few iterations.

You are reviewing themes. You need to read the codes and data associated with each theme and revise them considering your assumptions, position, literature, and research question.

Defining and naming themes. This step is essential, as your research data tells the story. Here you define and name each theme so that the reader can get insight into your thinking and process.

The final step is writing up your research; here, you do another analysis where you pick the best examples to support your themes. Again, you want to let the data speak to the reader and provide rich, thick descriptions of your themes relating to the literature and research question. You might be tempted to put in too many quotes from your participants in your first draft, so careful editing is required.

When you carry out thematic analysis, it provides trustworthy and insightful findings. You can ensure that consistency is maintained and have a thread connecting your themes by ensuring your positioning; your epistemology will coherently underpin the empirical research claims. To sum up, you need to keep audit trails of how you worked with the data and at all stages be reflexive and give a self-critical account of the research process to enhance trustworthiness (Nowell et al., 2017). Coding and developing themes is a flexible and organic process and will evolve throughout. It is an active and reflexive process that will always bear the mark of the researcher (Braun and Clarke, 2021).

Using software to support your thematic analysis can allow you to code non-textual data such as pictures, videos, drawings, songs, poems, and other texts (see, for example, Glaw et al., 2017). Then, you can assign codes to these materials in the same way as you do to other qualitative data and use these codes to develop themes. In this way, your themes can be made up of pictures, quotes, video clips, and so on.

Thematic analysis has a lot to offer you in your data analysis. Its great strength is its flexibility. It is a gratifying process deciphering the key messages your data is telling and sharing this with others in a rich, thoughtful way.

8.3.4 Content analysis

Qualitative data obtained from, for example, scripts, historical documents, dialogues, or an open-ended question of a survey can be analysed using content analysis, which aims to synthesise data and describe its content. This is a valuable way of combining qualitative and quantitative methodologies in research (Mayring, 2014). Its objective is to systematically analyse content, quantify it, and create a new meaning. There are three main techniques for analysing content, reflecting different epistemological and ontological positioning (Hsiu-Fang and Shannon, 2005). The first one is a *conventional content analysis* in which a study begins with an observation, reviewing all data, and then identifying what codes are derived from your data. Therefore, as you read participants' responses, you make notes on the present themes, re-read your data, and keep reducing the themes until they succinctly represent your data. This is an inductive approach.

The second technique is a *directed-content technique*, whereby a theory drives findings. This means that before you analyse data, you have defined your codes and checked your data for the frequency of their occurrence. For example, you may search the content of your students' essays for evidence of growth, fixed, or mixed mindset (Dweck, 2006). Therefore, your starting point is the three mindsets, and as you go through the data for each participant, you put them into one of the three categories. This is a deductive approach.

The third approach is a *summative content analysis* whereby you identify keywords that you search for in your data before you analyse your data. These keywords may have been derived from your literature review, and you can also add them in the course of your analysis. For example, one of our students performed a content analysis on mental health policy documents relating to workplace relationships. She analysed documents gathered from many organisations and searched for words such as "workplace relationship", "high-quality connections", and "organisational belonging". In the middle of her analysis, she added more words and phrases as she continued to familiarise herself with the content of the documents. This is a mixed deductive and inductive approach.

The process of content analysis begins by identifying data you wish to analyse. Then, break it down into manageable units. For example, if you are analysing the content of an online chat forum, your unit will be the chat from each individual. Then, you decide on your data coding by selecting one of the three options, as suggested by Hsiu-Fang and Shannon (2005). As you read the chat from the forum, you can search for categories in the text and then count how many times they occurred. For example, you may identify that the most frequently occurring topic concerns self-awareness (120 times), the second most frequently mentioned topic was cyberbullying (85 times), and so on. Then, in the final step, you compare all the frequencies across the analysed units (Figure 8.3). This process amalgams Denscombe's (2014) and Hsiu-Fang and Shannon's (2005) models.

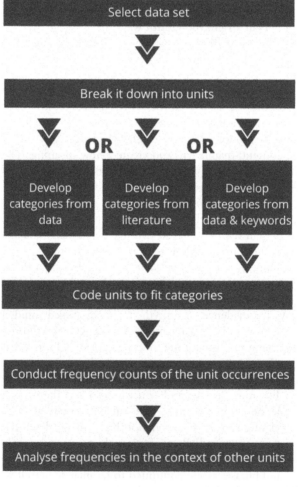

Figure 8.3 Content analysis process. *Source:* Adapted from Denscombe (2014), Hsiu-Fang and Shannon (2005).

8.3.5 *Interpretative phenomenological analysis*

Phenomenology is concerned with the lived experience and the meaning for the individual. It is idiographic in nature where the motive is to understand the personal experience, with many researchers using a single-person case study in their research (Eatough and Smith, 2017).

In an Interpretative Phenomenological Analysis (IPA), we are interested in an individual's experiences of phenomena, and "we treat this experience as a thing, something we encounter, but also as a process, something we are active in" (Shaw, 2019). The focus is idiographic and therefore suits single-person case studies. Where IPA differs from Grounded Theory (Section 6.1.7) and Narrative (Section 6.1.5)is in how data are analysed. In IPA, you do a complete analysis of a single case and then move on to a second case and so on. In Narrative and Thematic analysis, you work with the complete data sets (Shaw, 2019). This very in-depth look at single cases can be challenging for some researchers and takes a lot of time at the data–gathering stage. As the whole process is data-dependent, meticulous planning at the design stage of your research is essential. You will need to carefully plan how you gather the data and get to the detailed experiences. Consult Smith and Osborn (2003) for some pointers on developing interview questions for IPA. Petitmengin's work on micro-phenomenological interviewing is also very rich (see, for example, 2006, 2007, 2019).

The steps in IPA are as follows:

- Familiarising yourself with the data – It is essential that you document and reflect on the process of collecting your data. It may take multiple interviews to get the data you need. In familiarising yourself with the data, read and re-read transcripts and your notes and reflections. Listen to the interviews and then note down what you think is the person's meaning of their experience. Pietkiewicz and Smith (2012, p. 7) suggest that you note "distinctive phrases and emotional responses" at this stage.
- Transforming notes into initial themes – At this stage, you will work with your notes rather than the transcript. Here you are interpreting the participants meaning from their descriptions of the experience. Shaw (2019) suggests that it is good at this stage to make three columns and insert the transcript into the middle column and to do phenomenological coding (themes) in the left-hand column and interpretive coding (descriptions of the content) on the right-hand side. You do this for the entire individual sample before moving on to the next stage. It is essential to look at the entire data set before interpreting the meaning of the experience. Shaw (2029) brings you through the process of looking at the phenomenon of friendship for one person. First, you are doing phenomenological coding, writing descriptive summaries of the phenomenon being researched. This is followed by interpretive coding, where you try to make sense of the participant's story.
- Seeking relationships and clustering themes – You are looking for connections between themes at this stage. You will group them according to conceptual similarities and, when doing this, develop a descriptive label (Pietkiewicz and Smith, 2012; Shaw, 2019). You work in this way until you establish final themes. These will be presented in the results section of your research report.
- Writing up an IPA research – In this stage, you will take the themes and explicate them using extracts from the data. These themes help to give meaning to the experiences. The narrative account is usually followed by a discussion section "which relates the identified themes to existing literature" (Pietkiewicz and Smith, 2012, p. 9).

In some projects, you may want to continue to other cases and repeat these steps for each case and then compare themes across cases. Meaning is central to the IPA process; you, the researcher, are trying to explicate the meaning of experiences through careful analysis. As Smith and Osborn (2003) remind us

The assumption in IPA is that the analyst is interested in learning something about the respondent's psychological world. This may be in the form of beliefs and constructs made manifest or suggested by the respondent's talk. The analysis may be that the respondent's story can itself be said to represent a piece of the respondent's identity (p. 66).

IPA is a fascinating methodology and a way to analyse your data. It is advantageous when answering questions around feelings and experience, questions that want to explore how people are making sense of their personal and social world (see, for example, Smith and Osborn, 2015). As with other forms of narrative analysis, the need to have a clear audit trail of your thinking and decisions at various analysis stages is imperative for this kind of analysis and to increase the trustworthiness of your claims.

Petitmengin (2019) suggests that the lived experience is the most personal and intimate thing to any person and that for many people, the lived experience remains unnoticed. She proposes that the main reason for this lack of awareness is that the majority of our attention is absorbed into what we do to the detriment of how we do the activity. She suggests that many of our activities are lived like this and, in general, are not open to verbal description. This, however, does not mean that our lived experience is out of reach, but that accessing it requires particular expertise. She described a method of the micro-phenomenological interview where the researcher helps the participant become aware of the unrecognised part of a particular experience. This process results in very fine-grain descriptions of experiences (Petitmengin et al., 2018). The researchers then can present these experiences through a particular kind of analysis.

8.4 Quantitative analysis

When analysing quantitative data, it is crucial to identify what we are looking for. Sometimes, what stops students from engaging in the analysis is that they have collected too much data, and it is hard for them to discern what data they should use. Therefore, the starting point for the analysis is to identify (1) what variables you need to combine and (2) the purpose of this.

Your research question comprises the variables you are interested in. For example, your research question stated, *What is the difference between male and female attitudes towards inclusion?* You have two variables to explore in this question: (1) gender and (2) attitude. Therefore, all you need for the analysis is these two variables. Consider that your research question was, *After controlling for age, is there a relationship between employees' job satisfaction and managers' leadership style?* In this example, you have three variables: (1) age, (2) job satisfaction, and (3) managers' leadership style. Therefore, the first thing you need to identify is the variables you require for your analysis.

Your second consideration when analysing data is the purpose of your analysis. There are two primary purposes for analysing your quantitative data: (1) to contrast variables or (2) to explore relationships between them. When you contrast variables, you search for differences between groups. For example, you may wonder about the differences in motivation between girls and boys in your school, or you may want to test the differences in performance between students who have been introduced to character strengths and those who have not. When you are curious about relationships between variables, you may wish to explore a correlation between individuals' self-esteem and their passion for work. Therefore, it is essential to consider the purpose of your study to select the best analytical technique.

The clarity associated with the variable you use and the purpose of your analysis will help you decide what statistical test you need to use when analysing your data. The test you use will depend on the type of variables you collected in your data – i.e. categorical or continuous. For more information about the difference between them, please go to Chapter 7. Given that quantitative research is a methodological underdog in education (Boeren, 2018), few institutions offer training in analysing data. However, there are plenty of excellent tutorials available online, which guide you to carry out your quantitative research analysis. What you need to know is what test you need to do. The rest you can obtain from the tutorials and books available to you. Table 8.4 provides a list of tests that can be used depending on your collected data. The tests are divided into parametric and non-parametric tests. The parametric tests are used when data you have collected is usually distributed, and non-parametric tests are used when data is not normally distributed. This is why you need to check the normality of your data distribution before you embark on analysing data.

In addition to the specific tests that provide us with the results of our research project inquiry, when analysing quantitative data, we need to provide descriptive statistics for all of the variables we correlate or contrast. They include mean and standard deviation, minimum and maximum scores, standard error, and other information relevant to the statistics you select.

Finally, over the years, research results relied on statistical hypothesis testing, meaning that the results had to be statistically significant – i.e. not occurring by chance ($p < 0.05$) – to be meaningful. However, the effect size results are increasingly needed to be reported in research. The effect size relates to the difference or relationship between variables (Cohen et al., 2018). For example, if you measure the difference in wellbeing between boys and girls, the difference might be reported as being statistically significant. However, the effect size might be small, meaning that the actual difference in wellbeing between them is not considerable. Therefore, we recommend you identify effect sizes for all your results, along with their statistical significance.

Reflection time

What sampling methods are you planning to use for your research and why?

What data analysis techniques do you consider for your research and why? What are the next steps you need to take to learn more about it?

Recap time

This chapter has listed some of the ethical guidelines you need to consider when designing an empirical research project. We also reviewed a range of sampling methods that can help you collect your data. Next, we asked you to decide which ones are most suitable for your research and available to you. Finally, we reviewed a range of non-exhaustive data analysis techniques you can use when analysing your project findings.

References

AERA, American Educational Research Association. 2011. "Code of Ethics American Educational Research Association." www.aera.net/Portals/38/docs/About_AERA/CodeOfEthics(1).pdf.

American Psychological Association. 2017. "Ethical Principles of Psychologists and Code of Conduct (2002, amended effective June 1, 2010, and January 1, 2017)." www.apa.org/ethics/code/index.html

Boeren, E. 2018. "The Methodological Underdog: A Review of Quantitative Research in the Key Adult Education Journals." *Adult Education Quarterly* 68(1): 63–79. doi: 10.1177/0741713617739347.

Boxall, K., and S. Ralph. 2009. "Research Ethics and the Use of Visual Images in Research with People with Intellectual Disability." *Journal of Intellectual & Developmental Disability* 34(1): 45–54. doi: 10.1080/13668250802688306.

Bracken-Roche, D., E. Bell, M.E. Macdonald, and E. Racine. 2017. "The Concept of 'Vulnerability' in Research Ethics: An In-depth Analysis of Policies and Guidelines." *Health Research Policy & Systems* 15: 1–18. doi: 10.1186/s12961-016-0164-6.

Braun, V., and V. Clarke. 2006. "Using Thematic Analysis in Psychology." *Qualitative Research in Psychology* 3(2): 77–101. doi: 10.1191/1478088706qp063oa.

Braun, V., and V. Clarke. 2013. *Successful Qualitative Research: A Practical Guide for Beginners.* London: Sage.

Braun, V., and V. Clarke. 2019. "Reflecting on Reflexive Thematic Analysis." *Qualitative Research in Sport, Exercise and Health* 11(4): 589–597. doi: 10.1080/2159676X.2019.1628806

Braun, V., and V. Clarke. 2021. *Thematic Analysis A Practical Guide.* London: Sage.

British Educational Research Association BERA. 2018. "Ethical Guidelines for Educational Research." Web published. www.bera.ac.uk/publication/ethical-guidelines-for-educational-research-2018-online

British Psychological Society. 2018. *Code of Ethics and Conduct.* London: British Psychological Society.

British Psychological Society. 2021. *Code of Human Research Ethics.* London: British Psychological Society.

Chase, S.E. 2005. "Narrative Inquiry: Multiple Lenses, Approaches, Voices." In *The Sage Handbook of Qualitative Research,* edited by N.K. Denzin and Y.S. Lincoln, 651–679. London: Sage.

Clarke, V., and V. Braun. 2014. "Thematic Analysis." In *Encyclopedia of Critical Psychology,* edited by T. Teo. New York: Springer.

Cohen, L., L. Manion, and K. Morrison. 2018. *Research Methods in Education.* Abingdon: Routledge.

Denscombe, M. 2014. *The Good Research Guide.* 4th ed. Maidenhead, UK: Open University Press.

Dweck, C.S. 2006. *Mindset: The New Psychology of Success.* New York: Random House.

Eatough, V., and J.A. Smith. 2017. "Interpretative Phenomenological Analysis." In *Handbook of Qualitative Psychology,* 2nd ed., edited by C. Willig and W. Stainton-Rogers, 193–211. London: Sage. ISBN 9781473925212.

European Commission. 2019. *Communication from the Commission to the European Parliament and the Council.* Data Protection rules as a trust-enabler in the EU and beyond – taking stock. Bruselles: Com(2019) 374 final. https://eur-lex.europa.eu/legal-content/EN/TXT/?uri=CELEX%3A52019DC0374

Freeman, L., and C. Sullivan. 2018. "Thematic Analysis." In *Doing Qualitative Research in Psychology: A Practical Guide,* 2nd ed., edited by C. Sullivan and M.A. Forrester, 161–184. London: Sage.

Glaser, B.G., and A.L. Strauss. 1967. *The Discovery of Grounded Theory: Strategies for Qualitative Research.* London: Routledge.

Glaw, X., K. Inder, A. Kable, and M. Hazelton. 2017. "Visual Methodologies in Qualitative Research: Autophotography and Photo Elicitation Applied to Mental Health Research." *International Journal of Qualitative Methods* December. doi: 10.1177/1609406917748215

Guillemin, M., and L. Gillam. 2004. "Ethics, Reflexivity, and 'Ethically Important Moments' in Research." *Qualitative Inquiry* 10: 261–280.

Hsiu-Fang, H., and S.E. Shannon. 2005. "Three Approaches to Qualitative Content Analysis." *Qualitative Health Research* 15(9): 1277–1288. doi: 10.1177/1049732305276687.

Iacono, T. 2006. "Ethical Challenges and Complexities of Including People with Intellectual Disability as Participants in Research." *Journal of Intellectual & Developmental Disability* 31(3): 173–179. doi: 10.1080/13668250600876392.

Iacono, T., and V. Murray. 2003. "Issues of Informed Consent in Conducting Medical Research Involving People with Intellectual Disability." *Journal of Applied Research in Intellectual Disabilities* 16(1): 41–51. doi: 10.1046/j.1468–3148.2003.00141.x.

Maher, C., M. Hadfield, M. Hutchings, and A. de Eyto. 2018. "Ensuring Rigor in Qualitative Data Analysis: A Design Research Approach to Coding Combining NVivo With Traditional Material Methods." *International Journal of Qualitative Methods* 17(1): 1–13. doi: 10.1177/1609406918786362.

Mayring, P. 2014. "Qualitative Content Analysis: Theoretical Background and Procedures." In *Approaches to Qualitative Research in Mathematics Education. Advances in Mathematics Education*, edited by A. Bikner-Ahsbahs, C. Knipping, and N. Presmeg. Dordrecht: Springer.

Nowell, L.S., J.M. Norris, D.E. White, and N.J. Moules. 2017. "Thematic Analysis: Striving to Meet the Trustworthiness Criteria." *International Journal of Qualitative Methods* 16(1): 1–1. doi: 10.1177/1609406917733847.

Pendlebury, S., and P. Enslin. 2001. "Representation, Identification and Trust: Towards an Ethics of Educational Research." *Journal of Philosophy of Education* 35(3): 361. doi: 10.1111/1467-9752.00232.

Petitmengin, C. 2006. "Describing One's Subjective Experience in the Second Person: An Interview Method for the Science of Consciousness." *Phenomenology and the Cognitive Sciences* 5: 229–269

Petitmengin, C. 2007. "Towards the Source of Thoughts. The Gestural and Transmodal Dimensions of Lived Experience." *Journal of Consciousness Studies* 14(3): 54–82.

Petitmengin, C. 2019. "Towards Mixed Methods in the Exploration of Subjective Experience." Interacting Minds Centre, Aarhus University, Denmark. www.youtube.com/watch?v=YFU9YVuNXQg&t=440s [accessed 10.04.2020].

Petitmengin, C., A. Remillieux, and C. Valenzuela-Moguillansky. 2018. "Discovering the Structures of Lived Experience." *Phenomenology and the Congitive Science* 18: 691–730. https://doi.org/10.1007/s11097-018-9597-4

Pietkiewicz, I., and J.A. Smith. 2012. "Praktyczny przewodnik interpretacyjnej analizy fenomenologicznej w badaniach jakościowych w psychologii." *Czasopismo Psychologiczne* 18(2): 361–369.

Polkinghorne, D.E. 2006. "Narrative Configuration in Qualitative Analysis." *Journal of Qualitative Studies in Education* 8(5): 5–23.

Saunders, B., J. Kitzinger, and C. Kitzinger. 2015. "Anonymising Interview Data: Challenges and Compromise in Practice." *Qualitative Research: QR* 15(5): 616–632. doi: 10.1177/1468794114550439

Shaw, R. 2019. "Intrepretive Phenomenological Analysis." In *Doing Qualitative Research in Psychology. A Practical Guide,* 2nd ed., edited by C. Sullivan and M.A. Forrester. London: Sage.

Smith, J.A., and M. Osborn. 2003. "Interpretative Phenomenological Analysis." In *Qualitative Psychology: A Practical Guide to Research Methods*, edited by J.A. Smith, 51–80. London: Sage.

Smith, J.A., and M. Osborn. 2015. "Interpretative Phenomenological Analysis as a Useful Methodology for Research on the Lived Experience of Pain." *British Journal of Pain* 9(1): 41–42. doi: 10.1177/2049463714541642

Union, Official Journal of the European. 2013. *Directive 2013/33/EU of the European Parliament and of the Council of 26 June 2013 Laying Down Standards for the Reception of Applicants for International Protection*. Brussels: EU.

Walford, G. 2005. "Research Ethical Guidelines and Anonymity." *International Journal of Research & Method in Education* 28(1): 83–93. doi: 10.1080/01406720500036786

Xu, W., and K. Zammit. 2020. "Applying Thematic Analysis to Education: A Hybrid Approach to Interpreting Data in Practitioner Research." *International Journal of Qualitative Methods* 19: 1–9. doi: 10.1177/1609406920918810.

9   Presentation

9.1 Artefacts

What makes capstone projects particularly exciting is the flexibility of the project application. Traditional research theses result in volumes that often gather dust on a library bookshelf. However, a capstone project relates to professional practice and may come in various artefacts. An artefact is an outcome of a capstone project that supplements a written project, which can be a tool (e.g. software for online coaching), work of art (e.g. sculpture that depicts affect), object (e.g. architectural model of the relaxation area), or document (e.g. policy update). Alternatively, it can be a research paper ready for publication, a book proposal, or a presentation. Figure 9.2 provides examples of artefacts that may derive from a capstone project.

Say a student would like to use their capstone project to update particular policy documents. Their artefact would be the new policy documents, which they will submit in their capstone project appendix. In contrast, the written part of the project will describe the process they engaged in and the literature they drew from when updating all the documents. Say another student would like to create a sculpture and use it as a prop for a focus group discussion which would be described in the written piece of work.

Each one of the artefacts is further described in Table 9.1. Please note that these examples are not exhaustive. Your practice informs your artefact, and your scope for imagination is the limit.

Artefacts are usually not a necessary feature of capstone projects, which is why in some educational institutions, they are not assessed. Your capstone project may produce no specific artefact and focus solely on completing a written piece of work. Consider, however, how this optional, albeit beneficial, aspect of your project can add value to your practice.

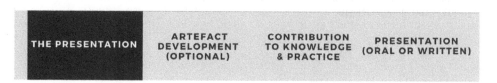

| THE PRESENTATION | ARTEFACT DEVELOPMENT (OPTIONAL) | CONTRIBUTION TO KNOWLEDGE & PRACTICE | PRESENTATION (ORAL OR WRITTEN) |

Figure 9.1 The outline of chapter 9.

DOI: 10.4324/9781003262428-9

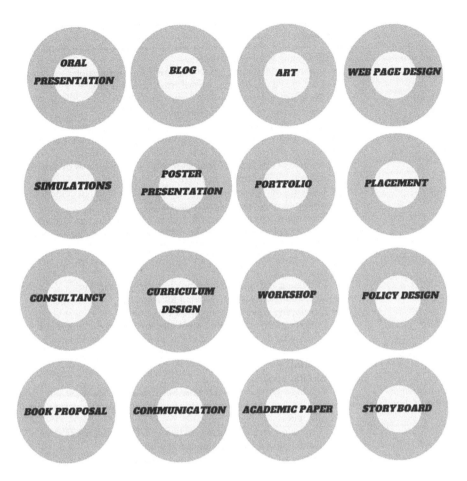

Figure 9.2 A range of possible capstone project artefacts.

Table 9.1 Examples of capstone project artefacts.

Artefacts	Examples
Oral Presentation	• Presenting a range of tools you have used when learning how to do peer coaching • Presenting to peers or a panel of academics what you have learnt during your programme • Presenting at a conference on your research project
Blog	• Developing a blog • Contributing to blog set up by the organisation where you work
Art	• Creating visual art – e.g. a sculpture, painting, drawing • Creating literary art – e.g. writing a book of poetry • Creating a set of dance moves and performing them • Creating a sound-art practice – e.g. a guitar tune • Directing an audio-visual performance – e.g. school's end-of-year theatrical performance • Creating an Animoto or a video

(*Continued*)

Table 9.1 (Continued)

Artefacts	Examples
Web page design	• Designing your own web page • Creating/redesigning a web page for your organisation • Developing a website as part of your art-based project
Simulations	• Designing video games • Testing devices created by students
Poster presentation	• Presenting an academic poster within or outside of your institution • Designing a series of wellbeing posters for your organisation
Portfolio	• A range of artefacts relating to your learning journey • A range of artefacts carried out in your organisation as part of the inclusion initiative you managed
Placement	• Undergoing a practical work experience in a work-placement capacity, reflecting on work-integrated learning
Consultancy	• Identifying a problem and offering solutions for an external agency's issue grapples. These could be made-up scenarios or actual consultancy work commissioned by external agencies
Curriculum design	• Developing a psychology course or module in a particular curricular area • Evaluating and redesigning a psychological curriculum • Developing assessment materials for a course • Developing artefacts to support a curriculum
Workshop	• Designing and presenting a workshop on your topic of interest • Developing a research-based curriculum support workshop on your topic
Policy design	• Reviewing existing policies and comparing them to the national standard • Writing a policy document
Book proposal	• Writing a book proposal for the book you have always wanted to write
Communication	• Writing and presenting a motivational speech to your demotivated colleagues • Designing a series of correspondence that you may use in your organisation when communicating with clients
Academic paper	• Writing an academic paper – e.g. a theoretical paper with an evidence-based model you created, an empirical paper that describes a unique study you have carried out, or a paper that describes a systematic review that you carried out as part of your capstone project
Storyboard	• Designing a storyboard to show how learning spaces can be developed in your organisation • Creating a psychology comic • Designing a poster on a psychological topic
Other	There are thousands of other artefacts that can be created as part of your capstone project. Please check with your supervisor about an innovative idea you have in relation to your project artefact

Reflection time

What "other" artefacts could you create as part of your capstone project?

What are the three artefacts of your choice and why?

Which artefact would add the greatest value to your educational practice and why?

9.2 Contribution to knowledge and practice

The traditional final year projects aim to create research findings that contribute to the current knowledge. Therefore, you need to compare and contrast the findings with other research. In addition to contributing to the current knowledge about the topic, students are expected to identify the contribution of findings to practice. However, the proportion of contribution to knowledge and practice in a traditional project is 70% to 30%. On the other hand, this proportion is reversed when designing a capstone project.

One of the differentiating features of capstone projects is their contribution to informing practice. However, the challenge you have is that most of the academic articles that you read focus primarily on the theoretical and research contributions, mentioning only briefly (a few sentences at most) the implications that the research has for practice. This imbalance in discussing research results makes some academics doubt their usefulness for practitioners (Bartunek and Rynes, 2010). This is one of the most fundamental differences that a capstone project offers to both the community of practitioners and researchers. In a capstone project, the contribution focus is reversed, as we pay more attention to the implications of research for practice than the implications for research or theoretical models.

When reflecting on the implications for practice, consider yourself and others. For example, your research showed that students do not like long-winded instructions. Therefore, your implications for practice may inform your practice, whereby you become aware of your instructions, and you consciously shorten them. In addition to this, you may consider who else will benefit from your findings. Of course, the most prominent group of people are fellow teachers. However, if you want to extend the impact of your capstone research project, you may also consider teacher education institutions, policymakers, or policy influencers, such as organisations that support policymakers.

Furthermore, when reflecting on the implications for practice, consider various actions you and others can take to improve educational practice. Informed by the most frequently cited implications for practice in academic articles (Bartunek and Rynes, 2010; Cuervo-Cazurra et al., 2013), they may include a call for you or others to start acting differently so that you will get different results, identifying additional resources that are required for enhancing your effectiveness as a practitioner, or redesigning your curriculum, pedagogical approach, or specific methods. Figure 9.3 will offer you a few examples of potential implications for practice. They are not exhaustive but will hopefully get you started finding a link between your research findings and how they can improve educational practice.

Reflection time

What aspects of your practice do you hope your project will help you improve?

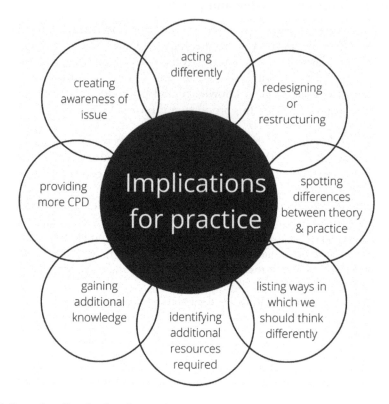

Figure 9.3 Examples of implications for practice.

9.3 Presentation

Every educational institution has its guidelines for the presentation of research projects. For some, an artefact may suffice; others request an oral and/or poster presentation. The vast majority of third-level institutions require a written presentation of the project, in addition to creating an artefact (if applicable). This section will first review the guidelines for oral/poster and written presentations. Given how challenging writing is for many students, we will also review some techniques to help you engage with writing effectively and efficiently.

9.3.1 Oral and poster presentation

You may be asked to design a poster representing your research either for a conference presentation, an assessment, or as part of the course requirement in your institution. Poster design and presentations are vital in academic work in many disciplines. The advantage of designing a poster is that it compels you to be succinct in the information you provide. In addition, it challenges you to present your research to a diverse audience, including those outside your discipline.

Think about the poster's purpose – you want to present precise information that the reader can understand and give an overview of the context for the research, the research question, methodology, methods used to collect data, and critical findings. You cannot put your entire research project on the poster or presentation, so you must make choices. These choices depend on the audience for your presentation.

When designing a poster, consider the following:

Purpose of the poster – to display the main points of your research project graphically

The audience for your poster – the general public, your academic advisor, fellow students, or more broad academic disciplines. For example, presenting your poster at a conference will be on display to all attending the conference. Therefore, it is best to avoid acronyms that your audience may not know.

Poster design – design will depend on purpose and audience. If the poster is presented in a virtual space, you might decide to include embedded links and so on. If it is a printed poster, you will need to consider many design aspects, including colour, font, and layout. You can use a template for the poster or design your own. Typically, people read text from left to right and top to bottom, so use this pattern for your design. Use blank space to frame content. Sometimes, it is good to use bulleted lists, pull quotes, or framed or box text to add interest. Don't overfill the poster with text.

A typical poster will contain the following sections:

Introduction section – this will read like an abbreviated abstract.

The literature section – this will give a brief overview of the critical literature linked to your research question/topic/area.

The methods section – this will present your positioning, methodology, and methods used. Here you might decide to use a graphic to represent the critical information.

Results section – here the key results are presented clearly. Consider graphics here also; a picture paints a thousand words.

Discussion section – here you present the headline conclusions from your research

Think about using alternative headings for these sections; for example, the methods sections could be *How I Did It*, and the findings could read *What Clients Had to Say*. Remember, you want your poster to be visually attractive and share the key messages from your research.

Colour and layout

Be as creative as you desire with colour and layout but remember *less is more* in most cases. Do not overuse colour or different fonts as it can make your poster look busy and distract from the vital message in the research. Colour is good to show relationships between sections. You can present the poster in two or three columns with crucial indicators for the logical sequence. Some students opt to use a visual metaphor as a background to the poster. Visuals can help communicate ideas faster, more effectively, and more memorably. Make sure to number and label visuals. However, they should supplement and complement your core message on the poster, not just be there for decoration. Specifically, visuals can serve the following purpose:

- arouse interest,
- save time and space,
- focus attention,

- reinforce ideas,
- explain the inaccessible,
- persuade, and
- prevent misunderstandings.

When presenting numerical data, use charts and graphs rather than tables, as these can be more effective for illustrating data trends. When designing charts or graphs, format them effectively by keeping them simple with clear legends. It is best to use two-dimensional graphics. Use a high-resolution JPEG (.jpg) for images and ensure that they will not be blurred when printed on the poster. Use the simplest possible typeface and avoid using the multiple different ones available. Avoid using underlining. Use contrast to distinguish between the different sections. Use alignment and proximity to help organise the material to clear the sequence to the reader. Don't put too much text on the poster. Remember it will be displayed on a poster board, so it should be legible from at least a metre away. Sans serif fonts work best for posters. Headings' font sizes should be between 36 and 48, with 30–36 for body text. Your title can be 90–120. As with all academic writing, details matter, so do a good proofread to check spelling, grammar, and sentence structure. Finally, remember to include bibliographic details.

Poster presentation

The following section is for people giving a formal poster presentation. You may be presenting at a conference on your research. Plan your presentation to ensure you are not repeating the information on the poster verbatim. Your presentation should reinforce the essential information on the poster and add to it. You will need to anticipate the questions you might be asked.

Tips for clear communication

- Know your audience
- Know what you want to say
- Find illustrations, examples, and pieces of evidence that support and clarify the central ideas you want to communicate
- Structure in a logical order
- Prepare for questions

How to prepare for a poster presentation

AHEAD OF THE DAY

- Identify your target audience. If it is an assessment, read the outline of the success criteria for the assessment.
- Start the process of collecting ideas, insights, and illustrations.
- Decide on how your poster will be used as part of your presentation.
- Plan your talk on paper and check the links to your poster.
- Think back to your purpose and audience, select trigger words.
- Make clear notes and rehearse.

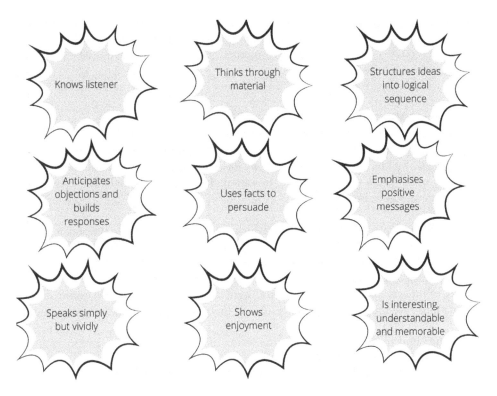

Figure 9.4 The characteristics of a good communicator.

On the day

Notes: Decide how you will use notes; it is good to have them but not rely on them.

Distractions: Manage outside distractions, check out the room where you will speak, decide if you need a window open, where you will stand, make sure you do not stand in front of your poster or presentation.

Body language: Think about your body language, how you will stand, how you will use your hands for gestures and how you will use eye contact and vocal cadence. It is best to stand in one position and avoid moving, as it distracts attention from what you are saying. Use hand gestures to illustrate and reinforce key concepts. Maintain eye contact with your audience as much as possible. This is an excellent way to see if your message is clear.

Nerves: Manage your nerves by practising box breathing ahead of the talk. Sit straight up in a chair with your hands on your lap and slowly exhale to the count of four, then breathe in (inhale) for the count of four, hold your breath in for the count of four, and breath out (exhale) for the count of four. Practising this in the days coming up to your talk for at least four rounds of box breathing will help you relax.

Mistakes: If you make a mistake on the day, own it and move on. We all make mistakes, and it is better to own them than to cover them up.

Pace: Pay attention to the pace of your talk, practice, and the amount of time that you talk. It is better to say less and be more explicit in your message than to try to put too much into the talk. It is good to signpost your talk for the audience; for example, "Now that I have discussed my methodological design, I'll describe briefly the instruments I used in the study".

Questions: Prepare for questions; if you do not understand the question, ask the person to repeat it. If you still are unclear, then restate or paraphrase the questions by saying, "What I think you are asking is", and then answer the question. It is good to expand on your answer and use it to build a bridge to a new point you wish to make. For example, if a person asks a question you do not know the answer to say, *"Thanks for this interesting question, I am unable to answer it at the moment because . . . but I will take note and look into it"*. It is always best to say you don't know something than prove you don't know it.

Think about how you might use questions during your talk to stimulate interest, for example, *"How many here today have grappled with the problem of positioning?"* This makes the audience feel part of your research journey. You might use questions to ensure your audience understood something, for example, *"Was I clear on how I analysed these data?"* It is good to think of three to five key points that you want to get across in your discussion after the presentation, have them clear in your head, and then use them to help answer questions.

Ending: End your talk by thanking the audience, inviting questions, and sharing your contact details if you are available to accept follow-up questions.

These presentation skills can be used when presenting a paper at conferences.

9.3.2 Written

In addition to the study design, you also have an essential decision about your research project's written aspects. Some educational institutions do not require any written outputs and are happy with the artefacts you produce, be it a theatrical performance or a piece of art. However, most research projects are assessed via a written report and/or an assignment (van Acker et al., 2014).

There are three options for the presentation structure of your capstone project

1 Artefact-informed structure
2 Traditional thesis structure
3 Ubiquitous structure

9.3.3 Artefact-informed

Some of your choices about the artefacts you select may inform your writing structure. For example, suppose you choose to write a policy document as part of your written assessment. In that case, the written structure of your project may resemble that of a policy document preceded by the assignment title page. Similarly, if your artefact were an academic paper, then the structure would resemble that of an academic paper from a journal, where you intend to publish it after graduation. The artefact-informed structure is unique to your research project. You should discuss the parameters within which you can design your structure with your project supervisor.

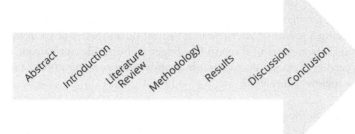

Figure 9.5 Traditional thesis structure.

9.3.4 Traditional thesis

Some students, especially those who choose to carry out an empirical research project, present it in a traditional thesis format. This means that their sections include abstract, introduction, literature review, methodology, results, discussion, and conclusion. Figure 9.5 provides a pictorial representation of the structure.

Abstract

A well-written abstract summarises the main points of your capstone project. It is usually 200–250 words long. It should not include citations unless your educational institution permits them by standard convention. The abstract structure is usually very concise and includes the following points:

- One or two sentences about the background of your research project, which provides the rationale for you carrying out research
- One or two sentences about your research design
- One or two sentences about your findings
- One or two sentences about the discussion and implications of your findings

The implications part of your abstract provides invaluable information for practitioners. Sometimes the authors provide a generic statement of the implications of their research – e.g. "Implications for the teachers are discussed". However, given that the fundamental part of the capstone project is to provide practitioners with a resource for their research-based practice, it must be carefully considered.

Introduction

This is a relatively short section of your research project. The objective of this section is to provide a reader with a brief rationale for your study. First, it offers a brief background to the topic of your project and then explains why it is relevant.

Literature review

The literature review is a well-structured series of arguments drawn from reading the literature about a topic of your choice. It is not enough to relay what you have read. Instead, the literature review chapter is about organising what you have read into a logical argument and taking a reader of your research project on a journey of your way of thinking about it. It usually consists of three to five larger sections relevant to your topic. Each section is then further divided into paragraphs that develop your argument. The objective of the literature review is threefold:

1   It aims to identify the past literature relating to your topic.
2   It aims to present the literature through the specific lens you choose to view it.
3   It helps you establish your research questions, which you present at the end of your literature review.

Methods

There are two objectives of writing the methodology section. The first one relates to rationalising your choices when designing your research; the second one conveys the practical design aspects of your research project. Your methodology chapter needs to provide the rationale for your methodological design. You need to demonstrate that other designs were considered and explain why you selected the design for your project. This relates not only to methodology but also to the methods applied in your research project.

The structure of the methodology varies according to your research design; however, here are some of the typical elements of it:

•   Research design – In this section, you explain your choices about the design of your study.
•   Participants – In this section, you explain the choices you have made about the sampling method and present the profile of your participants.
•   Instruments – This section is sometimes referred to as "Materials" or "Measures" and relates to the tools you used to help you carry out your research project. This may include the questions you have used and how you came up with them. If you used a set of pre-existing measures, you could describe them in this section, along with other pertinent information related to them and props or other implements you used in your study.
•   Procedure – This section of the capstone project refers to the steps taken when designing a study. If a study is complex, such as when you use an experimental design, care needs to be taken when describing it. This section includes the procedure of asking participants for consent, steps taken when carrying out your study, or the pilot studies you have conducted. The objective of this section is to present the step-by-step procedure you have used so that you can replicate the study in the future.
•   Ethical considerations – In this section, it is crucial to demonstrate what ethical issues you have considered when designing your study and the specific ethical guidelines you have used, which may be either your educational institution guidelines or a professional body's guidelines, such as American Psychological Association, British Psychological Association, Australian Association for Research in Education, Asia-Pacific Educational Research Association, or others that are relevant to your geographical area.

Results

This section provides the results of your study. The way you organise it depends on your research question and your study design. Usually, each research question or component of your research question is introduced one by one. The results mustn't deviate from your research question. However, you need to focus your results specifically on responding to your research question.

QUALITATIVE RESEARCH

There are at least ten ways to organise and present your qualitative data (Cohen et al., 2018). Table 9.2 provides the display types, along with examples for your research projects. Your presentation usually starts by identifying themes and subthemes, which may be placed in a table or a graph. It is followed by a systematic presentation of your data supplemented with participant quotes. Finally, we recommend reviewing several academic papers as examples of data presented for a specific qualitative methodology.

Table 9.2 Techniques for organising, analysing, and presenting data in qualitative research.

Organise, analyse, and present your qualitative data by	*Example*
Groups of people	If you carried out research that identified the psychological wellbeing of adults diagnosed with different chronic illnesses, you may want to divide them into groups associated with their diagnosis, the length of time they experienced it, or the severity of their illness.
Individual people	You present each participant and their stories one by one.
Issues or themes	You analyse all participants together and then present the findings as themes/issues with example quotes from each participant that relates to each theme/issue.
Research question	If you have two research questions in your study, you can divide your results into two sections, one relating to each research question. If you synthesise your data for both, two separate sets of themes will emerge for each one of the research questions.
Data collection method	If your research project design is complex and comprises several methods, you can divide your findings into sections devoted to each method. For example, the first section of your results may refer to a survey you analysed and the second to the action research you carried out.
Case study or studies	You can present the results of your case studies either by describing each case study, one by one, or by combining findings from all case studies that present similarities and differences among them.
Narrative	Presenting stories of participants one by one.
Event	If you wish to identify the impact of various events on children's lives, you may analyse and present data for each turning point event. For example, if your study is about children dealing with bereavement, you may either synthesise data from a number of children or present narratives from individual children relating to the death of someone close to them. Then the next event you describe may relate to the professional help they received. The following may even relate to the help they received at home. Therefore, your data analysis and presentation may be centred around events.

(Continued)

Table 9.2 (Continued)

Organise, analyse, and present your qualitative data by	Example
Sequence and time frame	You may wish to analyse the experience of first-year college students. You can therefore do it within a chunk of time you select (e.g. one year) or break it down into a time sequence (e.g. the first term, the second term, the third term). Your analysis would relate to each individual time frame.
Theoretical perspective	Changes in the inclusion policy may be reviewed from various theoretical perspectives, such as strength-based.

Source: Adapted from Cohen et al. (2018).

QUANTITATIVE RESEARCH

The quantitative results are usually presented by firstly listing descriptive data, such as mean (M) and standard deviation (SD) for the variables selected for the analysis. Therefore, if your research identifies a correlation between students' sense of belonging to school and performance, you will begin your analysis by presenting M and SD for both variables. Following on from this, for each statistical test, there are specific results that need to be mentioned. Finally, your results will need to be described in a paragraph, following the guidelines for each statistical test. Then you can provide an expanded version of your results in a table.

Discussion

The objective of the discussion section is to discuss your findings in the context of past literature and provide the implications for practice. The section, therefore, may include the following:

- A discussion about how your study compares with other research findings
- An explanation of your findings in the context of theoretical frameworks
- A contribution of your project to the existing knowledge base
- Limitations of your research project
- Implications for practice for you and others (e.g. fellow practitioners, policymakers)
- Implications for future research

Conclusion

This is an extended version of the abstract.

9.3.5 Ubiquitous structure

Despite capstone projects having an impromptu structure, some patterns emerge from the choices made by students when presenting their capstone projects. We have reviewed over 300 projects and created a frequently used structure. Figure 9.6 provides a pictorial representation of this ubiquitous structure.

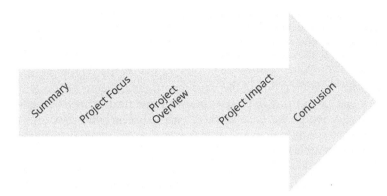

Figure 9.6 Ubiquitous capstone project structure.

Summary

The summary of the project provides an outline of your project design, findings, and implications for practitioners.

Project focus

There are two main parts of the project focus: rationale and objectives. The rationale delves into why the project was initiated and provides the background for it, which may include your personal experiences or the experiences of fellow practitioners. The project's objectives come from the rationale and are similar to your research aims, from which you draw your research questions.

Project overview

This project amalgamates the traditional literature review and the research design. This section needs to provide the theoretical and practical background to your project. You can do this by critically engaging with your literature review, arguing for the need for your project to improve practice, presenting your research question, and following on with a project design that best suits your question. In addition, the design of your project includes relevant aspects from the methodology section of a traditional thesis structure.

Project impact

The impact of your project section presents your results and your discussion. They can be presented either as separate parts or together. When they are presented as separate parts, you will start with reviewing your research questions and associated results, and then in the next section, you will discuss your findings in the context of past research and practice. When it is presented together, you will discuss each finding and follow it up with a discussion in the context of past literature.

Conclusion

The conclusion is a summary of the project.

9.3.6 *Writing process*

For many students, writing is one of the most significant academic challenges they experience, so they engage in many ineffective practices that further prevent them from producing high-quality work. We once worked with a student who took a 20-year break before enrolling in a master's programme. Her fear of writing became so intense that she was ready to quit two months after commencing her studies. Instead of withdrawing from the programme, she sat down with us, and we came up with a plan for building her confidence in writing. A year later, she graduated with a distinction. Academic writing is like making an omelette. Once you know what ingredients to put into your mixture and in what order to do it, you will be able to replicate it endlessly in the future.

9.3.6.1 *Obstacles*

This section will examine some of the obstacles that may prevent you from writing and explore potential solutions to your problem. The obstacles often result in procrastination, which ultimately puts you under more pressure as your deadline for the research project is looming. Procrastination refers to the process of postponing your writing and often ignoring thinking about it until the last minute when you have to do it. This last-minute work often results in mediocre output, which doesn't serve you well. More importantly, however, suppressing your thoughts about the project may keep you awake at night worrying about it. As Fyodor Dostoevsky put it, "Try to pose for yourself this task: not to think of a polar bear, and you will see that the cursed thing will come to mind every minute" (Dostoevsky and FitzLyon, 2013, p. 1).

Mind you, instead of procrastination; you may be engaging in incubation (Biswas-Diener, 2010), which is a process that resembles procrastination (see Section 2.5 for more). Individuals who incubate do their writing at the last minute, just like procrastinators. However, they usually receive better grades because instead of suppressing their thoughts about the project, they actively think about it and plan it.

For example, before writing this book section, I reflected on it for almost a week. I wondered how I could make it valuable and relevant for you. I wondered about its structure, what concepts I should include, and in what order. When I sat down to write it, my words flowed easily, and I wrote it relatively quickly. Therefore, if you are an incubator like me, continue doing it, as it is a valuable technique for carrying out your capstone project. However, if you pretend that the project does not exist for weeks and months, we recommend you try and overcome the obstacles that fuel your procrastination. Table 9.3 lists some of the main obstacles that may prevent you from writing and offers solutions to them. Please review them carefully and reflect on which obstacle is your biggest challenge and what you can do to overcome it.

9.3.7 *Writing guidelines*

What often helps students write is a routine and familiarisation with writing. It takes professional writers several drafts to produce the books and academic papers you read. The same applies to your research project. The first draft is usually a rough outline of your

Table 9.3 Reasons for procrastination and possible solutions.

Reason	Solution
Disorganised notes	Review Section 4.2.1 of this book, which discusses effective ways to organise your notes.
Unsure what to write	Speak with your supervisor and together try to come up with a structure for the section or a chapter you are writing. Alternatively, write in bullet points what sections you might require in your research project.
Perfectionism	Try to prepare a first draft which is "good enough". You can work on making it better later.
Not sure where to start	Come up with a plan. Start writing your first draft, and don't worry if it is incoherent. You will improve it later.
Need to do some more reading	Review Section 4.2.2, which discusses methods for conducting a literature review.
I am not interested in the project	Change your topic. If it is too late to change it, consider what strengths you have that you can practice when completing this project. Engaging with your strengths will help you enjoy it more.
Something is stopping me, and I can't figure it out	Research shows that in these situations, it is useful to do expressive writing. Take a piece of paper, and for the next 20 minutes, write about your feelings and thoughts associated with this project. You may have to repeat this process daily for three to four days to help you figure out the next steps.
Other reasons	List other reasons you have for procrastinating and share your concerns with your friends. They can help you come up with solutions.

project; once it makes sense to you, you create draft 2, draft 3, draft 4, and sometimes drafts 6 through 10 or more, if need be. Writing is a process of drafting and re-drafting your work until you and your supervisor are happy with it.

The more you practice writing, the easier it becomes. It is a myth that we need to wait for the muse to write. Most professional writers have a strict writing schedule, and their muse is their alarm clock alerting them they should start to write. For example, Graham Green sat down at his typewriter every morning and did not get up until he wrote 500 words. This regular habit of writing is essential when you embark on any writing project. Set up a schedule of writing, be it in the morning, afternoon, evening, or at night, whatever works for you, and devote at least an hour to writing daily. Treat your research project not as a sprint but as a long-distance run, to which you can contribute with small samples of writing regularly.

Before you sit down to do your writing, be clear about what section you want to contribute to. Is it the outline of your project or impact? Please make sure you are clear about it so that you don't waste valuable writing time deciding on it. Also, try not to postpone some sections of your project because they are too challenging to write or don't feel like writing them today. Again, this wastes your time and encourages procrastination. Instead, write your first draft steadily from section to section, without skipping any parts. If you don't have references for something, just put in brackets "(ref)" and move on. You will be able to fill in all the gaps in your next draft. It is easier to make changes to a draft than create it.

Everyone works differently when coming up with ideas for writing sections for their project. Some students incubate for a long time, create mind maps, or brainstorm their arguments and paragraphs. Others develop a skeleton structure of each section, where they note pertinent research they want to include in each paragraph. Finally, some students initially write their project as bullet points and treat each bullet point as a further paragraph. Each of these techniques is useful, as long as it works for you. If it doesn't, come up with an alternative.

As you write your research project, make sure you have a golden thread maintained throughout your entire project. This thread relates to the topic/research problem/research question. It is like a spine that keeps all the parts of your project together. It runs from the introduction to the literature review, methodology, and conclusion of your project. Now and then, remind the reader of your project focus and keep relating all your paragraphs and sections to it. An easy technique we often suggest to students is to ask yourself, "*So what?*" after writing each paragraph and section. "*So what that this is what the literature says? How does it relate to my overall project?*" Asking yourself this question will keep you on track and focused on maintaining the golden thread.

Structuring your project

Your project is structured into chapters, and each chapter has several sections. For example, you may divide your literature review into three to five sections that introduce your topic systematically. They are further divided into three to five paragraphs, all of which build your argument as you keep writing up your capstone project. Each of your sections and paragraphs needs to have a beginning, middle, and end. The end concludes your argument and helps you move it forward.

Some of the most straightforward structures for writing your paragraphs and sections in your project come from the inductive and deductive reasoning we discussed in Section 3.3 of this book. If you choose deductive reasoning, your paragraph should start with a *statement* – e.g. *Maths is students' favourite topic*. Then, the following few sentences go on a loop between providing *examples* from the literature of the evidence of this statement and *explaining* what it means. Finally, each paragraph needs to finish with a conclusion, either a summary statement or a bridging statement that connects this paragraph with the next one. Figure 9.7 provides a pictorial representation of this writing model.

Alternatively, you can employ inductive reasoning when structuring your paragraphs, whereby you omit the *statement* and begin your paragraph by providing *examples* that support your argument, *explain* them, and finish the paragraph with a conclusion. Whichever method you select will work as long as you provide clarity of your arguments and a cohesive and consistent presentation.

Figure 9.7 Example of deductive reasoning applied in writing a research project paragraph.

Reflection time

On a scale from 1 to 10, how confident do you feel about presenting your research project? If you woke up tomorrow and you realised your confidence was 2 or 3 points up, what is the first thing that you might notice yourself doing? Now come up with a few things you can do this week to help you get there.

Recap time

In this chapter, we presented you with a range of options for creating artefacts associated with your capstone project. Then, we asked you to decide which would add the most outstanding value to your practice. We have also reviewed several implications for practice that you may consider, as they are a crucial part of a capstone project. Finally, we provided you with tips on presenting your research project in both oral and written form and building your confidence in it.

References

Bartunek, J.M., and S.L. Rynes. 2010. "The Construction and Contributions of 'Implications for Practice': What's in Them and What Might They Offer?" *Academy of Management Learning & Education* 9(1): 100–117. doi: 10.5465/amle.9.1.zqr100.

Biswas-Diener, R. 2010. *Practicing Positive Psychology Coaching: Assessment, Activities, and Strategies for Success.* Hoboken, NJ: John Wiley & Sons Inc.

Cohen, L., L. Manion, and K. Morrison. 2018. *Research Methods in Education.* Abingdon: Routledge.

Cuervo-Cazurra, A., P. Caligiuri, U. Andersson, and M.Y. Brannen. 2013. "From the Editors: How to Write Articles That Are Relevant to Practice." *Journal of International Business Studies* 44(4): 285–289.

Dostoevsky, F., and K. FitzLyon. 2013. *Winter Notes on Summer Impressions.* London: Alma Books.

van Acker, L., J. Bailey, K. Wilson, and E. French. 2014. "Capping Them Off! Exploring and Explaining the Patterns in Undergraduate Capstone Subjects in Australian Business Schools." *Higher Education Research and Development* 33(5): 1049–1062.

10 Making impact with your research

The main objective of your research project is to complete your degree in psychology. However, apart from submitting it for assessment, some research projects may be suitable for publication. Publishing your research will ensure that other people can learn from your experience, and you can add value to the existing wealth of knowledge. We encourage you to work with your supervisor and decide on the best way to disseminate your findings. Next, you will find some options you have and advice on how to publish your research project to impact practitioners and future research.

- Conferences (oral and poster presentation)
- Educational institution online thesis/capstone project submission
- Professional and popular magazines and newspapers
- Peer-reviewed journals

10.1 Conferences

You may consider sharing your research project findings via academic and professional conferences. What is important is to disseminate your findings so that they can help other practitioners improve their practice and also assist researchers in progressing research. This is so much better than letting your hard work gather dust on a library bookshelf.

To speak at an academic conference, you need to determine which conference attendees may be interested in your research. Then, inquire into the dates you need to write and submit your abstract. Each conference announces its abstract submissions in advance, usually 8–10 months before the conference. Your abstract is written the same way you write an abstract for your final year project (see Chapter 9). You submit it along with additional information that the conference organisers require, such as your name, affiliation, and other pertinent details relating to the conference topic.

You can apply for either a conference presentation or a poster presentation. A conference presentation is usually short – i.e. 7–20 minutes, depending on the conference. Some well-known researchers are usually invited for longer talks, although this may vary. Please note the different options you have concerning the types of presentations you can do, depending on the conference you select. Some academic conferences encourage practitioners to share their research-based practice and, as such, may have an option of organising a workshop rather than a talk. If this is something you may be interested in, you should opt for it.

DOI: 10.4324/9781003262428-10

After you submit your abstract for either a talk or a poster, it will be peer-reviewed, and within a few months, you will find out whether you were successful at securing it or not. Sometimes, organisers may reject your oral presentation application and instead offer you a poster presentation. It is up to you if you wish to accept it. Acceptance of a conference or poster presentation means that you commit to attending the conference and speaking at it.

Please note that unless you have secured conference funding, you will be usually asked to pay for both the entrance fee to the conference and travel costs. Some conferences are free of charge; thus, the cost is waived. Other conferences, e.g. some professional membership conferences, may pay presenters an honorarium. Alternatively, you may volunteer at a conference that will allow you to attend and speak at a conference free of charge.

Finally, please review Chapter 9 for advice on how to prepare for an oral and poster presentation.

10.2 Educational institution

At some colleges and universities, capstone projects and other final year projects are published online and accessible either as an abstract or full version. You can usually opt-in or out of this facility during your submission or after receiving your award. The advantage of this type of publication is to ensure that your research is available to the general public and fellow psychologists and researchers. In addition, apart from ticking a box, you will not be required to do any additional work for it to be published.

10.3 Professional magazines and newsletters

If you are doing a capstone project, the obvious place to publish your findings is a professional magazine or newsletter. Their target audience is practitioners, and given that at the heart of the capstone project are practising psychologists, a professional magazine is your natural choice. This will allow you to share your experience of completing a project with other practitioners to improve their practice. In addition, your insights into how you used your research and applied it in practice will be invaluable for those who wish to try it out. Given that we are all part of the learning community, you must share your knowledge with others.

Many psychological organisations have a magazine, which they publish regularly. Some of these magazines may require diligent citations and a reference list. Others may opt for a summary of research without any references, some will ask you to write a popular article where you briefly mention your findings and then reflect on them in the context of practice. Before selecting which magazine you target, please familiarise yourself with their requirements and ensure you are satisfied with their brief.

10.4 Newspapers and magazines

You may also share your findings in newspapers and magazines with the general public. Psychology is of great interest to many; therefore, if you can find an angle and pitch your article in a way that the editors find appealing, you may be able to publish your research in the media and allow your research to help not only practitioners but also the general public.

10.5 Pitching for an article

When pitching for any magazine or newspaper article, the first thing to note is to ensure that the outcome of your project applies to their audience. Therefore, if your project relates specifically to cognitive psychology, there is little point in getting into a magazine designed specifically for educational psychologists. Instead, make sure that the magazine targets the audience that was part of your project and if not, try to make your study applicable to them.

For example, if indeed your study is related to cognitive psychology and you have found a great magazine that targets educational psychologists or a magazine devoted to health, identify which aspects of your findings will apply to their audience and pitch it bearing this in mind. Remember that you are trying to add value to the target group. Unless you do it, the editor will not be interested in your article.

Another thing to bear in mind is the style with which the articles are written in a magazine or newspaper for which you pitch. For example, consider the difference between a high-brow newspaper and a tabloid. Are their first paragraphs sensationalist, or are they measured? Do they develop arguments over longer paragraphs, or do they require short, one or two-sentence paragraphs? Whatever style they use is the style you will need to emphasise in your pitch.

When pitching an article, you need to provide a concise one-paragraph outline of your article. If the psychological magazine you are pitching for likes academic-style articles, then your abstract will suffice. However, if it is an article written in a non-academic style, start with a problem that you will try to resolve and finish with a solution you plan to offer. Pitches like this work very well for professional articles.

Once your pitch is successful, find out how many words you must write and when; this will help you plan your writing more efficiently. Make sure that you will deliver it on time if you commit to writing something. Editors rarely give second chances.

10.6 Peer-reviewed journals

In addition to magazines and newspapers, you may re-write your project to suit an academic, peer-reviewed journal. The "peer-review" aspect refers to how two or three academics review an article before it is accepted for publication. The target audience of peer-reviewed journals is academics rather than practitioners. However, while traditionally, journal articles were written by academics for academics, the contributors include many practitioners who have engaged in rigorous empirical research in recent years.

Each academic journal has a set of guidelines they follow. They may accept, for example, qualitative research only, with a specific focus on an aspect of psychology or a nexus between two parts of psychology. Unless your article (paper) fits their theme or research methodology, your article will be automatically rejected. Similarly, they may follow APA seventh edition referencing or Harvard referencing. You need to check which referencing style is required before submitting your paper. This is why reading the submission guidelines is worthwhile and deciding whether your paper fits the necessary standards and theme.

The peer-review process is usually long. The first screening process happens when a journal editor reviews your paper and decides if it is suitable for a peer review. If they deem it unsuitable, your paper is returned to you with a change request or rejected. If they deem it appropriate, it is sent out for peer review. This means that two or three academics will read your work and challenge it. They will ensure your arguments are strong, the research you present is up to date, and all aspects of your paper are in order. They may then accept it for publication, ask you to make small changes or significant changes, or recommend it to be rejected.

You are usually given a few weeks to make changes to your paper. You need to stick with the deadline provided by the editor and go through each reviewer's comments and alter your paper accordingly. It is helpful to trace your changes and send a letter to the reviewer addressing each comment. All the reviewers work free of charge, and the objective of the review is to help you improve your paper, so they must be treated with respect. As an editor of a journal, I have seen some students respond less than respectfully towards the reviewers; they were offended by the reviewers' comments instead of embracing them and learning from them.

Conclusion

Writing this book was inspired by our students, who through their openness, passion, and creativity shaped the contours of capstone and final year projects. They have fully engaged with the process of practice-based research as part of their capstone projects and shown us the great benefits it can offer to both the community of practitioners and researchers in this field. We hope this book eased the journey of completing your project and helped you establish an even more important pathway for autonomous research-based practice that will continue for years to come. After all, this is what engaging with capstone projects is all about.

Index

Page numbers in *italics* indicate a figure and page numbers in **bold** indicate a table on the corresponding page.